VETERAN
AMERICANS

A VOLUME IN THE SERIES

Veterans

EDITED BY
J. Ross Dancy and Brian Matthew Jordan

VETERAN AMERICANS

Literature and Citizenship from
Revolution to Reconstruction

Benjamin Cooper

University of Massachusetts Press
Amherst & Boston

ISBN 978-1-62534-331-4 (paper); 330-7 (hardcover)

Designed by Sally Nichols
Set in Adobe Minion Pro
Printed and bound by Maple Press, Inc.

Cover design by William Boardman
Cover art: Inscription of Andrew H. McWhorter, Central Park Hospital autograph
book, Wm. Oland Bourne Papers, Manuscript Division, Library of Congress.

Library of Congress Cataloging-in-Publication Data
A catalog record for this book is available from the Library of Congress.

British Library Cataloguing-in-Publication Data
A catalog record for this book is available from the British Library.

An earlier version of chapter 4 appeared as "Franklin H. Durrah, John William De
Forest, and the Varieties of Military Experience" in *Arizona Quarterly* 67, no. 2
(Summer 2011); a revised version here is printed by permission of the Regents of
the University of Arizona.

For Erika and Allegra

CONTENTS

PREFACE

There are those rare occasions for literary historians when the eyes dilate and the spine locks. *Veteran Americans* began in such a moment several years ago while I was listlessly poking around a database and by chance came upon an advertisement for "Left-Handed Penmanship," a writing competition for amputee veterans held soon after the Civil War. Eventually that contest would form the basis of my inquiry into nineteenth-century veteran literature (see chapter 4), but at the time, I was alarmed and bothered by questions about these hundreds of soldiers whose names and stories arguably had been lost to time. They were certainly unknown to me. Who were these veterans, and what did they have to say? Why were they compelled to write in such large numbers and from such a wide range of states? What were their purposes in writing so quickly about their military experience, and what, if anything, did they accomplish in asserting themselves as authors?

Eventually such questions led me to the Library of Congress, where the contest submissions are stored. There, I witnessed veterans who had written and drawn on envelopes, on scratch paper, and on stationery. They had copied in their own hand the Emancipation Proclamation and also composed their own verse. They had personalized their handwriting in striking calligraphy and also fallen into wild, nonsensical scribbles (as seen on the front cover). Having lost their dominant hand, some had written with retrained limbs, but if both limbs were lost, they wrote with pens clenched between their teeth. What I sensed was an unrelenting psychological and political need for early American veterans to write—that they might be seen (many included a *carte de visite*) and that they might be heard. At the same time, I realized that what I was staring at were veteran needs that had been unmet in the century and a half since they were written. Here, I thought, was a strand of nineteenth-century literature still in search of an audience, and that lack is what I set out to address with this book.

Eventually I would trace my reactions to "Left-Handed Penmanship" all the way back to the founding of the Republic. In the process, I discovered a constellation of veteran authors who struggled against civilian prejudice about their character, against shifting collective memories of nineteenth-century war that removed military experience from the nation's self-definition, and against a variety of headwinds in the unsure development of antebellum print culture. And yet, given all that, the nation's earliest veterans were nonetheless undeterred from demanding that their value as American citizens and authors be recognized. It is a remarkable story of protest and anger but also of beauty and resilience. I have tried to tell that story straight, but let me say up front that any errors or shortcomings are mine and mine alone. Any virtues the reader may find belong to the veteran authors and texts themselves and to those who helped me along the way.

The support of many places and people made this book possible. Early on, the Library of Congress and the Huntington Library provided me a vibrant intellectual space. Later, a Peterson Fellowship at the American Antiquarian Society (AAS) opened up for me the full breadth of nineteenth-century veteran literature. The staff at the AAS are so pleasant, helpful, and learned that one feels spoiled while working with them. Such places refresh one's sense of purpose, and I cannot thank the staff of these libraries enough for their support.

I had two institutional homes while writing. At Washington University in St. Louis, my learning community and support system included Philip Sewell, William Paul, Dan Grausam, Guinn Batten, Daniel Shea, Carter Smith, Brooke Taylor, Chris Boehm, Jian Leng, Wendy Love Anderson, Barb Liebmann, Heidi Kolk, Jennifer Gallinat, Randall Calvert, Angela Miller, Vince Sherry, and Peter Monahan. The Department of English, the Center for the Humanities, and the Program in

American Culture Studies were each and all incredibly generous with
their financial support of my research. Washington University Libraries, and Chris Brady in particular, always kept the books coming.

At Lindenwood University, my good luck with being around smart
and earnest people has continued. I could list the entire faculty of the
School of Humanities, but I want to give particular mention to a group
of colleagues who have welcomed me and who have encouraged this
project in ways large and small: Kyle Glover, Geremy Carnes, Ana
Schnellmann, Travis McMaken, Jill Clements, and Sarah Noonan. I
could not ask for better deans than Mike Whaley and Justine Pas, who
lead with great cheer and endless energy. Money certainly is not endless,
and I thank the Humanities Faculty Scholarship Advisory Committee,
Provost Marilyn Abbott, and President Michael Shonrock for providing
me the resources and the time to be away from the classroom to finish
this book—which is not to say the classroom has not been important.
To all the students who have sat in a room with me, know that I learned
(and continue to learn) more from you than you may realize.

I owe even more thanks to those who read various stages of this
book and reacted to it not only with patience and incisive commentary
but also with the conviction that I was onto something important. Rafia
Zafar taught me both rigor and how to find joy in what I was doing.
Without her time and encouragement, I would not have made it this
far. Gerald Early showed me that sentences should not only make you
think; they should also, by virtue of their elegance, break your heart (he
never said that, but read his sentences and you will see what I mean).
He has set a high yet liberating standard for what academic writing can
be, and I met him at just the right time. Bob Milder and Iver Bernstein
taught me more about the nineteenth century than anyone else has to
date. Randy Ingram never read this manuscript, but he did read plenty
of my middling prose when I was far younger. To him and to all my
teachers at Davidson, you shape me still.

Katherine Mooney stopped by my office one day to say I should talk
to Clark Dougan, then an editor at the University of Massachusetts
Press. Clark was an early enthusiast of this project and a helpful voice
in the process of making it into a book, but he was also set to retire. In
his place, Brian Halley has been a remarkable steward. Brian is all the
good adjectives one can think of—smart, responsive, good-natured,

cogent in his feedback. The entire Press has been as much, and if I had known that everything would have been this pleasant, I would have finished the book long ago. Nancy Raynor and her thoughtful copyedits improved everything you see here. Other sharp people have done their fair share in reviewing the merits of my argument, in particular Kathleen Diffley, James Dawes, Dana D. Nelson, Sandra Gustafson, and Alan Nadel. Thanks also to the hard work of my anonymous peer reviewers.

My parents, Karin and Dan, raised my brother, Matt, and me to love the world and each other as best we could. They sacrificed a lot for us and taught us how to be curious and persistent. As I look back on my childhood in Fairbanks, Alaska, and the entire cast of neighbors, teachers, and friends who cared for me, I feel humbled and fortunate. There are so many others whose presence also lines these pages, including Olimpia, Franco, Clara, Oskar, Amy, Dave, Meredith, Cinzia, and Claudio. Above them all, Erika Conti deserves her due, but I struggle with how. How do you acknowledge the person who makes your life possible? How do you compress all the things you want to say about your partner's generosity, wisdom, and humor into a crowded paragraph whose words already seem inadequate? I do not know, *buddina,* so I will only say this book in many ways is more yours than mine. The same is true for Allegra, who arrived smiling and has not stopped yet. Watching you become yourself has been the greatest joy of my life. Thank you for letting me be your dad.

ABBREVIATIONS

All references to the following texts are cited parenthetically in the text:

ATP   Thomas Painter, *Autobiography of Thomas Painter: Relating His Experiences during the War of the Revolution* ([Washington, DC?]: Printed for private circulation, 1910).

BP   Herman Melville, *Battle-Pieces and Aspects of the War,* ed. Hennig Cohen (New York: T. Yoseloff, 1963).

C   Royall Tyler, *The Contrast: A Comedy in Five Acts,* ed. James Benjamin Wilbur (Boston: Houghton Mifflin, 1920).

D   Henry Adams, *Democracy* (New York: Penguin, 2008).

J   William H. Richardson, *Journal of William H. Richardson: A Private Soldier in the Campaign of New and Old Mexico, under the Command of Colonel Doniphan, of Missouri,* 3rd ed. (New York: Published by William H. Richardson, 1848).

MR   John William De Forest, *Miss Ravenel's Conversion from Secession to Loyalty* (New York: Penguin, 2000).

N   Joseph Plumb Martin, *A Narrative of a Revolutionary Soldier: Some of the Adventures, Dangers, and Sufferings of Joseph Plumb Martin,* intro. Thomas Fleming (New York: Signet, 2001).

PS   Thomas Dring, *Recollections of the* Jersey *Prison-Ship: Taken, and Prepared for Publication, from the Original manuscript of the Late Captain Thomas Dring,* ed. Albert Greene (Providence: H.H. Brown, 1829).

S   James Fenimore Cooper, *The Spy: A Tale of the Neutral Ground,* intro. and notes Wayne Franklin (New York: Penguin, 1997).

VETERAN
AMERICANS

INTRODUCTION

What We Talk about When We Talk about Veteran Americans

"Well, right now," she said, "I'm *not* dead. But when I am, it's like . . . I don't know, I *guess* it's like being inside a book that nobody's reading." "A book?" I said. "An old one. It's up on a library shelf, so you're safe and everything, but the book hasn't been checked out for a long, long time. All you can do is wait. Just hope somebody'll pick it up and start reading."

　—*Tim O'Brien,* The Things They Carried *(1990)*

The story goes that during a diplomatic trip on behalf of the Massachusetts governor to New York City in March 1787, Royall Tyler for the first time saw professional theater. Tyler's experience with the stage jolted a month-long creative frenzy culminating with *The Contrast,* a short five-act play that opened at the John Street Theater in New York City on April 16, 1787. Widely credited as the first dramatic comedy written by an American and performed by professional actors, *The Contrast* was well received by critics and audiences alike. The play's list of private subscribers includes many prominent readers, among them George Washington (two copies of the play were found in Washington's personal library, one of them autographed by Tyler); Aaron Burr, then secretary of war; Henry Knox; as well as a myriad of other Continental Army officers, from captains to majors and colonels.[1] That there were so many military readers of Tyler's first play should come as little surprise. Only a month after the play's initial run, the Constitutional Convention would begin in Philadelphia populated with recent heroes of the Revolution. That the play took as one of its central concerns "the contrast between a gentleman who has read Chesterfield and received the polish of Europe and an unpolished, un-travelled American" soldier is also of little surprise, given Tyler's recent military life (*C* 112).

Only a few months before *The Contrast*'s swift composition and production, the gentlemanly Tyler had joined the army for the second time in his life, on this occasion as a major under General Benjamin Lincoln during Shays' Rebellion.[2] Tyler was at Harvard in 1775 when the Battles of Lexington and Concord took place only a few miles away. After taking his degree in 1776, he joined the Revolutionary Army in Boston under the generalship of John Hancock. At the request of his mother, who already had lost her husband to the war in 1775 and who had another son serving as a spy for Washington, Tyler spent most of the Revolution a safe distance from the front.[3] Regardless of their intensity, Tyler's intermittent experiences as a soldier visibly left their imprint on his play and its "native themes" (*C* 20). Written by a veteran who would come to carry more social capital than most of his fellow veterans, *The Contrast* stands as the first dramatization of the latent anxieties that military experience produced for early Americans. *Veteran Americans* is about how that unease took hold during the early Republic and throughout the nineteenth century, and moreover, how veterans wrote back.

Explaining how American culture has both embraced and marginalized its veterans starting with the nation's founding is one of my ultimate concerns in this book. In its most basic form, ambivalence surrounding veterans during the nineteenth century is tied up in questions of who and what makes an American citizen and who has the authority to write about and remember war (it is also the product of how the nation repeatedly chose to deny military violence and its attendant political crimes— against Native Americans, Mexicans, Filipinos, among others—in its self- definition). My other primary concern here is to chronicle how veteran authors of the early Republic and throughout the nineteenth century challenged, resisted, and protested their cultural and political exclusion in prisoner-of-war narratives, memoirs, magazines, newspapers, novels, and, as the case of *The Contrast* documents, on stage. Within the specific context of the nation's early years, martial experience threatened an inchoate system of American democracy that thrived on discourses of peace, consensus, and solidarity. Such a system could not incorporate the various forms and contents of veteran experience and found a willing accomplice to exclude such in civilian print culture, which was largely protective of these values. As a result, veterans were diminished in early American literature as lazy and shallow, liars and confidence men, criminals all. Beginning with the nation's first "native" drama, we have a problem that has never gone away: the veteran American.

The veteran American is an unresolved identity that is somehow more American (a *veteran* American) at the same time it is always less. That is because the veteran is also a hyphenated identity (a veteran-American), one who, in the words of W. E. B. Du Bois, "ever feels his twoness" and whom our cultural and political institutions have historically marginalized.[4] Apply for a job today and on the "voluntary demographics" page next to race, disability status, and criminal history is a question about veteran status. Each of these categories on its own defines the margins of American citizenship, and while it is possible that employers ask (and the law requires they ask) because they care about diversity and want to help a historically underemployed group, it is also just as possible that governments and businesses identify veterans, racial minorities, and criminals so as to (illegally) discriminate. We screen out veterans as we weed out other political minorities because you can never be too sure about them.

Although most of this book is about the United States before the twentieth century, I take it as a central premise that the intellectual history of nineteenth-century veteran representation and authorship informs the nation's modern relationship with veterans and the military. That is to say, readers should be able to recognize the veteran American in Royall Tyler's play as well as in William Faulkner's *Absalom, Absalom!* or in Kathryn Bigelow's *The Hurt Locker*, because, just as in the nineteenth century, veterans today claim our admiration and sympathy at the same time they incite prejudice, fear, and distrust. Consider the rising rejection rate of Veterans Administration (VA) disability claims or think about the paranoid plotline of Showtime's early seasons of *Homeland* that could never make up its mind whether Nicholas Brody, the decorated Iraq War hero, was a terrorist or a patriot.[5] The veteran American supposedly knows something nonveterans (and also non-Americans) cannot know, something Gnostic, transformative, and

singular that only service can teach. Yet the nation is always on guard
for being tricked by that mysticism. The veteran American is a cultural
trope who is wise at the same time he is untrustworthy, marriage material but also a danger to your daughter. He is hardworking yet lazy, traumatized but quick to make his trauma an excuse—always victim and
villain and hero all at once. *Veteran Americans* is not an explicit exon-
eration of "veterans," nor is it an outright denunciation of "civilians,"
yet it argues that we need to be more precise about the long history
of skeptical vacillation that surrounds military experience. Doing so
causes us to reconsider the putative differences we imagine separate not
only veteran from civilian but also citizen from alien, combatant from
noncombatant, war from peace, and the nineteenth century from today.

Discomfort over veterans was a central feature of *The Contrast,* although
it did have other plotlines. For the audience, the play probably would
have registered first and foremost as an American take on the English
comedy of manners. The crowd quickly comes to learn that the gentleman with European sympathies, "who has read Chesterfield," is Billy
Dimple, a smooth-talking New York dandy. As the curtain opens, Dimple is engaged to be married to Maria Van Rough, a woman from the
same social caste, but one who is having nagging doubts about his character. He is, in her eyes, "a depraved wretch, whose only virtue is a polished exterior; who is actuated by the unmanly ambition of conquering
the defenceless" (*C* 38–39). Subsequently, the audience becomes
acquainted with Henry Manly, the "un-travelled American," whose role
in the play will be to protect and uphold "probity, virtue, [and] honour"
(*C* 114–15). Manly is a taciturn and somewhat melancholic Revolutionary War hero from the countryside. He has never before been to the
city, "never nearer than Harlem Heights, where he lay with his regiment" (*C* 42). The two men could not have been more different.

The Contrast proposes there is a choice to be made in the representation of post-Revolutionary New England and that Dimple and Manly
illustrate competing alternatives. On the one hand was the libertive
Dimple, a con man and a rogue, but a con man and a rogue whom
people liked. He is loved by three women, among them Maria, Charlotte (Manly's sister), and Letitia, the richest of the three and therefore
Dimple's real marital interest. As the scoundrel so succinctly puts it:

"I must break with Maria, marry Letitia, and as for Charlotte—why, Charlotte must be a companion to my wife" (C 66). The play offers an alternative to Dimple in the silent but principled honesty of the veteran Manly. After Dimple is exposed and pilloried in the last act, Maria's affections are cleared for Manly to court and, in the final scene, win. During every stage of the action's development, Tyler's characters and narrative structures clearly telegraph where the audience's sympathies should lie, and so when Maria selects Manly over Dimple, the central tension is resolved and the play may end. She has wisely chosen in Manly something more "American" than his counterpart, Dimple, and presumably, Manly is as much Maria's pick as he is Tyler's and the audience's.

But what precisely does everyone get when we get Manly? The question has occupied much of the play's scholarship, most of which has often focused on the uneasy contradictions Manly posed for post-Revolutionary America as the country was transitioning into a market economy and trying to articulate for itself where its republican principles stood. A hardworking farmer and a loyal patriot, Manly is the "overdetermined signifier of American virtue"; at the same time, both he and his artless virtue are constant objects of satire. Dimple mocks his naivety. His sister mocks his stubbornness. Even some contemporary reviewers mocked the ways in which he spoke (often in soliloquy).[6] As Robert Pressman puts it, "Everything that he says, the audience is intended to approve . . . How, then, are such powerful messages to be reconciled with the ironic distancing of the satire?"[7] What has been overlooked in the critical interpretations of *The Contrast* is that the play's indecision regarding its hero's civic virtues and social value is, in truth, a reflection of a yet larger, and for Tyler more personal, rift between literary representation and martial experience.[8] The primary contrast of the nation's first drama is not between American and British, not between egalitarianism and decadence, not even between rural and modern, but between veteran and civilian. It is the military distinction that hangs over all other tensions in the play.

"Sir, there is no character so respectable as that of a soldier," Dimple exclaims when he first runs into Manly in Act III. The sarcasm fails to land. Instead, Manly gladly internalizes what should have been taken as a backhanded insult. "I declare (it may be my weak side) that I never hear the name of soldier mentioned with respect, but I experience a thrill of pleasure which I never feel on any other occasion" (C 81). The pleasure Manly takes in his military service is of course not real—at the very least, with the war now many years removed, it is not current—but maintaining the mantle of the war-weary veteran locates Manly, if not also Tyler, in a comforting memory of their recent military past. Manly never feels more alive, more American, than when he feels a soldier, and though their fighting days had also just passed, the veterans in Tyler's audience must have sympathized with the sentiment of fading glory. Only five years after the war, they were already creatures of a different age and already feeling the exclusion from the nation's larger political communities that such men as Dimple controlled. War had not compelled the newly formed nation to listen to its veterans when they spoke (in soliloquy or otherwise). Instead, the Revolutionary War had created a discursive difference, one that continues to be felt—these veterans, they aren't like you and me.

They are, like Manly, noble and respectful men of principle (of course), yet at the same time (also like Manly) they elicit our public scorn. *The Contrast* will reward the old veteran with a wife at the end, but not before repeatedly ridiculing him for the audience's amusement. Dimple mocks Manly in the above scene because the war hero is walking down the street in his old soldier's uniform. He does not belong here, Tyler keeps telling us, and, indeed, throughout the play Manly looks out of place and out of joint, not only to his romantic rival but even to his own family. When Manly first arrives in the city in Act II, his sister, Charlotte, begs him to take off his uniform: "brother, positively I can't introduce you in these clothes." The veteran will not listen. "This coat was my regimental coat in the late war . . . I can only say, sister, that there was a time when this coat was respectable, and some people even thought that those men who had endured so many winter campaigns in the service of their country, without bread, clothing, or pay, at least deserved that the poverty of their appearance should not be ridiculed" (C 50). Manly demands undying respect from his sister on the grounds that "there was a time" when his coat represented service and sacrifice. The play seeks to answer whether that time has expired or if it still endures. Manly's regimental coat is a tactile argument for what he sees as the continuity of a true American character: the military garment is as timeless as the national virtues it carries within its folds. The coat goes with anything, anywhere, but Charlotte, who has lived in New York City for some time by now, is quick to refute her brother's attitude. "In the time of war, when we were almost frightened to death, why, your coat was respectable, that is, fashionable; now another kind of coat is fashionable, that is respectable" (*C* 51). Times have changed, she claims, but Manly refuses to incorporate the new fashions of the day. He will wear his soldier's coat for the remainder of the play.

The Contrast divides veterans and civilians in the early Republic. Without fail, what one group said was not what the other heard. Manly performs his character as if the war was still happening, and by so doing, he underscores what has long since been a central problem in the tradition of American war literature: Which speakers control the conversation, and why? Is the war over and Manly no longer a soldier simply because Charlotte and Dimple stop recognizing him as one? Or, by virtue of Manly's military experience, does he (and implicitly Tyler) have a claim to the immediacy and meaning of war that outweighs the protests and social niceties of a people who just want to move on? Which group in the play finally gets the last word (and the final silence) on the Revolutionary War? Who, for that matter, may speak for any war? When is the right time? Scholars have tended to believe that nineteenth-century Americans shied away from these questions altogether during the immediate heat of war, opting instead to relegate the task to later generations.

To wit, Stephen Crane is often credited today as the most notable author of the Civil War for *The Red Badge of Courage,* except his novel was not published until 1895, and Crane was not even alive during the Civil War; in a similar fashion, James Fenimore Cooper took hold of popular memory of the Revolutionary War with *The Spy,* first published in 1821. Following Daniel Aaron's influential *The Unwritten War,* our received wisdom suggests that American war in the eighteenth and nineteenth centuries was often a delayed trigger, "accounted for by . . . the reticence of veterans, the fastidiousness of lady readers, the alleged indifference of the most gifted writers . . . or simply by the general rule that national convulsions do not provide the best conditions for artistic creativeness."[9] If war was central at all to the lives of early Americans, it was only long after the fact, and only then by such civilian artists as Crane and Cooper whom we have come to accept as accomplished and authoritative artists. My purpose here is not to remove Crane or Cooper or anyone else who did not serve in the military from their place in the canon of war literature but rather to point out that despite our pretensions, there actually were early Americans who did serve in the military and who documented their experience and sought to make art of it in print. Manly has been defiantly standing there wearing his uniform waiting to be noticed for more than 200 years.

Veteran Americans privileges the voices and representations of nineteenth-century veterans themselves. From prisoner-of-war narratives and sensational adventure pamphlets to memoirs and novels, military men and women were active members of early print culture. This narrative of veteran production has not been told enough, and while I am careful not to say that early veterans know best, I do want to suggest that they know *something*—specifically in their perpetual critique of the civilian monopoly in defining American citizenship and the ways in which early literary practices helped to facilitate that monopoly—and that these early veteran voices have been neglected in the conversations we have about war and the United States in the nineteenth century.

Contrary to Aaron's claims, early American veterans did not avoid the writing of war. For the civilian players of *The Contrast*, war could not have been further from their minds, yet Manly will not be denied his chance to constantly remind them of it. Here is Manly once again, telling the crowd why he has come from the country to New York in the first place: "I came hither to solicit the honourable Congress, that a number of my brave old soldiers may be put upon the pension-list, who were, at first, not judged to be so materially wounded as to need the public assistance. My sister says true [*to Maria*]: I call my late soldiers my family. Those who were not in the field in the late glorious contest, and those who were, have their respective merits; but, I confess, my old brother-soldiers are dearer to me than the former description. Friendships made in adversity are lasting; our countrymen may forget us, but that is no reason why we should forget one another" (*C* 94). Manly's address underscores a prevailing tension in nineteenth-century veteran literary culture between, on the one hand, wanting to be recognized and reintegrated into American society and, on the other hand, refusing that same desire to conform to civilian notions of citizenship and instead continue the rhetorical fight against the perception of injustice alongside "my old brother-soldiers" who "are dearer to me than" civilian citizens.

Indeed, no full and fair pension system would be established by Congress for Revolutionary War veterans until 1832, almost fifty years after Tyler wrote. The regular United States Army and Navy remained small and largely unfunded organizations until well after the Civil War—a choice as much about a limited budget and weak federal government as it was about what the nation wanted to be. In the period between the early Republic and Reconstruction, many veterans who lacked social capital dwelled in a living tomb, what Caleb Smith calls in his study of the early American prison a kind of "civil death."[10] They were excluded, silenced, and in various ways made unwelcome by the world they oftentimes begrudgingly engaged via print. Like the larger constellation of veteran authors that *Veteran Americans* explores, Manly's martial presence on stage demands from his audience members their acknowledgment of the veteran, his suffering, and his sacrifice. That the audience failed to do so only speaks to the prescience of the play and the larger social and political issues it raises about early American literature and culture.

First and foremost among those issues is the nature of early American citizenship, about which *Veteran Americans* makes two important contributions. First, military service has long carried with it the promise of bestowing citizenship and belonging, especially for traditionally marginalized populations, yet that promise was imperfectly met. This implicit contract has been true throughout the twentieth century (to which I will return), but it was even more alive during the nineteenth century. From Deborah Sampson in the Revolutionary War to Sarah Emma Edmonds in the Civil War, women passed, fought, and capitalized on their celebrity. Paul Foos makes the case throughout *A Short, Offhand, Killing Affair* that immigrants and the working-class poor joined the Mexican War effort in the hopes of making a better life for themselves.[11]

Perhaps the most elegant spokesmen for military citizenship was Frederick Douglass speaking before a crowd of African American recruits in Rochester in 1863: "The chance is now given you to end in a day the bondage of centuries, and to rise in one bound from social degradation to the place of common equality with all other varieties of men . . . Let us win for ourselves the gratitude of our country, and the blessings of our posterity through all time."[12] The disconnect between the allure of early military service and its reality was exacerbated by what I frame as my second intervention dealing specifically with how literature helps manufacture American citizenship. Citizens recognize and inhabit their citizenship in part through the telling of their lives. To be a citizen means you have the right to narrate your own story and to have it heard by others. Moreover, you have the right to be the hero of your own story and to write it as you see fit independent of the pressures and biases of others. None of these privileges were permitted to early American veterans. Citizenship is constructed and maintained through the production and reception of the literary lives of authors who argue for their belonging, and early American veterans were largely unsuccessful in their advocacy. To borrow the words of Vietnam veteran Tim O'Brien (albeit in a different context), the early American veteran became an author without an audience, "inside a book that nobody's reading."[13]

In the chapters that follow, I emphasize early veteran representation but do not defer to it, and there are consequences to such a methodology, especially as that preference disrupts common twentieth- and twenty-first-century assumptions about genre, ethics, and authority in the representation of war. There is a certain irony to Tim O'Brien's line—"inside a book that nobody's reading"—because O'Brien is most definitely read today, as are other contemporary veterans, such as Robert Stone, Karl Marlantes, Brian Turner, Colby Buzzell, and Phil Klay. Today, Americans read veteran literature more than they ever have before, and although today's veterans still struggle for political redress and civilian recognition, they nonetheless have a presence in literary and cultural marketplaces that did not exist for much of American history. We listen to veterans now, even if inadequately, and so I want to make clear that reading veterans may feel like a social practice that has always been with us, but historically it is the exception rather than the rule.

Scholars of the twentieth century, all of them veterans, have made distinctions between literature written by veterans and war literature more broadly speaking (the genre Daniel Aaron had in mind) with the assumption that such distinctions have no connection with the nineteenth century. I argue they do. Gulf War veteran Alex Vernon began his book on Ernest Hemingway, James Salter, and Tim O'Brien by announcing that "the difference between war literature and veteran literature is important, one that is too often overlooked. To study war literature does not necessarily restrict one to texts by veterans, while to study veteran literature means that in addition to fictional and nonfictional accounts of their war, we also study their texts not directly about war."[14] I acknowledge Vernon's distinctions, but I argue they do not go far enough. What I want to underscore here is that this scholarship—like the entire field of what could be considered veteran studies more broadly—has limited itself once again to the twentieth and the twenty-first centuries and as a result missed an opportunity to consider the full history of the American veteran in print.

Princeton literature professor emeritus and World War II and Korea veteran Samuel Hynes began *The Soldiers' Tale* (1997) with World War I and concluded with Vietnam on the grounds that the twentieth century reflects what he thought were still "our wars."[15] Early American soldiers of the Revolutionary, Mexican, and Civil Wars have not been afforded the same designation as "our" concern, and as a result Manly and his cousins have largely remained disenfranchised in the current scholarship that has long assumed veteran literature in the United States somehow miraculously begins with World War I. Yet beginning in the late eighteenth and early nineteenth century, veteran authors developed tropes of representational partition and political estrangement long before the more familiar twentieth-century veteran authors did the same.

Of the modern veteran critics, one of the most prominent is the late Paul Fussell, who as a scholar often argued for the veteran's proprietary ownership of the genre we call "war literature." World War II is prominent in Fussell's work because the war was prominent in his own life. He was a foot soldier in the European theater and makes no qualms in *Thank God for the Atom Bomb* (1988) for basing his critical (and ethical) stance—the atomic bomb was necessary because it ended the war and saved the lives of American soldiers—on the authority of his personal military experience. In a move that could be considered disrespectful and arrogant, his title essay was written on the forty-second anniversary of the bombing of Hiroshima and Nagasaki. In it, Fussell argued for "the importance of experience, sheer, vulgar experience, in influencing, if not determining, one's views about that use of the atom bomb." His critical voice was aggressive, and he refused to listen to civilian dissent from men such as "Michael Sherry," who "was safe at home," or "John Kenneth Galbraith," of whom Fussell writes, "I don't demand that he experience having his ass shot off. I merely note that he didn't."[16]

It has been tempting for critics to recoil at Fussell's chauvinism because he was not alone among veteran critics in claiming the exclusive rights of veteran authority. Vernon declared that "as for my own experiences of war and the military, I sincerely believe that they help me understand these writers and their works on a certain level."[17] J. Glenn Gray remarked in *The Warriors* (1959) that "no outsider has a moral right" to judge the actions of soldiers.[18] Raymond Williams, who served in the British Army during World War II, complained of the impersonal "distance" manufactured by the media coverage of the Falklands War: "I have not heard any talk of that distant calculating kind from friends who had been in actual battles."[19] *Veteran Americans* recasts the grand twentieth-century narratives we have about veterans and military experience—that they are an isolated "band of brothers" who are exceptional, bitter, often drawn from the underclasses of American life yet always capable of "making something of themselves"—as but the latest symptom in a larger turf war that veteran authors have waged since at least the Revolutionary War over who they are and what value their identity carries.

As such an early text as *The Contrast* well illustrates, to talk about the experience of war in the United States has always been a struggle over semantic differences and an argument slanted by the politics of group identity and civic duty. Who, after all, is a veteran? What behaviors and ideologies characterize his power, his personality, and his political status?[20] Since the American Revolution, soldiering has been for the nation a prominent and ongoing site of cultural anxiety for noncombatants.[21] Thomas Jefferson and his coalition of Democrats worried over the possible creation of an aristocratic military class. Their solution was to dilute the soldier's strength by bestowing his title to all able-bodied white males, to in effect limit the soldier's sphere of influence by making military practice a universal expectation of citizenship. As

Jefferson wrote, "I think the truth must now be obvious that our people are too happy at home to enter into regular service, and that we cannot be defended but by making *every citizen a soldier,* as the Greeks and Romans who had no standing armies."[22] Each American war has largely been conceived in the popular mythology as the people's war, from the Revolution to the War on Terror. John Adams would proclaim as early as May 1776, "We must all be soldiers."[23] Following September 11, 2001, commentators were all too willing, albeit for different fears, to align themselves with Jefferson's and Adams's sentiments, declaring as did Peggy Noonan in the *Wall Street Journal* that "we are all soldiers now."[24] Paul Kahn's recent scholarship on post-9/11 terrorism likewise echoes the sentiment of an American state protected by a citizen brigade, "always on call for the sacrificial act."[25] Regardless of the reason, this strand of inclusiveness in our terminology of military service has come at a cost. It is imprecise theoretically and also disregards how the meaning of military service within American culture has shifted over time.

"Being there" in Jefferson's and Adams's republican model meant an active identification of soldiering as fundamental to the operations of citizenship. In this version, military service should be central to the identity of all American citizens, just as it was for Cincinnatus—a model echoed, for example, in both the life of Royall Tyler and in the character of Manly.[26] Cincinnatus (and the society he inspired after the Revolutionary War) finds a strong pattern in American culture because the image of the reluctant soldier who lays down his plow (only to return to it once war is over) represents the veteran in terms that deny his permanence. The veteran should become, as much of *The Contrast* caricaturizes, a transient identity thrust upon a people in a time of need, nothing more than an emergency duty that fades when it is no longer required.

Removed from this militia mindset is the notion that there are actual historical actors who would disagree that military service was only a temporary burden and one that was shared equally when it came. Similar to Jefferson's sense of veteran impermanence, John Casey has more recently argued in *New Men: Reconstructing the Image of the Veteran in Late-Nineteenth-Century American Literature and Culture* that it was not until after the Civil War that military service was regarded as anything other than an "episode in a man's life"; yet *Veteran Americans* disagrees that veterans only awoke during the Civil War and for the first time began thinking about themselves as veterans.[27] As the following chapters will demonstrate, memories of war throughout the nineteenth century lingered for veterans and disappeared for nonveterans—a distinction that could only be possible if a substantial and qualitative difference developed between veterans and nonveterans throughout the nineteenth century over the place of military experience in American life.

Furthermore, Noonan and Kahn's words reflect an alternative model wherein the veteran difference has been imagined away. "Being there" in a liberal conception of citizenship becomes a much more passive affair: "we are all soldiers now" on 9/11 insofar as "we" were all targets, not because every American citizen was expected to enlist. The adjunctification of the modern professional military from civilian life has had many consequences, among them the growing separation of military service from its putative foundational purpose to help form citizens. Today there are "other people" who will do the fighting for us, but never "other citizens." To put it that way would remind the civilian nation of its Jeffersonian failures to act collectively. Moreover, within the narrower context of men and women who identify themselves as veterans, the issue of what counts as military service does not become much clearer.

Only a "true" veteran such as Fussell would claim that "indeed, unless they actually encountered the enemy during the war, most 'soldiers' have very little idea what 'combat' was like. As William Manchester says, 'All who wore uniforms are called veterans, but more than 90 percent of them are as uninformed about the killing zones as those on the home front.'"[28] The supposed ontological distinction produced by combat and "the killing zones" distinguishes green "veterans" (as well as noncombatants) from bona fide soldiers. For Fussell, among others, the twentieth-century imagination of military experience was too broad. Were some who were there not really there? Citing Lloyd B. Lewis's study of Vietnam nonfiction narratives, *The Tainted War* (1985), Vernon noted that "by excluding texts written by anyone above company grade (lieutenants and captains), by sailors and airmen, and by soldiers in support roles who did not see combat, it attends to 'less than 5 percent of all the GIs connected with the tragedy of Vietnam.'"[29] This stratification of soldier communities and what "being there" actually signifies likewise posed a problem for veteran authors throughout the nineteenth century. At issue in the territoriality of these veteran debates are the very criteria by which we measure American citizenship—who belongs and who is excluded? What behaviors, identities, and experiences are rewarded and which are left out? How, finally, do veteran Americans affect the ways in which the people of the United States relate to one another, to their armed forces, and also to their enemies abroad (and within) who are the casualties of American war?

Different voices have different answers to these questions, and it should be noted that in the early years of the Republic there was no coordinated set of answers from veteran writers. *Veteran Americans* shows that "veteran literature" is a specific literary and cultural tradition but not a deliberate one—even though there is almost always in early veteran texts an awareness of a veteran past, a sense of veteran neighbors in the present, and a fear of what will come for veterans in the future. Ultimately, veteran literature is not an impenetrable category, nor is it blessed with an ontological distinction that renders it impossible for the nonveteran mind to understand. But it often imagines itself to be both, and that self-awareness deserves serious study. *Veteran Americans* interrogates the body of early and nineteenth-century American veteran literature through the lens of the oftentimes contradictory isolationist terms it sets for itself, and while veterans surely have a strong interest in how they choose to represent themselves (more often as victim than as perpetrator), I do not see how their self-interest prevents us from thinking critically about the cultural and political problems they raise.

My critical posture is the same courtesy we afford Native American literature, women's literature, and numerous other categories of literature that have been forged through the bonds of group identity and common experience. When we talk about African American literature, for instance, what we are really talking about is the creative work written by and subsequently about African Americans, albeit with some arguable exceptions, such as Harriet Beecher Stowe and William Styron. Inevitably, war experience falls into a familiar trap in defining what exactly it encompasses. One could imagine that a woman refugee noncombatant subject to numerous rapes and displacements would have much more to say about war than a career infantryman who was never in a live theater. The earliest of American veteran writing was acutely sensitive to the unsure dynamics of what "counted" as war experience and veteran identity. Such twentieth-century veterans as Fussell fetishized combat as the sole determinant, but the nation's earliest veterans emphasized their invisible suffering and political isolation rather than killing. To paraphrase Drew Gilpin Faust, the cultural work of the nineteenth-century soldier was not to kill but rather to strive, suffer, and die, often anonymously, and almost always for a nation like Manly's that quickly wanted to move on.[30]

Like many sentences in this book, that last sentence may come off as accusatory. The nation quickly moves on, I claim, but implicitly my argument will not. There is more than a suggestion there of moral superiority, that I get it but other critics and readers have not, and so let me admit the tonal risks involved in coming off as the voice of incessant critique. The particular methodological challenge of *Veteran Americans* resides in its overlapping nests of skepticism and distrust—terms that not only describe the dynamic between civilian and veteran but also, potentially, between this book and its audience. The United States of America today is a nation that does not require its citizens to serve in the military. Less than 1 percent of its citizens choose to do so at any given time, and that population is not necessarily picking up this book.[31] More likely, I am writing to the civilian 99 percent of which I am myself a member. I am not a veteran. Given my age and station, I probably will never become one. Instead, I am a part of the civilian structure of bad faith that I often critique and from which I cannot escape. If at times the reader feels resistance to my prose when the temperature of my analysis is rising, I can only say that such heat is itself a product of *my own resistance* to thinking about the nation's default civilian settings whose privileges I enjoy every day. *Veteran Americans* is about veteran literary culture in the United States from the Revolution to Reconstruction, but it is also necessarily about the historically ingrained prejudices of American civilian society because it was written through them and it will likely be read through them.

The first chapter, "Revolutionary Captivity," explores the origins of veteran detachment in Revolutionary prisoner-of-war narratives.

Captivity narrative scholarship of the eighteenth and nineteenth centuries has assumed that literary tropes of captivity have always worked to transform Anglo captives such as Mary Rowlandson into enlightened political subjects. When scholars have written about Revolutionary prisoner-of-war narratives at all, they have quietly subsumed military captivity within larger narratives of sympathy and war propaganda. Yet prisoner-of-war narratives written by Ethan Allen and Thomas Dring (among others) deserve to be read somewhat apart from this established tradition of Anglo captivity narratives. Contrary to our nationalist expectations that military imprisonment makes captives resilient and somehow more American rather than less, Revolutionary captivity narratives reveal the veteran captive's ultimate foreclosure from psychological and political freedom. Veteran representations of their own military captivity do not celebrate their isolation but rather worry over how their experience will affect their political standing once the war is over. Ultimately, I argue that the early association with political imprisonment worked not to discipline veterans into coherent American citizens but instead separated them from the larger political communities burgeoning during the first decades of the nineteenth century. Even veterans who were never imprisoned increasingly became involved in a print system that represented veterans as yet another identity on the margins of American citizenship—alongside slaves, prodigal sons, confidence men, and wayward criminals.

The subsequent failure in Jacksonian America to trust, let alone read, veteran representation organizes the second chapter, "Civilian Memories and Veteran Memoir," about how veteran memoir beginning in the 1820s engaged with overlapping and conflicting generational memories of the Republic's founding. Veteran authors contested the civilian memories of the Revolutionary War, represented in James Fenimore Cooper's novel *The Spy* (1821), which memorialized the war as a narrative of spies and martyrs—most notably in the figure of John André, the British attaché executed for his complicity in Benedict Arnold's treason. By representing veterans as disloyal spies and confidence men rather than as suffering victims, *The Spy* (alongside other literary and cultural texts) worked to erase "regulars" from the collective memory of American war and, subsequently, from the shade of early American citizenship. Revolutionary veterans began publishing their war memoirs only in the late 1820s in response to these shifting memories of the Revolutionary War that privileged either the exemplary hero or the shared sacrifice of "the people." There was little rhetorical room for the regular Continental soldier to stake his claim.

Still, some fought to correct the record. Aging Revolutionary veteran Joseph Plumb Martin published his *Narrative* in 1830 after repeated applications for a federal pension were denied. Martin's memoir inaugurates a moment in American life writing dating from the 1820s through the Mexican War that forges a kind of veteran appeal, a genre of voices that I argue is an understudied literary archive of veteran political protest and dissent. Not only did such first-generation veterans as Martin have to contend with the repeated rebukes of their aging Revolutionary generation, but they also were at odds with a new generation of peacetime veterans such as Edgar Allan Poe (and later Mexican War "volunteer" veterans) with whom they shared little sense of a common history.

Soldiers for most of the nineteenth century were located on the frontier where they skirmished with Native Americans and conducted imperialistic campaigns such as the Mexican War. The geography of their deployment affected the nature of their literary production, which became less about public protest and more about private experimentation. Having not inherited a coherent identity and civic presence from the earlier Revolutionary generation, veterans during this time period were more adrift than they had ever been before. By analyzing archival material that includes military newspapers, inexpensive periodicals and pamphlets, and other ephemera, in the third chapter, "A Bunch of Veteran Amateurs," I argue that frustrated veterans had their voice vanquished in the decades leading up to the Civil War. Veteran literature became temporary and disposable, an amateur activity unfit for national consumption and unconfident in securing political redress.

American writers, such as Herman Melville, subsequently exploited veteran experience by ventriloquizing and writing over that experience, which interfered in the already fragile process of reintegration. A crucial example of this dispossession is Israel Potter, who was a survivor of Bunker Hill and eventually ended up a tramp in London. His begging continued in his self-authored 1824 memoir, but his plight was not truly legible until Melville refashioned his veteran voice in *Israel Potter* (1855), a novel of limited commercial success yet still a text that represents how little in control veterans were of their stories at mid-century. Melville would continue his appropriation of veterans in *The Confidence-Man* and, during the Civil War, *Battle-Pieces and Aspects of the War*. This chapter ultimately concludes that Melville was symptomatic of the nation's paradoxical fascination with and fear over the role of veterans as the amateurs of American life. Military experience was subsequently distorted and romanticized, and as a result, veteran voices were mostly obscured in much of the print culture of the time. Such an absence would prove impossible in light of the Civil War and its unprecedented number of citizens who were turned veteran.

In the final chapter, "The Real and Written War," I recognize the myriad soldier authors who wrote about the Civil War as it was happening and immediately after. Only months after Appomattox, *Harper's Weekly* held an essay-writing contest for disabled veterans of the recent war. The contest was a great success, but none of the entries were ever published. This suppression serves as the capstone to the nineteenth century by asking how veterans came once again to be discounted even after the most traumatic war of the century. A more visible veteran author, John William De Forest, wrote while still in the service what would become the 1867 novel *Miss Ravenel's Conversion from Secession to Loyalty*. Readers likewise did not read him, and I attribute his anonymity to the fact that De Forest wrote the fragmented and disillusioned war experience he knew, not the national memory others quickly condensed, bought, and sold in the popular romantic fiction of national reconciliation. At this point, the argument expands its critique to implicate "professional" officers, writers, and contemporary critics in the suppression of veteran voice—for example, Daniel Aaron remembers Ulysses S. Grant's *Memoirs* in *The Unwritten War*, but not the thousands of combatant narratives published in *Harper's*, *Atlantic Monthly*, *Century*, and *Galaxy*. Furthermore, De Forest's emotionally detached gaze at battlefield gore, I conclude, is a more significant factor than we usually acknowledge in the subsequent rise of American realism. How one acquires authority at the end of the nineteenth century to write "realistically" about war frames the conclusion, in which *Veteran Americans* opens up the stakes of what early and nineteenth-century veteran writing could mean to American literature and war writing in the twentieth century.

The conclusion, "Veterans in Outer Space," offers an alternate strain of veteran representation that privileges fantasy and science fiction rather than verisimilitude. Through the lens of Henry Adams's 1885 political novel, *Democracy*, I argue that civilian realism emerges at the end of the nineteenth century as a cover-up for the failures of Reconstruction-era America to defer to veteran experience and expression. Increasingly throughout the twentieth century, veteran literature became more and more synonymous with combat literature, a genre that audiences were supposed to recognize by its claims to authenticity, yet I position realism—as it came to be practiced by figures such as William Dean Howells and Henry James—as a literary strategy of denial rather than of earnest sympathy. As a result, veteran authors of the twentieth century, such as Edgar Rice Burroughs, Richard Heinlein, and Joe Haldeman, rejected realism in favor of science fiction and outer space, contexts that operate for veteran authors as alternate sites to their lived military experience. Veterans in outer space are not fantasizing or daydreaming but rather subverting yet another civilian appropriation of their lived military experience.

The scope outlined here is ambitious but also limited. For all that *Veteran Americans* includes, it also leaves out prolonged discussions of gender and race. Each appears (albeit briefly, as earlier in this very introduction), and yet the scant treatment is a result less of indifference than of the belief that how race and gender affect veteran literary culture are separate books unto themselves. Indeed, each construct often has been taken separately in scholarship that challenges the white male monopoly of war. In the early 1990s, Lynne Hanley protested the aura of definitiveness the public had placed on someone such as Paul Fussell after his influential *The Great War and Modern Memory* (1975) was published.

Hanley's critical objection was that all Fussell's literary examples were written by white British soldiers: "None [of the reviewers] challenged Fussell's omission of all literature by women and civilians, none challenged his assumption that war literature is written by and about soldiers at the front." Her argument assumed, not without merit, that since war is such a convoluted phenomenon, affecting not only the home front but also future generations in untold ways, it could not possibly be narrated on the shoulders of soldiers alone. "Without, I believe, a single conscious thought on the matter, Fussell and the critics and anthologists he draws on stake out a territory for war literature that excludes every account but that of the literate, British or American soldier. The locale of war literature is the front, the battlefield. The author of war literature has to have been there. If we accept this definition, there is little we can do but choose among the stories of soldiers."[32] The objections Hanley raises are understandable, as are similar objections from others, yet these complaints are in truth about more than Fussell and the implicit patriarchy in his choices.[33] They are really larger objections about the nature and organization of the war canon (objections that *Veteran Americans* shares), about what texts get read and the reasons for how and why they should be read at the expense of others. They are also not books that are explicitly interested in women who claim a veteran identity and who turn to authorship as a way to negotiate their undefined status as American citizens.

That is not to say there were not such women veterans who did. Sarah Rosetta Wakeman enlisted as a private in the 153rd New York State Volunteers for a period of two years during the Civil War until she died from disease in June 1864.[34] Passing by the male sobriquet of Lyons Wakeman, Sarah was rhetorically careful in letters to her family. "I like to be a soldier very well," she asserts in December 1862. Similarly in September 1863, "I am well and enjoy myself first rate for a soldier." As was true for many male veterans, her profession of veteran identity coincides with the articulation of her innate literacy and capacity for self-representation: "Father, you needn't be a feard to write any[thing] private to me for I can read all you can write. I suppose you thought that I would have to get Somebody to read it for me but I read it all my self."[35] Wakeman's indignation at her father's sexism, her frustration at not being taken seriously both as a soldier and as a reader, echoes the resentment and annoyance of many veteran voices that appear throughout this book.

As was also true of many male veterans, Wakeman feels separated from the civilian world she left. "I don't care anything about Coming home for I [am] aShamed to Come, and I sometimes think that I never will go home in the world. I have enjoyed my self the best since I have been gone away from home than I ever did before in my life. I have had plenty of money to spend and a good time asoldier[ing]. I find just as good friends among Strangers as I do at home."[36] The point should be made again: in voicing protest (against her father and authority) and alienation (feeling she can never go home again), Private Wakeman's writings do not differ substantively from those of her male counterparts. From the position of my argument, gender works to accentuate and intensify the perennial crises of confidence and citizenship that are the main (not necessarily the male) subjects of this book.

Take, for instance, an experience such as military captivity that suggests more similarity than difference between men and women: "Over to Carroll Prison they have got three women that is Confined in their Rooms. One of them was a Major in the union army and she went into battle with her men. When the Rebels bullets was acoming like a hail storm she rode her horse and gave orders to the men. Now She is in Prison for not doing aCcordingly to the regulation of war."[37] Shirley Samuels has argued that "as war provokes risks, it also releases women [such as this female major] from ordinary social roles," which rings as a true statement in need of complication.[38] In Wakeman's appraisal, the female soldier is exemplary in her valor but also remarkable for her transgression in commanding male subordinates. The woman major may be "released" from her gender roles, but at the same time that she experiences something like freedom and gender equality, she also experiences captivity and inequality. She remains in jail because, like the male Revolutionary captives of chapter 1, she is an undesirable and undisciplined subject in need of reform. So are the other women soldiers who have been unmasked: "The other two is rebel Spies and they have Catch them and Put them in Prison. They are Smart looking women and [have] good education."[39] Wakeman had a good education as well, but there was no writing your way out of being caught. The constant threat compelled her to masquerade always as a man, and such anxieties of being exposed are reflected not only in prisoner-of-war narratives but also in the civilian fiction of chapters 2 and 3.

Indeed, most women veterans of the early Republic were forced to pass as male—in actual military service but also in print (Wakeman's private letters were not published during her lifetime). Again and again throughout antebellum America, civilian male authors cross-dressed as well as co-opted female veteran representation.[40] *The Female Soldier, or the Surprising Life and Adventures of Hannah Snell* (London, 1750) narrates the exploits of the cross-dressing sailor (Snell) but in the third person. That is, her military experience was "Printed for, and Sold by R[ichard] Walker," a man, as well as authenticated by the mayor of London, another man. The memoirs of Deborah Sampson, perhaps the most famous woman veteran of the Revolutionary War, who also passed as male, were penned and authorized not by Sampson but by her aptly named protector, Herman Mann. In his play *She Would Be a Soldier,* Mordecai Manuel Noah imagined a cross-dressing woman running to the front lines of the War of 1812 not out of patriotism but as a way to escape an undesirable suitor.[41] The romantic plotline might not seem very "manly," yet the male veteran voices found in the following chapters would recognize a similar struggle in the rhetorical constraints of a text such as *She Would Be a Soldier.*

Women and their military experience were spoken for by men in the early Republic similarly to how veterans, regardless of gender, were spoken for by skeptical civilians. Such a dynamic presents itself in sharp relief in a representative text such as *She Would Be a Soldier,* for example during one revealing scene that intersects gender with race. Two white prisoners, Pendragon and La Role, have disguised themselves as Native Americans so convincingly that their captor, Lenox, believes them to be Native Americans in fact. His conviction offends Pendragon. "Why what the devil, sir, do you take us for Choctaws? Can't you tell a man of fashion in masquerade?" That question might as well be asked of the play's audience and its ability to discern the supposed essence of a military man—or is it woman? White or Native American? "Who and what are you?" Lenox demands in reply. Is the person before him truly "the *honorable* Captain Pendragon, and taken prisoner fighting in the ranks with the Indians, and in disguise? A man of rank and fashion, and a soldier, changing his complexion, his nature and his character— herding with savages—infuriating their horrid passions, and whetting their knives and tomahawks against their defenceless prisoners? Impossible!"[42] The civilian nervousness over gender and race in early veteran literary culture are indices of a more fundamental unease surrounding veteran character more broadly—whether it be temporary or permanent, incoherent or stable, desirable or decrepit; here, only the clothing is different. Put another way, early veteran texts that are explicitly gendered or racially marked ask questions that all early veteran literature engage. "Who and what are you?" gets asked not in opposition to the largely white male voices in this book but in concert with them.[43]

Who and what am I? In the extensive scholarship that has been written about African Americans in the military, the principal way to read black veterans' response has been "a citizen and a man." Jennifer James opens *A Freedom Bought with Blood: African American Literature from the Civil War to World War II* with the scene of Crispus Attucks's death at the start of the Revolutionary War. Attucks fought because he "imagined himself as a citizen," and moreover, his martyrdom was "a definitive argument for black citizenship rights."[44] James joins other critics who have long argued that enslaved black men imagined citizenship to be the reward of military violence. As Bernard C. Nalty notes in *Strength for the Fight: A History of Black Americans in the Military,* slaves were enlisted into colonial militias as early as 1703 to fight against hostile Native Americans. If a slave killed or took a Native American prisoner, "and could produce a white person who had witnessed the deed," that slave would be granted freedom. Even before Attucks then, there was precedence "linking manumission to battlefield heroism," which meant that enslaved people were incentivized to fight for their freedom (others such as Denmark Vesey and Nat Turner took violence out of a military context and into their own hands).[45] No one seems to disagree that African Americans fought out of "principle," namely, to secure their "liberty."[46] Such has been the perspective of contemporary and nineteenth-century Americans alike.[47]

Attention has often been paid as well to how military service for African Americans promised not only citizenship but also manhood (a surrogate for whiteness). Thomas Wentworth Higginson, the white colonel of the all-black 1st South Carolina Volunteers during the Civil War, documented in *Army Life in a Black Regiment* how the putative savagery of the black race melted away before white eyes. "Camp-life was a wonderfully strange sensation to almost all volunteer officers, and mine lay among eight hundred men suddenly transformed from slaves into soldiers, and representing a race affectionate, enthusiastic, grotesque, and dramatic beyond all others." Repeatedly, Higginson seems shocked that "they seem the world's perpetual children, docile, gay, and lovable, in the midst of this war for freedom on which they have intelligently entered."[48] Higginson's paternalism is off-putting, but it is appears to be sincere. Civil War African American veterans themselves often represented themselves similarly as having been rehabilitated and "made a man" in the army because, as James argues, doing so allowed them to believe in their social mobility. William Cooper Nell wrote *The Colored Patriots of the American Revolution* (1855, with introductory notes from prominent abolitionists Harriet Beecher Stowe and Wendell Phillips) so as to fabricate a political "passport . . . the proper 'papers' allowing black Americans *entry* into a nation they have nonetheless occupied since its beginnings."[49] Inherent in this consensus view is the widespread belief in the military as a promise that delivers to make (in this case, black) boys into American men, and citizens at that. While that may have been true for some, the opposite has been true for many of the veteran voices that *Veteran Americans* leaves out.

I will end with two such voices. William Apess, a Pequot, before becoming an advocate for Native American rights and an ordained Methodist minister, joined a New York militia while a teenager to escape his indentured master who was abusing him. He enlisted as a musician but was soon impressed into the regular ranks as the War of 1812 ramped up. Apess felt conned in the beginning of his military service, just as he felt tricked at the end over unpaid wages.

> As soon as it was known that the war had terminated, and the army disbanded, the soldiers were clamorous for their discharge, but it was concluded to retain our company in the service—I, however, obtained my release. Now, according to the act of enlistment, I was entitled to forty dollars bounty money and one hundred and sixty acres of land. The government also owed me fifteen months' pay. I have not seen anything of bounty money, land, or arrearages, from that day to this. I am not, however, alone in this—hundreds were served in the same manner. But I could never think that the government acted right toward the "*Natives*," not merely in refusing to pay us but in claiming our services in cases of perilous emergency, and still deny us the right of citizenship; and as long as our nation is debarred the privilege of voting for civil officers, I shall believe that the government has no claim on our services.[50]

Race condenses the veteran question. As a Native American veteran, Apess confronts what the prisoners of war, veteran memoirists, ama-

teur writers, and penmanship contestants of chapters 1, 2, 3, and 4 are
also confronting (albeit not through the lens of race), that the "the government" has continued to "still deny us the right of citizenship" in refusing to recognize veteran service and make reparations—be it for "the
'*Natives*,'" poor whites, or African Americans.

Apess's memoir challenges the very optimism of the promise which
military service purports to hold, as does the memoir of Susie King
Taylor, an African American woman who served alongside Higginson's
regiment as a nurse. At the end of her 1902 memoir, King looks back at
how the Civil War did not improve the lives of African Americans, even
though nearly 200,000 of them had served. The black veteran's assur-
ances of manhood and citizenship met the reality of Jim Crow America:
"In this 'land of the free' we are burned, tortured, and denied a fair trial,
murdered for any imaginary wrong conceived in the brain of the negro-
hating white man. There is no redress for us from a government which
promised to protect all under its flag."[51] Social mobility and political
progress were fantasies for Apess and King, and race works to unmask
what I think the other voices in this book also reveal. To be a veteran
American from Revolution to Reconstruction was to be mired in a
political and literary system of unrelenting displacement and deferral,
to be condemned to what Paul Fussell diagnosed as the abject condition
of the veteran of World War I, who always carried with him that weary
feeling of a "hope abridged."[52] What follows is the story writ large of
early veteran hope and its expressed disappointment in the literature of
the United States.

CHAPTER 1

Revolutionary Captivity

1776–1820: Mary Rowlandson, Ethan Allen,
Lemuel Roberts, Thomas Dring

Of the war I did partake;
With anxious care, and hardships there;
My nature I did break.

Full eight long years, I served there,
My country to defend;
Now I'm forsook, my nature broke,
May all appear, my friend.

   —Benjamin Fowler, "The Lamentation of Poor Benjamin Fowler, Who
   Served Faithfully in the American Army . . ." (ca. 1783–1800)

To my knowledge, no work of scholarship has tried to take Revolutionary prisoner-of-war texts as a significant ripple in the captivity genre, nor has scholarship recognized the troubled voices within these texts that reflect the early American veteran's foreclosure from social and political life—no Revolutionary War literary history, no work on early American autobiography, no study of captivity narratives.[1] It is the Revolutionary captive's perceived status as a political prisoner that is the tale I tell here, because that part of the story has not yet been told. The captivity narrative during the Revolutionary War was a nationalistic form, yet many veteran captives did not feel part of an emergent nation even as they wrote in the genre. A public skeptical of veteran complaints made matters worse; moreover, many veterans often suffered the traumatic return of their own injurious memory that writing about military captivity after the fact so often solicited.

This incredible civil-military strain has yet to find traction in early and nineteenth-century literary studies, which is remarkable given that twentieth-century American literature addressed such drift quite frequently. To this absence, Revolutionary prisoner-of-war narratives represent what could be called the first gasps of an American veteran literature. Furthermore, these veteran narratives recalibrated the dynamics of North American captivity, which up until the Revolution typically had involved a member of the majority in power (a white woman, such as Mary Rowlandson) being taken by powerless members on the outside (such as a displaced Native American tribe). American prisoners of war discovered that they were the powerless outsiders, and moreover, they soon came to realize that no one was coming to repatriate them despite their narrative protest.

Between its initial publication in 1682 and the years leading up to the American Revolution, Mary Rowlandson's captivity narrative was reissued only once, in 1720. It was republished three times in 1770, once again in 1771, and twice more in 1773. What was it about the captivity narrative, and this one in particular, that resonated with a people about to wage the Revolutionary War? Critics who have taken note of the resurgence have attributed Rowlandson's wartime popularity to the resonances between her kidnapping and that of colonial North America. Revolutionary readers returned to the Native American captivity narrative because they could easily identify in Rowlandson a captivity analogous to their own. Greg Sieminski has pointed out that in 1770, when Rowlandson first reappeared in circulation, the city of Boston had already been occupied by the British for two years.[2] Political subjection exacerbated the colonists' growing *rage militaire*, reaching its boiling point in the Boston Massacre in March the same year. Rowlandson became a patriot, so to speak, on the title page to the 1773 edition published in Boston by John Boyle with a rifle, defending her homestead from an approaching horde of white-faced British invaders.[3] The short answer to why captivity narratives became popular during the Revolutionary War was because the captivity trope was good for American nationalism—just take out Wampanoag Indians and insert General Thomas Gage.

A

NARRATIVE

OF THE

CAPTIVITY, SUFFERINGS AND REMOVES

OF

Mrs. *Mary Rowlandson,*

Who was taken Prifoner by the INDIANS with feveral others,
and treated in the moft barbarous and cruel Manner by thofe
vile Savages : With many other remarkable Events during her
TRAVELS.

Written by her own Hand, for her private Ufe, and now made
public at the earneft Defire of fome Friends, and for the Benefit of the afflicted.

BOSTON:

Printed and Sold at JOHN BOYLE's Printing-Office, next Door
to the *Three Doves* in Marlborough-Street. 1773.

1773

FIGURE 1. Mary Rowlandson, *A Narrative of the Captivity, Sufferings and Removes of Mrs. Mary Rowlandson.* Courtesy, American Antiquarian Society.

The nation-building possibilities of this villain substitution from Native American to British were enticing. In a letter to his longtime friend and member of Parliament David Hartley from 1780, Benjamin Franklin disclosed a recent "order of congress" instructing him to publish a "schoolbook" of British cruelties in taking Americans captive "and to have thirty-five prints designed here [in Paris] by good artists and engraved, each expressing one or more of the different horrid facts, to be inserted in the book, in order to impress the minds of children and posterity with a deep sense of your bloody and insatiable malice and wickedness."[4] That children's book never materialized, but its congressional motivation was the same as the martialization of Rowlandson in 1773. The war captive on the Revolutionary page—be she historical, such as Rowlandson, or contemporary such as the multitude of prisoners-of-war whom Franklin worked to liberate from British prisons during the war—was more abstraction than actual person, a faceless rhetorical instrument by which the developing nation might imagine itself as victim to, while also different from, British depravity. No matter that cruelty toward prisoners went both ways in actual fact during the war, each textual remembrance of past and present Revolutionary captivity worked to help wartime colonial readers rationalize their real acts of violence against the British. Such claims about captive texts and impressionable readers have usually been made because they coincide with larger critical investments related to sympathy in early American literature.[5]

According to this consensus in the scholarship, Revolutionary prisoner-of-war narratives operated the same as Native American captivity narratives. Rowlandson and Franklin were separated by time but not ideology in their joint assault on tyranny and depravity. Robert Denn has more or less subsumed the two genres, arguing that prisoner-of-war narratives were a logical and popular subset of the Native American captivity narrative because both forms worked within a fairly overt system of propaganda that confirmed the "image of the American . . . in simple, homely virtues—loyalty, perseverance and honesty."[6] This critical conflation is understandable because soldiers, sailors, and their editors were clearly aware of their close collaboration with the established tradition of Native American captivity narratives.

Soldier Nathaniel Segar's publisher made the connection explicit in 1825, claiming "Mr. Segar's case is the more memorable as being the last, and marking, as a distinct monument, the termination of that long line of barbarities which commenced at the memorable era of Philip's war."[7] Well before Segar, the *Narrative of Colonel Ethan Allen's Captivity* (1779) was the first and, along with another anti-British invective, the *Narrative of John Dodge* (1779), the most widely read prisoner-of-war narrative of the late eighteenth century, going through eight printings before the Revolutionary War was over.[8] Dodge's editor from the second edition published in 1780 announced his politics quite clearly: "The Narrative of John Dodge is one of the records of frontier life during the period of the American Revolution that displays the intense feeling of hatred and unfairness evinced by the British soldiers to the American rebels."[9] While one of my primary objectives here will be to articulate the important differences within the mélange of Revolutionary-era captivity narratives and what those differences reveal about civil-military relations and the struggles of early American veterans, let me not deny at the outset the significant similarities in how the most popular of these texts circulated.

Rowlandson and Dodge in particular were successful with a segment of the Revolutionary audience because both repressed American complicity in atrocity. Whig readers responded to these texts because they focused on British violence and, as a result, did not focus on the violence that American forces waged on their British counterparts and Native Americans. Narratives such as Dodge's and Rowlandson's therefore appealed to liberal readers because such narratives manufactured difference between themselves and the British while also erasing American racism and imperialism against Native Americans. Before being taken captive in 1775, Dodge lived and traded peacefully with Native Americans "half way between Pittsburgh and Detroit," but then the British army began to offer "the Indians twenty dollars a [rebel] scalp, by which means they induced the Savages to make the poor inhabitants, who they had torn from their peaceable homes, carry their baggage until within a short distance of [Fort Detroit], where in cold blood, they murdered them, and delivered their green scalps in a few hours after to those British Barbarians, who on the shrill yell of the Savages, flew to meet and hug them to their breasts reeking with the blood of innocence, and shewed them every mark of joy and approbation, by firing of cannon & c."[10] Native Americans in Revolutionary captivity narratives had "the blood of innocence" on their hands as they had in earlier texts, although for Dodge, the Revolutionary Indian was less a savage than he was the regrettable dupe of "British Barbarians." The grotesqueness of this alliance became the warrant for Dodge's dismay and confirmed for him the justness of the cause for American independence. Dodge and his country were victims, never perpetrators, and indeed one would be hard pressed to find any explicit trace of guilt or remorse in Dodge's captivity narrative for his actions. Instead, he and several other Revolutionary captives vilified the British axis of evil in order to help discriminate a separate and (they hoped) coherent political identity for their colonist North American audiences that was underwritten by the moral clarity of American liberalism.

Up to this point, I have tried to outline the usual ways literary historians have understood how captivity narratives during the Revolutionary era were produced and consumed as Whiggish propaganda. Such interpretations are useful but ultimately incomplete because they neglect the larger archive of Revolutionary captivity narratives written by American soldiers and sailors, many of whom did not hide behind Dodge's mask of American exceptionalism but rather struggled with the political emergencies produced by their various states of captivity. The Revolutionary War marks the first time when North American captives were detained under the prospects of liberal democracy, and a new identity—the American veteran—began to emerge in print. While no one would deny that Rowlandson suffered greatly while a captive during King Philip's War, as did Dodge during the Revolutionary War, was Rowlandson a soldier? She was abducted at home. Was Dodge? He was a trader on the frontier. Would either have imagined themselves to be an American veteran?

These days the United States seems to care very much about who lays claim to military identity. Congressional actions such as the Stolen Valor Act of 2005 reflect how post-9/11 civil society considers the impersonation of military service so disrespectful as to be unlawful; that act (subsequently overturned in 2012) presumed American veterans undergo an experience so insular and sacred that nonparticipants have no right to speak to it. The usual focus on the nonveteran likes of Rowlandson and Dodge as the authorities of Revolutionary captivity suggests that a sense of separation between civil and military life did not exist for the early Republic and its readers. If, in fact, one were to end the story of Revolutionary-era captivity narratives with Rowlandson and Dodge, one would have the impression that civil-military relations were uncomplicated and that veteran voices (that is, people who were aware of themselves as having undergone a military experience that others had not) did not exist in early national print culture. Yet neither assumption is true.

Early American veterans and their citizenship have always been belated concerns, mostly because both have usually been seen through civilian eyes that tend to remember the Revolutionary War often as "the people's war." Not only is "the people's war" an incomplete if not outright inaccurate record of how American warfare has been distributed among the population of the United States, but, more important, this collective memory disregards the long-standing exclusion of the soldier, sailor, marine, and airman from the public sphere. This compartmentalization has been noted by contemporary military historians such as Jeremy Black, who more recently argued that the professionalization of the modern military has relegated the armed forces "an adjunct of society," and by political scientists such as Samuel P. Huntington in *The Soldier and the State* (1957).[11] Scholarship aside, anyone who has clapped for the troops at a baseball stadium or after an airplane lands only then to turn to the game or busily disembark has felt, on some level, the petty citizenship I am describing here (and which the Stolen Valor Act made into law).

To borrow Lauren Berlant's sentiments from a different context, these condescending civilian "moments of oppressive optimism in normal national culture" have an affective history that begins with the textual lives of Revolutionary captives.[12] Captivity ultimately empowers Rowlandson and Dodge—she rediscovers her faith, and his hatred for the British becomes entrenched. Yet the Revolutionary captives whom I consider here were embittered and enfeebled by their ordeals, not empowered. At the same time that these earliest of veteran American voices imagined themselves to be the victims of British cruelty, they also lamented the ways in which they and their fellow veterans became the scapegoats to an inchoate and exclusionary system of civilian citizenship that was predicated in part on the sequestration of military experience from public life.

* * *

An untold number of soldiers and sailors were detained in one way or another during the Revolutionary War because the fragmentary nature of military records and reports makes it impossible to come to a final reliable number.[13] Ethan Allen supposes some 11,000 prisoners died, while various other sources estimate 11,000 died on board the prison ship *Jersey* alone. Historians since have put the number closer to 18,000 Americans captured by the British between 1775 and 1783. Of that number, about 8,500 died from disease or starvation. Edwin Burrows's recent accounting has revised the total number of prisoners to 30,000, of which he believes approximately 18,000 died during confinement.[14] What can reliably be said is that between 1779 and 1830, more than twenty Revolutionary soldiers and sailors published narratives detailing their experiences as prisoners-of-war. Hundreds more who were never detained (among them such generals as Henry Lee and James Wilkinson and regular Continental infantrymen such as Joseph Plumb Martin, who appears in chapter 2) published their journals and reflective memoirs mostly after the War of 1812.[15] Revolutionary prisoner-of-war narratives cover a range of conditions and circumstances. Soldiers and sailors were held in Native American villages under British control, in commandeered churches and makeshift prisons in American cities, on board prison ships such as the *Jersey* off the coast of New York, and in large detention centers in England.

Old Mill Prison in Plymouth, England, was one of the largest of these bases and home to William Widger, an army private early in the war and a naval privateer later on, who was captured at sea in February 1779 and held as a prisoner of war until Cornwallis's surrender two years later. His diary, of which only portions from 1781 remain, is a text without a country. The England where Widger lives is an unsettled transnational space with inmates brought in from both sides of the Atlantic: "*Sunday 28the.* Cloudy, Guards as Usual, raind hard last Night, day before yesterday, 33 Dutchmen were brought to prison the Numbr. of prisoners now confined in these prisones are as follows, vizt. Americans 202,—Frenchmen 437,—Spaniards 50,—Dutchmen 180."[16] The commingling of nationalities in prison unsettles and confuses Widger. Anticipating the ways in which Benedict Anderson would imagine communities centuries later, he subsequently attempts to repatriate himself by reading American newspapers and keeping track of the war's developments back home.[17] He knows, for example, George Washington's troop numbers and movements; he is overjoyed by Ethan Allen's successful siege at Ticonderoga.[18] Despite these moments of private comfort while pining for his country from afar, the diary's most revealing feature is a dream sequence near the end wherein Widger teleports himself back home to North America.

The fantasy of national reunion begins where he was born and where his family still resided: "Last Night I Dreamed I was in Marblehead [Massachusetts]." At first Widger encounters several old acquaintances who mean well and want to welcome him back into the fold, but having been separated by time and place for so long, Widger laments to one friend how his captivity has blurred his memory of the old countryside. It was too "damd hard now . . . you See I am this Side of the weay." Widger feels separated from the America of his own mind, and this nervousness is made worse once he runs into another apparition who stops him "and Shock hands with me and Said he Was Glad to See me he Said my Wife was Just Deliver'd a Boy I thout I Started at that and Said it was a damn'd Lye it was imposable for I had been Gone tow years and leatter and it was imposable." Incredulous that his wife could have become pregnant while he was held captive, he becomes frantic. "I met my Mother and Stopt and talked with hur She asked wheir I was not a Going home to see my wife I tould hur no I was dam'd if ever I desired to See hir a Gain She Said the Child was a honest begotten Child and it was Got before I went to See and it was mine I said it was imposable for the Child to be Mine for I had been Gone Mour then two years . . . I tould hur I was a dam'd foule to Coum home but I Could go back in the Brig I came in."[19] Today we might recognize the paranoid soldier anxious about his wife's promiscuity in his absence a cliché, but Widger's fear of being cuckolded speaks as much to the infidelity of the body politic as it does to that of his wife. The perceived loyalties of both have been strained in Widger's vision. He imagines himself as having been forgotten back home during his period of military detention and subsequently replaced. His paternity has been implicitly usurped by unknown civilian men, the progenitors, he fears, of the coming generation of Americans soon to be born like his bastard son, without any memory of displaced Revolutionary captives such as himself. Faced with the erasure of his bloodline, Widger insists he would rather return to "the Brig I came in" than face such an insult from his countrymen. This point is worth repeating: the Revolutionary captive would rather stay in a military prison abroad than feel a "dam'd foule to Coum home." Written in 1781, the same year the Articles of Confederation were ratified and something like the United States could be said to exist, William Widger's diary already worried those United States would never exist for him.

That the emerging nation had forsaken and marginalized its soldiers was a common private complaint of military men. At Valley Forge, Joseph Hodgkins wrote to his wife, Sarah, about the civilians back home who had "Lost all Bowls of Compassion if They Ever had any"; they "have Lost all there Publick Spirit I would Beg of them to Rouse from there stupidity and Put on som humanity and stir themselves Before it is too Late."[20] Ebenezer Huntington entered the Continental Army as a private soon after the war began, and by 1780 he was a lieutenant colonel who had experienced a wide array of military life.

> The Rascally Stupidity which now prevails in the Country at large is beyond all description . . . I despise my Countrymen, I wish I could say I was not born in America. I once gloried in it but am now ashamed of it . . . The Insults and Neglects which the Army have met with from the Country, Beggers all description, it must Go no farther and they can endure it no longer . . . I am in Rags, have lain in the Rain on the Ground for 40 hours past, and only a Junk of fresh Beef and that without Salt to dine on this day, recd no pay since last December, Constituents complaining, and all this for my Cowardly Countrymen who flinch at the very time when their Exertions are wanted, and hold their Purse Strings as tho' they would Damn the World, rather than part with a Dollar to their Army.[21]

Huntington grew "ashamed" of his "Cowardly Countrymen" for being skeptical about military hardship. Notably, however, Huntington's complaint was not a public affair. Like Widger's diary and Hodgkins's letters, the implied audience was confidential—veterans like him. Taken together, such familial documents are a counterpublic to how Revolutionary soldiers and sailors such as Dodge (if not also Rowlandson) were represented in print as loyal soldier-citizens.

Scholarship from Michael Warner, Bruce Burgett, and Russ Castronovo has argued that citizenship in the early Republic was characterized by "privatization and disengagement," which is to say by the quiet withdrawal from public life rather than by visible agitation and loud activism.[22] Burgett summarizes Warner's premise in *The Letters of the Republic* thusly: "Citizens . . . gained political power only insofar as they were able to represent their *local* and *embodied* experience as *universal* and *disinterested* through the mediation of print."[23] The embodied subjectivity of a Revolutionary captive did not abstract all that well for a nonveteran audience because military experience is not universal (only a few fight for the many) and certainly not disinterested (on the contrary, it lobbies for recognition and reparation). Rowlandson's sudden reappearance in the 1770s demonstrates that the captivity narrative was a commercially successful wartime genre of American liberalism that preferred its readers not make too many demands on an inchoate nation. As a result, veterans who were motivated to publish accounts of their military experience in captivity had to submit to the demands of a public print culture, which at the time meant working within the captivity genre. Yet even while working within such a nationalistic form that was indifferent to the fates of veterans such as Widger, Hodgkins, and Huntington, Revolutionary prisoner-of-war narratives nonetheless expressed anger and confusion toward their readers, the nation, and themselves. I want to underscore those textual moments where veterans lose their citizenship "cool" and begin making demands for redress in print.

The political reality for Revolutionary soldiers who volunteered was the same for those who were impressed. All effectively relinquished their natural rights during the duration of their military service, and many soldiers imagined such a surrender to be a political crisis.[24] If soldiers were subsequently captured while in military service, the heightened fear became that there would be no end in sight to their term of service and thus no hope of ending their subjection and restoring and securing political rights. What might have been an at-will contract instead became a life sentence. As Charles Metzger has argued, Revolutionary prisoners on both sides were "divested of all rights by capture"; neither their treatment nor the conventions for exchange were ever standardized. Denied rights and a political process for appeal, soldiers, sailors, and other war-time prisoners were held in listless "custody rather than punishment," a distinction in language that speaks to a larger distinction in the kinds of captivity at play during the end of the eighteenth century.[25] In contrast to its textual relatives, the Barbary captivity narrative and the Native American captivity narrative, Revolutionary prisoner-of-war captivity was uniquely defined by its extrajuridical deferral of humanitarianism. Unlawful enemy combatants taken on the field (or sea) of battle were spared death (presumably a sign of the combatant's humanity and the captor's restraint) at the same time they were denied due process and legal standing (an open-ended deferment of their humanity as well as the captor's responsibility for their well-being). Revolutionary captives subsequently did not feel dead, but neither did they feel fully alive.

Perhaps no Revolutionary prisoner-of-war appears to be more alive than Ethan Allen. Early twentieth-century biographers of Allen emphasize his self-aggrandizing bravado, how he endured grave injustices and gross maltreatment from the "barbarous" British.[26] I concede that it would be foolish to deny that the *Narrative of Colonel Ethan Allen's Captivity* was conceived and most likely consumed as Whiggish war propaganda. Yet the text resists such a unilateral reading because Allen also uncovers the political emergency captivity created for his fellow prisoners. The narrative opens while Allen is a militia officer at the siege of Fort Ticonderoga in New York in 1777. His captivity begins, as does Rowlandson's, in a moment of localized and racially charged violence, here following the Battle of Longue-Pointe near Quebec.

> I handed him [a British officer] my sword, and in half a minute after a savage, part of whose head was shaved, being almost naked and painted, with feathers intermixed with the hair of the other side of his head, came running to me with an incredible swiftness; he seemed to advance with more than mortal speed (as he approached near me, his hellish visage was beyond all description, snakes eyes appear innocent in comparison of his, his features extorted, malice, death, murder, and the wrath of devils and damned spirits are the emblems of his countenance) and in less than twelve feet of me, presented his firelock . . . [Allen manages to escape] but in less than half a minute, I was attacked by just such another imp of hell.[27]

Allen represents the encounter as an exaggerated contest of race and nation, in which the white patriot honorably gives up his sword in rhetorical contrast to the dark and depraved "imp of hell," no better than a mercenary, whose heart lacks any humane compassion. This storyline seems predictable enough, yet soon Allen begins to internalize his racial Other. Shortly into the incarceration, Allen feels his captors are not treating him with the respect due an officer: "to give an instance upon being insulted, in a fit of anger I twisted off a nail with my teeth, which I took to be a ten-penny nail."[28] One could argue that as Allen is slowly transforming into a Revolutionary captive, he merely embellishes his descriptions for the sake of his readers, but if that is the case, why must he act throughout like an animal? Why must he describe himself so similarly to the "naked and painted" savage who has just made him a prisoner?

Here and elsewhere, Revolutionary captivity becomes a scene of subjection. As his captivity lengthens, Allen wants to imagine himself as above the fray, still the detached gentleman concerned with Parliamentary procedure and the legal likelihood of his execution once he arrives in England for his incarceration.[29] But even when he is trying to remain civilized, emotional fissures of fear and loathing betray the text's cultured airs. His captors cannot empathize: "humanity and moral suasion would not be consulted in the determination of my fate."[30] Appeals to humanity fail Allen because such transactions take place only between lives that de facto are recognized as human, and the Revolutionary War had changed the politics of recognition. His existence while a military prisoner constitutes what Judith Butler has meant by "precarious life," or how it is that the apprehension of "life" in the context of war depends upon the frames in which other people are viewed. One is only alive if your life is considered by your enemy to be worth living and consequently worth mourning.[31]

In Allen's captive world, only military captives mourned other military captives because the rest of the world did not apprehend their dignity. "For I reasoned thus, that nothing was more common than for men to die, with their friends round them, weeping and lamenting over them, but not able to help them, which was in reality not different in the consequence of it from such a death as I was apprehensive of; and as death was the natural consequence of animal life to which the laws of nature subject mankind, to be timorous and uneasy as to the event or manner of it, was inconsistent with the character of a philosopher or soldier."[32] For sympathy to operate as it did in other captivity texts, two human beings whose lives were both recognized and valued as human must interact—Rowlandson and her reader, for example. Martin Heidegger once compared the condition of captivity to a stunned animal existing somewhere between consciousness and unconsciousness, "within an environment but never within a world," and Allen's soldiers "of animal life" lack a similar sense of mutual recognition in which compassion provided access to the psychic life of others.[33] Mourning for dying soldiers was an unfinished affect since the watcher was "not able to help them." Allen writes his own plight as a stoic bid for sympathy from his American audience, yet the spectacle of his fellow prisoners, both for Allen and for his civilian readers, is a sympathetic proposition ultimately frustrated by the Revolutionary captive's fundamental anonymity amid the multitude. Every soldier and sailor would die inhuman, which was to say nameless and unknown, somewhere off Allen's page.

Allen spends his captive life trying to understand the violence such a silencing has done to his ability to feel community. He never knows what to write and how to feel about his captors. When he is not insulting them ("As a nation I hate and despite you"), he is praising their "munificence . . . so unexpected and plentiful" and wondering about "the generous enemy" who took time to save an American "wounded by a Savage with a tomahawk." He similarly does not know how to represent his fellow prisoners. At first, he "remonstrated against the ungenerous usage of being confined with the privates, as being contrary to the laws and customs of nations." He understandably hates being placed alongside "murderers, thieves, and every species of criminals." But then Allen encounters a huddled mass of American prisoners of various ranks, from common soldiers to officers. Political hierarchies disappear amid the captives' diminished capacity for speech. "I saw some of them sucking bones after they were speechless; others who could yet speak, and had the use of their reason, urged me in the strongest and most pathetic manner, to use my interest in their behalf."[34] This crowd of Revolutionary captives anticipates the grotesque "inarticulate and indescribable cries" of the Civil War soldier missing his lower jaw in Ambrose Bierce's "Chickamauga," whose deformity transforms his voice into "something between the chattering of an ape and the gobbling of a turkey—a startling, soulless, unholy sound, the language of a devil."[35] Likewise, these disenfranchised Revolutionary captives, anonymous and silenced, "sucking bones" in a savage manner, cannot compete for audience with Rowlandson and Dodge.

Revolutionary captivity produced silence, and in response when conditions became "deplorable" enough, Allen takes it upon himself to speak for the group by complaining and "writing to the Captain [in charge of the prisoners], till he ordered the guards, as they told me, not to bring any more letters from me to him."[36] Allen's furious entreaties to his captor, metonymically reflecting the larger aspirations of the written text as a whole to testify to the Revolutionary captives' shared helplessness, did nothing to remedy the soldiers' condition, since, as James Dawes suggests, the "mere accumulation of words bears no fixed relationship to the processes of liberation and peace: the expansion of discourse is itself sometimes a form of violence, as thinkers from Antonio Gramsci to Michel Foucault have observed."[37] Dawes begins his study *The Language of War* with the Civil War, but his meditations on the dynamics of traumatic representation could benefit from looking even further back. Rather than liberate the captive as we might say of Rowlandson and Dodge, writing for the Revolutionary captive could also harm when his words did not deliver the community and freedom their author desired.

The majority of Revolutionary captivity texts were published in New England by small printers with limited distribution and paid for by the authors themselves or their families. More often than not the landscapes of the authors' imaginations were similarly regional, restricted to the immediate environments and movements of their individual detentions. Such local engagements subsequently would have convinced readers who were already convinced—veteran authors themselves, their families, and their immediate communities—but fail to reach federal ears. Even if these texts had been distributed and read widely, they would have run into deeper currents of civilian resistance. Given his class and social standing before the war, Allen reintegrated into life after captivity better than most, yet the skepticism inherent in his relationship with Revolutionary captivity was representative of early

American veteran life. Any demand the Revolutionary captive made for political recognition unsettled narrowly held notions of civilian citizenship because being captured during the Revolutionary War also invited questions for both captives and their potential readers about racial identities and national loyalties.

Who am I? Where do I stand? Some like Ethan Allen insisted on their Anglo-American identity, but others were more forthcoming about their uncertain loyalties, especially when military captivity was over- seen by Native Americans—a situation that created a confusing context of power and subjugation.[38] The soldier's proximity to Native American identity was a matter of some anxiety to veteran Lemuel Roberts in his captivity narrative. While plotting an escape from a Montreal prison, Roberts joins forces with none other than John Dodge.[39] The pair is joined in their escape attempt by three other soldiers named Holmes, Blackman, and Pue. Temporarily free, the men come upon a Native American village where they are soon captured and sent back to the British camp. "On our way [back to prison] one of the Indians began to deride and pester Pue, calling him [I]ndian, and placing his wampum cap upon his head, the long feather of which almost reached the ground, Pue being very low stature. For a while I thought all was going well, but Pue being angry, called to me, engagedly, to fight."[40] June Namias writes about the white Indian as a figure who comes to welcome assimilation and identification with his captor's culture (Mary Jemison's 1823 *Narra- tive* is perhaps the best known example of this type).[41] Pue is not a white Indian who willingly accepts the mores of his new culture. Rather, he "becomes Indian" insofar as the political status of Native Americans and military prisoners were similar. Both were under the orders of the British (in this case), and both were populations that had no clear political recourse against their powerful wardens. Pue is insulted by the association with being Native American, yet the association is prescient insofar as the Revolutionary captive had no recognizable rights.

In another case of veteran resistance to Native American identity, Luke Swetland's prisoner-of-war narrative begins near the Susque- hanna River in July 1778, where he becomes "cut off by the Indians, and with my family was captivated with many others." After a quick and fortuitous escape, he comes upon "a party of continental soldiers" who "were going back to retake the place and also to harvest the grain."

Unfortunately for him he is caught again, and this time while in the company of soldiers—thereby rendering him a combatant by association. All are subsequently ordered to be executed. Swetland is treated by Native Americans operating under British orders with prolonged abuse and intimidation. Speaking for the absent British commander, the Native American overseer "would often call to me and say come in my dog, as much as to say come here my dog, and when I was come to him would cock his firelock and put it to my breast and grin and put his finger to the trigger with an air of much fury, at first I thought it was the last moment of my life"; then, he would "put it to my forehead with the same furious motions as before, and so went on all that day doing every thing he could invent to afflict me." Swetland's torture ultimately opens him to the suggestion, as his Native American captain tells him, that he has entered into a new Native American family: "this old squaw is your grandmother, and pointing [to] the biggest of the little ones said that is your sister, and then two little ones are your cousin, and so went on through the town telling me who were my relations, and said I should soon be an Indian." After having "lived twelve months and two days" in this community, Swetland begins to act the part his captor prophesies, after which "the Indians were remarkably kind to me."[42] Luke Swetland would come to accept the cultural and political limbo that Lemuel Roberts resisted, yet regardless of whether they accepted their precarious political indeterminacy or fought it, veteran authors were always aware of it.

While a prisoner onboard the British prison ship *Jersey*, veteran Ebenezer Fox describes his defection to the British army after extensive psychological and bodily torture. "Many were *actually starved to death*, in hope of making them enroll themselves in the British army," he notes; moreover, "as every principle of justice and humanity was disregarded by the British in the treatment of their prisoners, so likewise every moral and legal right was violated in compelling the prisoners to enter into their service." Like the transformations of Roberts and Swetland, the experience of switching sides traumatizes Fox. He cannot sleep while stationed in a lazy British garrison in Jamaica, far removed from the vagaries of the war. "I still felt myself in a state of servitude,—a prisoner, as it were, among the enemies of my country—in a thralldom, from which I was desirous of being released."[43] Technically free but nonetheless still unsure of his freedom, Fox spends time with a number of black slaves whose state of captivity he imagines to be similar to his own. The slave and the soldier would often dream together of a joint escape: "I had become acquainted with several negroes in Kingston, and always found them kind and willing to give any information that was in their power to furnish. They appeared to feel a sort of sympathy for the soldiers and sailors; seeing some resemblance between their own degraded condition and that of the miserable military and naval slaves of British despotism. Whatever might be the cause, I always found the negroes in and about Kingston ready to give every facility to a soldier or sailor who wished to desert."[44] Although the term "brainwashing" would not be coined until the Korean War in the middle of the twentieth century, the fearful logic of civilian citizenship in 1800 and 1950 is similar. If Fox could not only turn British but also imagine himself as black, then who knew what other soldiers and sailors had become under the coercion of the enemy while a Revolutionary captive. How a Revolutionary soldier "passed" or failed to pass fascinated readers during the early years of the Republic, most notably in the figure of Major John André (a key figure of Revolutionary memory in chapter 2), who was Benedict Arnold's liaison in the conspiracy to hand over West Point to the British.

One could not tell what was in the Revolutionary captive's heart, and that opaqueness was a difficulty his writing could not overcome. Was André an honorable enemy combatant doing his duty when he was caught on shore in civilian clothes carrying false papers? A spy? A common criminal? The questions attendant to Revolutionary captivity *unmade* American national identity, not least because the same questions could easily apply to American "rebels" themselves. A civilian early Republic was largely shaped by what Dana D. Nelson has theorized as the collective fantasy of national manhood, a "functional community that diverted [white male] attention from differences between them" by locating instead external markers of difference such as race and gender.[45] Revolutionary captives and their narratives erased much of that difference, consequently disrupting the Anglo male fantasy of community that Nelson describes. The adaptability of the Revolutionary captive's racial associations and national allegiances therefore had no firm place in American democracy because they were fluid in ways liberal civilian readers feared. Many prisoners of war consequently masked the political inconveniences their captivities had produced, especially in narratives that were published in the anti-British run-up to the War of 1812.[46]

Yet even in these later captivity narratives, veterans had difficulty fully repressing how military captivity had in truth transformed them in the years after the Revolutionary War, which is to say that not only were they politically undefined but also many were traumatized, broke, and confused. Lemuel Roberts eventually "found the prevalence of humanity" in his Native American captors, yet after being subsequently returned to British hands in Montreal, Roberts sounds as if he suffers from Stockholm syndrome: "Mr. Jones, the provost master, was one of the best men in the world, and during near three weeks that we remained under his charge, treated us with great generosity, but this was so far from being the case with others, that it gave me a very lasting idea of the difference between man and man."[47] Like Ethan Allen before him, Roberts does not know how he feels about his captivity and his captors, nor is he comfortable with whether or not his writing about his military experience has helped clarify his confusion.

When the war is over, Roberts is plagued by what we would probably label post-traumatic stress disorder today. Similar to William Widger's vision of self-annihilation, Roberts encodes his traumatic past in an apocalyptic dream:

I dreamt that I was in a house in Old Canaan, in Connecticut . . . I thought that I was standing looking out of a west window towards Salisbury hill. On a sudden, a dreadful and tremendous blaze burst out of the south end of the hill, full in my sight, a blue and terrible blaze, and flashed from end to end of the hill, and as far as my eye could extend. On observing this most dreadful scene, my first impressions were, that the world was coming to an end; that my fate was fixed and my doom sealed forever; on which my sins, even my secret enormities, as well as my open violations of solemn covenant with Heaven, stared me in the face, and filled my soul with fear and trembling. Even the glass of the window seemed to melt close to my face, and the sulphurious scent emitted from the blaze, almost choaked me; on which I threw myself on the bed crying for mercy, mercy! When I awoke and found it was a dream.

For Roberts, the Revolutionary captive's self-effacing shame cannot be undone by writing about it. His ontological crisis while a captive contributes to his religious crisis when he is no longer a captive. "My secret enormities" find no confessor, neither from his "beneficent Creator" nor from his country full of reluctant readers. Roberts's narrative finally concludes a page after this dream with an italicized plea to Congress to pay him for his military service and concomitant disability: "*I am rendered almost totally unable to attend to bodily labor of any kind.*"[48]

Entreaties for help were a common tactic for many Revolutionary veterans to highlight their impotence and exclusion from American life and letters. Indeed, the growing number of literary appeals in the early decades of the nineteenth century marked a significant shift in veteran self-understanding from forlorn to defiant. As the years wore on, begging in print became a way to flip the citizenship question and put it instead on the civilian reader—a way of saying, "I have been loyal to you, but you have not been loyal to me." Perhaps no sign of disloyalty was more offensive than unpaid pensions and what they represented not only about veterans' standing as loyal citizens but also about the political value of their written testimony. This suppression will be a focus of chapter 2, but let it be said here that regular Continental soldiers did not receive any formal recognition until 1818 when Congress passed the first War Pension Act, but even then a veteran had to prove his suffering through sworn affidavits.

This initial bill provided better terms for officers than for infantrymen, and militia soldiers were expressly excluded from the act's 1820 amendment that stipulated pensions were reserved only for those Continental soldiers who were in "such reduced circumstances of life as to need the assistance of their country for support" and who could prove their disability and poverty were tied to the war.[49] When Congress passed the original bill, they did not fund it, and the groundswell of needy veterans met empty coffers. By the end of 1818, some 20,000 soldiers had already applied. Subsequent amendments in 1820 and again in 1823 created harsher standards that were even more discriminating. Over the course of the various pension programs the government would receive more than 80,000 applications.[50] Considering that at least 200,000 men and women had served in the Revolutionary military and "some fifty thousand of them were still alive in the 1820s and

1830s," the percentage of veterans demanding recognition and reparation was extremely high.[51]

The narrative I have been constructing of veteran exclusion and its literary response is easy to oversell. Let it be remembered that at this time the United States was a new polity, its institutions immature and sometimes fragile, and its ideological basis uncertain. Furthermore, the debt from the Revolutionary War was substantial, and then as now, budgets constrained by very limited resources were sure not to please everyone. Veterans demanding pensions were but one group making demands on a relatively weak federal government. They were also decentralized themselves, usually writing in isolation from one another. While the financial troubles of the United States might make the unpaid pensions more understandable, they do not negate the consequences these decisions had on the lives of the petitioners.

Whether or not Congress had good reason to pay, whether or not we agree with their self-representations as misunderstood victims rather than as perpetrators, these soldiers and sailors nonetheless imagined themselves to have lost out in the struggle over who was represented and what was valued in American democracy. After the Revolutionary War, the federal army was severely cut—a calculation as much about what the nation wanted to be as it was about money. Civilian citizens would feel no real sense of obligation to military identity until after the Civil War when the unprecedented number of combatants and casualties helped revise the inherited image of the veteran as subhuman and untrustworthy, an image that I am arguing begins its expression in Revolutionary captivity narratives many decades earlier.[52]

It should further be noted that although not all veterans were captives, the genre of American veteran literature nonetheless began in captivity. Coming out of the prisoner-of-war narrative, the remainder of antebellum veteran literature was deeply affected by the distrust and neglect Revolutionary captivity had wrought. Veterans—and veteran authors in particular—were presumed to always be on the make. Some veteran authors celebrated their association with confidence men, including *The Memoirs of the Notorious Stephen Burroughs* (1798), *A Narrative of the Life, Adventure, Travels and Sufferings of Henry Tufts* (1807), and *A Narrative of the Life and Travels of John Robert Shaw* (1807). Many others (such as Lemuel Roberts) could not make the criminal stereotype work for them and instead angled to represent themselves as honest beggars in need of honest charity.

David Perry, a veteran of the French and Indian War as well as the Revolutionary War, brought his 1822 memoir to a printer because he was "too poor to bear the expence himself." Alas, "it was not in the Printer to do it; and he now looks to a liberal public for some trifling remuneration of his labor and expence, from the sale of this little volume."[53] Veteran of Bunker Hill and one-time captive Israel Potter was exiled from the United States and forced to beg in the streets of London in his 1824 *Life and Remarkable Adventures of Israel R. Potter,* a tale so pitiful for Herman Melville that he "redeemed" the veteran beggar in his 1855 novelization. Civilian pity, however, was an ambivalent desire within early veteran literature, something that would put food on the table but also injure veteran pride. Consequently, veteran authors increasingly wrote out of a confidential sense of their own Gnostic brotherhood, pitted against their imagined noncombatant readers. The descendants of Revolutionary captivity would eventually come to locate their political life not in civic institutions and deliberative democracy but in the imagined and confidential bonds of commiseration their war memories helped forge even decades after the Revolutionary War was over.[54]

John Quincy Adams's presidential election in 1824 was the first in which all free white men, regardless of property, could vote, yet Revolutionary captives were still writing about the imbalances of power that held many veterans in political limbo even decades after the war had ended. The year 1824 was also when former prisoner-of-war Captain Thomas Dring began writing his Revolutionary captivity memoir. In 1782 at the age of twenty-five, Dring had been for the second time in three years "confined on board the prison ships of the enemy," where he would stay for five months (*PS* 5). *Recollections of the* Jersey *Prison-Ship* is one of the last Revolutionary captivity narratives, and the desperation Dring describes on board the notorious British prison ship *Jersey* was as much a record of 1782 as it was a reflection of 1824.

Forty years later the swarming "multitude" (*PS* 10) of "skeleton carcasses" (*PS* 13) were still a "crowd of strange and unknown forms, with the lines of death and famine upon their faces" (*PS* 15). Like Ethan Allen's earlier narrative, this late-generation Revolutionary captivity often dwells

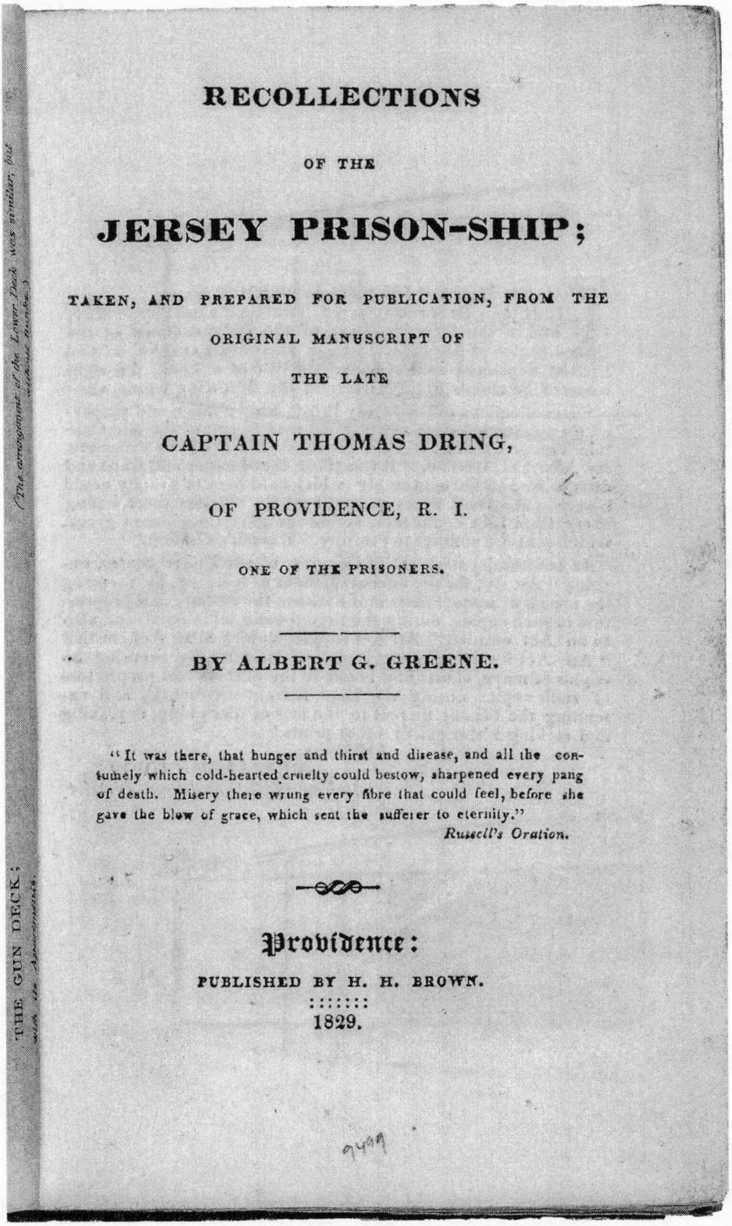

RECOLLECTIONS

OF THE

JERSEY PRISON-SHIP;

TAKEN, AND PREPARED FOR PUBLICATION, FROM THE

ORIGINAL MANUSCRIPT OF

THE LATE

CAPTAIN THOMAS DRING,

OF PROVIDENCE, R. I.

ONE OF THE PRISONERS.

BY ALBERT G. GREENE.

"It was there, that hunger and thirst and disease, and all the contumely which cold-hearted cruelty could bestow, sharpened every pang of death. Misery there wrung every fibre that could feel, before she gave the blow of grace, which sent the sufferer to eternity."

Russell's Oration.

Providence:

PUBLISHED BY H. H. BROWN.
: : : : : : :
1829.

FIGURE 2. Thomas Dring, *Recollections of the* Jersey *Prison-Ship,* ed. Albert Greene. Courtesy, American Antiquarian Society.

on the hellish vision of communal incarceration wherein human beings have been reduced to mere "other objects" (*PS* 17) passing by one another unacknowledged. Wartime captivity had enervated civilization but not completely. Dring soon finds himself crossing over into the prisoners' ad hoc society. As would most who made their way on board, Dring immediately locates a prisoner in the early stages of smallpox and exchanges blood with him in the hopes of being inoculated. Sharing antibodies was one kindness. Shaving each other was another. Captives soon organized themselves into messes that regulated and administered rations of food (*PS* 22–31). Such moments of generosity among the prisoners are juxtaposed with painful betrayals. There were "among the prisoners . . . about half a dozen men, known by the appellation of '*Nurses*'" (*PS* 53), who were traitors to their fellow inmates. "They were all thieves," Dring notes, and though they were as much prisoners as were their patients, the nurses stole from the sick and the dead (*PS* 53–54). Similarly, the "Working Party," composed only of officers, gained fortune and favor by working closely with their overseers (*PS* 45–47). The apathetic multitude—the most frequent word used to describe the gathering of captives—often behaves in the text without allegiance, concern, or fraternal bond.[55] Indeed, his fellow countrymen who should be his equals were no better than the actual enemy, as in the case of "the notorious *David Sproat,* the Commissary of Prisoners" (*PS* 9).

Sproat is the only overseer whom Dring names, and like John Dodge's and Ethan Allen's ambivalent vilifications of their own captors, Dring is suspicious of Sproat because he represents a crossing over of national loyalties. "This man was an American Refugee, universally detested for the cruelty of his conduct and the insolence of his manners" (*PS* 9). As with the traitorous nurses and the turncoat officers who composed the Working Party, Dring internalizes the betrayal of his fellow countrymen more acutely than he does the others. "We always preferred the Hessians, from whom we received better treatment than from the others. As to the English, we did not complain; being aware that they merely obeyed their orders in regard to us; but the Refugees or Royalists, as they termed themselves, were viewed by us with scorn and hatred" (*PS* 70). Dring tolerates being held captive by other ethnicities and even by other nations—the Hessians as well as the British—but not by the mercenary American refugees whose behavior and motives were unpredictable. These lawless and mercenary men had turned the prison ship into a separate and forlorn world—a "republic of misery" (*PS* 82) he calls it at one point.

Dring expected that their version of a prisoner-of-war democracy would prevent him and the few other like-minded prisoners from becoming like Sproat. They formed political community as best they could by mimicking the hierarchies of civilian society. All officers, Dring included, lived in the gun room above deck where men of civility "who humanely tendered us such little services as were in their power to offer" (*PS* 25) were a contrast to the common seamen living in much worse conditions in the lower decks. Sproat had eliminated distinctions among men, and Dring wanted to bring them back. "I was never under the necessity of descending to the lower dungeon," he notes, since "its occupants appeared to be mostly foreigners" (*PS* 40). The prisoners also consented to a rudimentary system of law and order, establishing "a code of By-Laws" which were "chiefly directed to the preservation of personal cleanliness, and the prevention of immorality" (*PS* 84). Prohibitions included foul language, drinking alcohol (if they could get it), stealing, smoking, and shaving on the Sabbath. "There were many foreigners among our number, over whom we had no control, except so far as they chose voluntarily to comply with our regulations; which they cheerfully did, in almost every instance" (*PS* 85).

On Sunday mornings, "Our Orator," a common sailor by the name of Cooper, would stand and deliver the equivalent of a sermon; he would "read us our By-Laws . . . [and preach] that these laws had been framed in wisdom, and were well fitted to preserve order and decorum in a community like ours: that his present object was to impress upon our minds, the absolute necessity of a strict adherence to those wholesome regulations" (*PS* 91). This ritual impressed on captives a local government whose ultimate aim was to translate their "republic of misery" into a redemptive republic of recognition and remembering, for Cooper always "closed with a merited tribute to the memory of those of our fellow sufferers who had already paid the debt of nature. 'The time,' said he, 'will come, when their bones will be collected; when their rites of sepulture will be performed; and a monument erected over the remains of those who have here suffered, the victims of barbarity, and died in vindication of the rights of Man'" (*PS* 93–94).

The irony for Dring, writing in 1824, could not have been lost. During the war, the people of New York could plainly see British prison ships from the coastline. A poem by a former prisoner was published in the *New Hampshire Gazette* on January 19, 1779, and Philip Freneau published "The British Prison-Ship" (which Dring cites as epigraphs to almost every chapter) in 1780. Several letters attributed to the "Prison Ship, New York" were also published in the *Pennsylvania Packet* from 1781 to 82.[56] The wartime prominence and visibility of the Revolutionary captive's plight, however, quickly vanished once the war was over and the prisoners of war were prisoners no more. No one thought much about the *Jersey* until 1803, when Wallabout Bay was dredged to build the city's navy yards and workers came across the unexpected large cache of bones Cooper had predicted. The bodily remains prompted the city to seek appropriations from Congress to build a memorial, but the federal government denied funding. In 1808, the Tammany Society privately paid to have the bones entombed in Fort Greene Park (then called Washington Park). When the cornerstone was laid on April 13, more than two thousand civil and military figures paraded the streets of New York with a pageantry "unprecedented for splendor and impressiveness, and which was witnessed, as then estimated, by upward of thirty thousand persons." The grand festivities "proved, as grand in promise as it was empty in result," for soon "the bubble burst—the tide of popular enthusiasm . . . was well nigh forgotten." Money to complete construction dried up until 1855, when the Martyr's Monument Association was formed to construct a memorial.[57]

Even then, no construction would begin until 1908 on the one hundredth anniversary of the prisoners' initial interment. A New York historian speaking before the Daughters of the Revolution in 1895 noted the long history of these soldiers' neglect. "No monument marks the spot where they rest. No inscription informs the visitor where they repose on that lovely hill. All efforts have failed. Congress has failed. The Legislature of New York has failed. Military and civic organizations have failed. Man has failed."[58] Now an obelisk stands in Brooklyn to memorialize Revolutionary captives, but what exactly do we remember when we remember Revolutionary captivity today? As the protracted history of the *Jersey* memorial promises, no monument will ever recognize the Revolutionary captive's endemic exclusion from national memory and

the American veteran's subsequent struggles to secure political recognition. The self-effacing logic of military captivity insures that there is no
enduring image of the Revolutionary captive, and because second-class
citizens get second-class memories, the *Jersey* memorial consequently
stands as a faceless reminder that something significant must have happened there long ago.

Dring's prisoner-of-war narrative stands as a transitional document of
the 1820s that bridges first-generation veterans with second-generation
Americans born after the Revolutionary War; it also reflects two lingering headwinds that veteran authors (regardless if they were prisoners of
war or not) faced during this transition—a problem of credibility and
an association with indignity. Increasingly as the nineteenth century
unfolded, civilian authors controlled and colored veterans' voices, and
Dring was no exception. Cut short by his death in 1825, Dring's manuscript found its way to his eventual posthumous editor, Albert G. Greene,
who happened to "discover" Dring's journal and publish it in 1829.

Greene claims in his introduction that his hope was to recover the
veteran's lost experience. Most of the men who had endured the prison
ships were now gone, "hence, so little that is authentic, has ever been
published upon the subject, and so scanty are the materials for information respecting it, which have as yet been given to the rising generations of our country, that it has already become a matter of doubt, even
among many of the intelligent and well informed of our young citizens,
whether the tales of the Prison-Ships, such as they have been told, have
not been exaggerated beyond the reality" (*PS* 2). Greene assures his
readers, "They have not been exaggerated . . . And so few of those who
suffered in these terrific abodes remain alive, that as a matter of precau-
tion, it seems to be required that some one possessing actual knowledge
of the facts, should embody them in a form more permanent than the
tales of tradition, and more detailed than can appear on the page of the
general historian" (*PS* 2–3). Indeed, "in a very short time, there will be
not one being on the face of the earth, who can, from his own knowledge, relate this tale; though many still live, who although not among
the sufferers, yet well know the truth of the circumstances which I have
written" (*PS* 4). At the same time that Greene extols the value of Dring's
lost and "authentic" account, he also questions whether the veteran

should be the one to tell his own story. Dring inaugurates a recurring problem for subsequent generations of veterans. Do they author their own stories, or do civilian editors?

The original text Greene found was, in his words, "thrown together, without much regard to style, or to chronological order. Not being intended for publication, at least in the form in which he left it, he appears to have bestowed but little regard on the language in which his facts were described" (*PS* v). In light of the original author's countless and "useless redundancies" (*PS* v), Greene maintains it was "necessary, that the work should not merely be revised, but re-written, before its publication" (*PS* vi). And so, in 1829, Green published what he presented as Dring's slightly retouched manuscript, the *Recollections of the* Jersey *Prison-Ship*. Not surprisingly, some have questioned the credibility and reliability of the text's voice. Edwin Burrows claims that Greene did not know Dring at all and merely came upon his disorganized journal and personal effects near his death, only to then "borrow" certain features from Andrew Sherburne's narrative (1828) while fabricating Dring's narrative. When sailor Ebenezer Fox wrote his memoir later in 1838, he copied Dring and Greene's details of the *Jersey* in his own account.[59] Burrows cites as evidence for his claim the following description from Sherburne of the English Old Mill prison: detainees "adventured to form themselves into a republic, framed a constitution, and enacted wholesome laws, with suitable penalties."[60] Such a passage seems remarkably similar to the makeshift democracy on board the *Jersey*.

This argument is an old one, that veterans could not possibly have had the time, the intelligence, or the inclination to organize themselves into a protodemocratic alternate society "of suffering." Because these veterans sound so alike, Sherburne must be quoting Greene, who must himself be embellishing Dring's words with his own brand of civilian republicanism. Like slave narratives during the same period, the mid-nineteenth-century veteran's appeal was often said to be spurious. Such speculation is too dismissive because it overlooks the aggregate patterns of suffering within veteran authorship during the early Republic. When smallpox was ravaging the *Jersey* and Dring finds he must depend on the disease of his fellow prisoners to inoculate himself, he pricks the webbing "between the thumb and fore-finger" with a needle contaminated by "a man in the proper stage of the disease" (*PS* 20). The wound festers, settles, and then scars, and Dring is protected from smallpox for the rest of his life. Lemuel Roberts likewise describes fellow captives who "privately inoculated" themselves from smallpox. Abner Stocking also talks about how while confined to the hospital the prisoners were left to regulate themselves.[61]

Dring, Roberts, and Stocking all describe a similar social response to disease, yet rather than defraud veteran literature, such patterns of representation suggest a common experience and a common reaction in the literature of the early Republic's veterans. Unavoidable questions still remain: Are these Dring's words, or are they Greene's? Would the impact be any less if the memories of Revolutionary captives were not, in fact, written by Revolutionary captives? Would contemporary authors and readers even ask such questions? Within the context of the early nineteenth century, authorship and authority were typically unstable affairs independent of the "veteran" distinction I am applying here, yet within the argumentative framework of the following two chapters, these questions matter very much. Many veteran voices of this period were fragile attempts at reintegration that were set back by the interference of civilian editorial oversight.

As a result, veteran authors often internalized their identity as a cultural transgression in need of forgiveness from a civilian audience. Consider Mrs. Deborah Gannett (née Sampson), the most famous female soldier of the Revolutionary War and the subject of the widely popular "romanticized memoir" ghostwritten by Herman Mann, *The Female Review* (1797).[62] Sampson's violations of gender were well known and well circulated in the immediate aftermath of the war, and with Mann's financial backing in 1802, she began delivering public lectures throughout New England in which she detailed the eighteen months she served as a cross-dressing soldier in the 4th Massachusetts Regiment. Her speech sounds like a prison-house confession full of guilt in need of repentance. Sampson describes herself as possessing a "juvenile mind," and her decision to lie about her sex and join the army under false pretenses "an *error* and *presumption,* because I swerved from the accustomed flowery paths of *female delicacy,* to walk upon the heroic precipice of feminine perdition!" Her self-flagellation peaks just as the address comes to a close while comparing her story to the Biblical parable of the Prodigal Son. "Who, for example, can contemplate for a moment, the *prodigal*—from the time of his revelry with harlots, to that of his eating husks with swine, and to his final return to his father—without the greatest emotions of disgust, pity and joy?" The compelling reason, she claims, to make the rounds of the lecture circuit was to redeem herself and walk as "a penitent for every wrong thought and step."[63] She wants redemption, though for what is not exactly clear.

Sampson's supposed guilt is undefined, as is Joseph Ritter's. Ritter defines his military experience in the same image of the Prodigal Son, even though his text, like Sampson's, has no indication of profligate or sinful ways. Regardless, his posthumous civilian compiler Joel Laire notes, "It appears from his own account that, at one period of his life, he was like the prodigal son who had strayed far from his father's house, and had wasted his substance in riotous living; but in great mercy and loving kindness he was brought back again to the banqueting house, where the Lord's banner over him was love." Ritter was just sixteen when he found himself serving in the Pennsylvania militia at the Battle of Brandywine. As that skirmish is about to take place, an overwhelming sense of wrong descends on him: "An awful pause preceded the engagement and some of us stood in solemn silence. I then remembered what I had seen and felt of the mercies of God, and was afresh convinced that it was contrary to the Divine Will for a christian to fight. I was sensible in my own heart that I had done wrong in taking up arms, and the terrors of the Lord fell upon me. I then secretly supplicated the Almighty for preservation, covenanting that if he would be pleased to deliver me from shedding the blood of my fellow-creatures that day, I would never fight again."[64] Ritter internalizes his guilt over the impending violence as sin and looks to the Lord for deliverance. Redemption would become a popular narrative strategy among veterans, especially as the years passed and memory continued to weigh heavily on them.[65]

Ritter knows he has done some undefined wrong. "I knew I had sinned in entering into the war, and no man going to execution could have felt more remorse." At the same moment he is describing himself as a sinner and a criminal deserving execution, "a party of Hessians came in and took me prisoner." In Ritter's retelling, his self-verdict is thus confirmed, and his subsequent imprisonment in Philadelphia was punishment for his crime of participating in the war. He looks back upon the chastening of his soul in prison with some relief, and when Ritter is finally paroled, he makes his way back home as had the Prodigal Son. "My relations and friends were rejoiced to see me, for they had not heard of me after the battle, and had supposed me dead; but my dear mother had maintained a belief that she would see me again, and would often say, 'my child is yet alive.'"[66] This image of redemption, shared by other veterans in the first decades of the nineteenth century, reflected contemporaneous theories surrounding the prison.

Prison reformer Benjamin Rush conceived of the prison as a space of self-reflection for the convict, from which he could return like the prodigal soldier to reenter society, as "one who 'was lost and is found—was dead and is alive.'"[67] Caleb Smith has documented how the rhetoric of American penitentiaries after the Revolutionary War emulated the democratic virtues of the nation's founding. Alongside other prison reformers such as Cesare di Beccaria, Rush imagined the modern prison to be "a living tomb," a place where the convict's self could become enlightened.[68] The purpose of the military prison for the criminal is not discussed by Smith, nor for that matter is the military prisoner a concern for Rush, who described soldiers as afflicted with a widespread "madness" and "Military Mania" that made it "impossible to understand a conversation with these gentlemen without the help of a military dictionary.— Counterscarps, morasses, fosses, glacis, ramparts, redoubts, abbatis, &c. for the beginning, middle, and end of every sentence. They remember nothing in history, but the detail of sieges and battles, and they consider men as made only to carry muskets."[69] The Revolutionary captive was a prisoner whose soul and self were not deemed suitable objects of reform (even if Sampson and Ritter sought it).

Prisoners of war were thus doubly damned. They were not generally considered topics of humanitarian reform because their custody was not technically a punishment for a crime; yet soldiers had always been associated even before the beginnings of the American Republic with a direct threat to law and order. Legal debate over the soldier's moral failings dates back as early as William Blackstone in *Commentaries on the Laws of England* (1765–69).[70] James Wilson of the first United States Supreme Court cited Blackstone in his decision to Hayburn's Case, one of the first cases brought before the court, in which the issue was whether the courts had jurisdiction to hear pension claims from veterans of the Revolutionary War (justices concluded the courts were no place to hear soldiers plead their case).[71] Early veteran texts attest again and again to episodes of the clandestine lawlessness within military life, as well as to the questionable punishments (or lack thereof) that resulted.

New York soldier Abraham Leggett was captured and made a prisoner of war in late 1776. Faced with no other alternative, his regiment agreed to the conventional terms of surrender only to be stripped naked and robbed by the British: "But the moment we Surrender'd they Crowded in upon us and began to Strip and Pillage what Ever we had on or about us. I spoke To Tu[r]nbull myself Sir you Promist us Good Quarters—your Soldiers are stripping us and leaving us naked—his answer was They have Captur'd the Fort at the Risk of There lives and I Cant Restrane them."[72] Leggett looked at war and wanted rules and recourse, but American jurisprudence at this point was still unformed.[73] Soldiers were left to their own moral compasses, for good or bad. While Sampson and Ritter share the sentiment of penitence with other self-described prodigal texts, such as *A Narrative of the Life and Travels of John Robert Shaw* (1807) and the *Interesting Journal of Abner Stocking of Chatham, Connecticut* (1810), lasting transformation rarely happened. Many veterans did not atone at all.

In *The Autobiography of a Criminal* (1807), Massachusetts militiaman Henry Tufts documents his time as a soldier, thief, deserter, and con man. He fornicated, swiped food, stole horses, and cheated fellow soldiers out of their money. His life as a soldier was a revolving door of arrest for desertion and subsequent escapes from jail. When once held long enough to force a formal military trial, Tufts "shuffled and prevaricated so dismally" that his "attorney, taking the proper advantages, overthrew the whole testimony, and procured my discharge" immediately.[74] Tufts never apologizes, nor for that matter does the persona within *The Memoirs of the Notorious Stephen Burroughs* (1798), "the first full length rogue narrative" in the United States according to Daniel Williams and a bestseller throughout the nineteenth century, "published nearly thirty times in fourteen different cities." Williams's accounting of early American criminal literature notes that Burroughs is unique in the tradition that dates as least as far back as Cotton Mather's *Pillars of Salt* (1699) insofar as "Burroughs made little pretense of moral instruction."[75] Partially modeled after the European picaresque, the veteran

and the criminal alike came to be popularized in their positions as outsiders looking in. Most likely readers of prisoner-of-war narratives in
the 1790s and early years of the 1800s were readers of other captivity
and criminal literature as well.

Seaman Joshua Davis, for example, shared the same Hanover, New
Hampshire, publisher as Burroughs (Benjamin True). The veterans
who wrote and the printers who shaped their texts often associated the
responsibility for war's evils with the individual veteran's moral failings,
which included not only racial mixing and gender crossing but also
opportunistic rape and pillaging. In this way, the impression of veteran
criminality helped to justify the alienation and segregation so many
Revolutionary captives felt from their local communities. Some reacted
by wanting to be welcomed back into the fold as had the Prodigal Son.
Others were less willing to repent for the supposed transgression of
their military experience. For them, the real crime lay in the unfolding sanitization of civilian memory of the Revolutionary War that was
unable or unwilling to accommodate the complexities of veteran experience which captivity had revealed.

CHAPTER 2

Civilian Memories and Veteran Memoir

1820–1830: James Fenimore Cooper, John André, Joseph Plumb Martin, Enoch Crosby, Thomas Painter

I have this consolation, that I have labored for the benefit of my beloved country and posterity. I hope the results of my toils and sufferings will be acknowledged by my country, and prove a lasting blessing to it, and be handed down unsullied to the latest posterity.

—*Nathaniel Segar*, A Brief Narrative of the Captivity and Sufferings of Lt. Nathan'l Segar, Who Was Taken Prisoner by the Indians and Carried to Canada during the Revolutionary War, Written by Himself *(1825)*

James Fenimore Cooper's Revolutionary War novel *The Spy: A Tale of the Neutral Ground* (1821) begins with two mysterious travelers who find themselves adrift in the Neutral Ground of Westchester County, New York, a no-man's-land situated between the British-occupied Bronx and the American line further north along the Hudson River. This is the same neighborhood that animates "The Legend of Sleepy Hollow" (1819–20), a place that Washington Irving described as "one of those highly favoured places which abound with chronicle and great men. The British and American line had run near it during the war; it had, therefore, been the scene of marauding, and been infested with refugees, cow boys, and all kind of border chivalry." For Irving as for Cooper, writing from the vantage point of the 1820s had made it so that "just sufficient time had elapsed to enable each story teller to dress up his tale [about the war] with a little becoming fiction, and in the indistinctness of his recollection, to make himself the hero of every exploit."[1]

The entirety of *The Spy*'s action will be contained in this lawless and precarious terrain that is patrolled by heroes "of every exploit" and roving bands of irregular soldiers who continually assault the schemes and properties of the novel's main characters. These bands include the Skinners—guerrillas who maraud for profit—and the Cow-Boys—opportunists in their own right albeit with marginal claims to the Loyalist side. The Skinners and the Cow-Boys constantly work to undermine each other, and as the plot unfolds, regular British and Patriot troops vie against the loosely organized militias. Everyone will skirmish with one another in an effort to control the novel's geography. "Who do you call the enemy?" is a life and death refrain in *The Spy*, and indeed the novel's frequent turns of fortune justify the paranoia inherent in the question (*S* 40).[2] The anxiety over how to identify allegiance and loyalty makes every soldier in Cooper's world an occasion for suspicion. It is into this context that the two travelers arrive incognito. On the last page of the novel, Cooper will reveal that the first of them, a detached and austere observer going by the nom de guerre of Harper, is none other than George Washington.

Memories surrounding veterans of the early Republic shifted as the Revolutionary generation faded and gave way to the United States of the 1820s, an era that increasingly ignored the living memory of veteran suffering found in Revolutionary captivity narratives and veteran memoir in favor of a collective memory of military experience as a site of disloyalty, subterfuge, and suspicion. Memories change as generations change, a fact no doubt illustrated by Cooper's representation of George Washington as a spy. Such an image would be sacrilegious today, yet contemporary readers were not taken aback by the characterization. W. H. Gardiner in his review of the novel for the *North American Review* noted the irony which surely had made other readers similarly smirk, that Washington was in fact (but not in our collective memory today) a master spy: "It is a matter of notoriety, that no military commander ever availed himself of a judicious system of *espionage* with more consummate address, or greater advantage to his cause, than General Washington."[3] Washington would be forgiven (if not praised) for his trickery, whereas others would be condemned; it is this double standard that unsettles the novel. The last page reveals not only the true identity of George Washington but also that of Harvey Birch, *the* spy of the title. We come to learn that Birch has been working as a double agent for Washington all along, and this revelation is almost as disturbing as our discovery of Washington's own double life, because for the bulk of the story Birch has been portrayed as the main villain and traitor to the Americans by allegedly providing supplies and information to the British army.

Washington's target in the beginning is the prominent Wharton family, whose home, The Locusts, is an important interchange of loyalties within the Neutral Ground. Throughout the war, the patriarchal Mr. Wharton has tried to remain impartial to both sides, yet his children do not share his neutrality. The youngest daughter, Frances, sympathizes with the Patriots, no doubt owing to her love affair with the American officer and primary warden of spies, Captain Dunwoodie. The older daughter, Sarah, remains a Loyalist, in large measure the result of her love affair with Dunwoodie's military rival, Colonel Wellmere. The family's only son, Henry, is a captain of dragoons in the regular British army who has been away from his family for more than a year; furthermore, he is the second traveler from the novel's beginning, dressed, like George Washington, in elaborate disguise.

Cooper published *The Spy* in 1821, the same year "the remains of Major [John] André were disinterred, and transported [back] to England," where they have resided in Westminster Abbey ever since.[4] Without question, *The Spy* was a retooling of the famous story of André, who was caught behind enemy lines in civilian clothes, but in Cooper's telling, everyone played the André role. The precedent from André's trial and execution dictated that either Washington or Henry Wharton would have been tried and executed as a traitor if caught out of uniform. As was true in the case of André, Captain Wharton's plainclothes will be the seal to his death sentence (but not his death) once he is discovered by the Patriot Captain Lawton. Because Washington and Wharton were no different in the eyes of the law, the novel acknowledges the contingency and luck involved in surviving and also winning the Revolutionary War. There but for the grace of God goes George Washington and the United States.

The ghost of André is thus split in *The Spy* between the unlucky Wharton, who gets caught, and Washington, who never does; furthermore, André's ghost tarnishes our memory of Washington, who presided over André's case and let him be executed despite popular outcry to spare him. In contrast to first-generation veteran representation that privileged individual trauma, confinement, and grief, second-generation civilian representation such as *The Spy* emphasized collective escape, luck, and relief at having survived.

According to his testimony at his military trial in Tappan, New York, André had been tapped by British general Henry Clinton to be the secret emissary for negotiations at West Point with Benedict Arnold about his defection. Much to his misfortune, on the night of September 29, 1780, André was captured behind enemy lines in upstate New York dressed in civilian clothes and possessing incriminating papers written in Arnold's hand.[5] On him were found a "pass from general Arnold to *John Anderson, which name* Major André *acknowledged he assumed.* Artillery orders, September 5, 1780. Estimate of the force at West Point and its dependencies, September 1780 . . . Return of ordnance at West Point, September 1780. Remarks on works at West Point. Copy of a state of matters laid before a council of war, by his Excellency general Washington, held the 6th of September 1780." The court quickly ordered André to hang, yet after the sentence André implored Washington by letter to give him his due as a gentleman. "Sympathy towards a Soldier will surely induce your Excellency and a military Tribunal to adopt the mode of my death to the feelings of a man of honor." Honor here meant death by firing squad, and André would have suffered his penalty gladly if he could be "informed that I am not to die on a gibbet" and also if Washington could assure him he was a "victim of policy and not of resentment."[6] Washington, however, refused to intervene, and André hung from the noose like a common criminal on October 2 before a large crowd.

Robert Ferguson has noted that "the military trial of André offered a substitution of type (André for Arnold) and of offense (espionage for treason) rather than a more slippery comparison of degree for the same crime . . . André filled the role of a useful sacrifice." Washington made clear and conscious decisions not to save André when he met the accused

The Unfortunate DEATH of MAJOR ANDRE
(Adjutant General to the English Army) at Head Quarters in New York, Oct.r 2. 1780,
who was found within the American lines in the character of a Spy.

FIGURE 3. John Golda, "The Unfortunate Death of Major Andre." Courtesy, Yale University Art Gallery.

with silence and refused Arnold's letters in absentia in support of André.[7] Indeed, it was Arnold, the greatest criminal and most infamous soldier in America, who not only escaped the whole affair unpunished but whose persona in the trial was noticeably suppressed. Despite the court's judgment, André's stoic rhetoric and soft personal manner swayed public opinion to his side. Alexander Hamilton recalled how André's composure during his trial and execution "melted the hearts of the beholders . . . Among the extraordinary circumstances that attended him, in the midst of his enemies, he died universally esteemed and universally regretted." "My feelings were never put to so severe a trial," he went on. "Never, perhaps, did any man suffer death with more justice, or deserve it less."[8]

Even those who were not there personally identified with André. The historian Hannah Adams remarked in 1807 how André was a man "in whom were united an elegant taste and cultivated mind, with the amiable qualities of candour, fidelity, and a delicate sense of honour . . . he was condemned and executed as a spy. His behaviour, during his trial, was calm and dignified, exciting the esteem and compassion even of his enemies, who deeply regretted the cruel necessity of sacrificing his life to policy and the usages of war."[9] Even Washington's chief spy, Colonel Benjamin Tallmadge, recounted how in the days leading up to André's execution, "I became so deeply attached to Major André, that I can remember no instance where my affections were so fully absorbed in any man. When I saw him swinging under the gibbet, it seemed for a time as if I could not support it. All the spectators seemed to be overwhelmed by the affecting spectacle, and many were suffused in tears. There did not appear to be one hardened or indifferent spectator in all the multitude."[10] Contemporary artists were likewise sympathetic in their work. In his play *André* (1798), William Dunlap contended, "Thou didst no more than was a soldier's duty, / To serve the part on which he drew his sword."[11] There was never any malice in André's heart, only duty, and for Anna Seward, there was also song. In *Monody on Major André* (1781), she rendered André into a "firmer Lover" and poet, a gentleman momentarily forced to

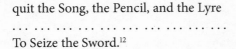

quit the Song, the Pencil, and the Lyre

. . .   .

To Seize the Sword.[12]

To be sure, other writers passed more severe judgment. General Nathanael Greene, for example, condemned André for his "supposed want of self-possession in so brave a man."[13] That being said, André's critics were largely outnumbered by his champions, in large part because André's predicament was usable for a nation in need of a sacrificial veteran.

The anxieties detailed in the previous chapter surrounding Revolutionary captives surrounded André as well. Was he a criminal? A victim? The ambivalent legacy and meaning of his death underscored the lingering remorse Americans felt over the Revolutionary War for their own treason. Washington Irving's Sleepy Hollow is also André's haunting grounds, a place where the ghosts of spies return with unfinished business. The legend of the headless horseman in the story is "said by some to be the ghost of a Hessian trooper, whose head had been carried away by a cannon-ball, in some nameless battle during the revolutionary war." What was more, the soldier's specter returned each night to commune with the national and painful symbol of the captured spy: "mournful cries and wailings [were] heard and seen about the great tree where the unfortunate Major André was taken."[14] Caleb Crane has read Irving's affection for André as the signaling cry of an era of American sympathy that would endure until the Civil War.[15] Indeed, the "sympathetic" figure of such spy martyrs as André and Nathan Hale was expressed in post-Revolutionary literary imaginations as a regrettable but necessary casualty of the war for which the nation's writers felt compassion and guilt but not any sense of injustice or outrage.

The case of André was not clear at all, yet in *The Spy,* his death legitimized the legal and social precedent for an American sovereignty "that inflicted punishment without the actual existence of crime" (*S* 312). In the carrying out of his lethal judgment, Washington invents the government's monopoly on violence (what Max Weber defines as the criteria for the state), and as such, André's verdict becomes a primal articulation of national power.[16] To complicate the nation's affective investments with André even further, early Americans continued to recognize a part of the themselves in the stylized image of the spy even decades after the war was over.

Indeed, *The Spy* is populated with a whole cast of conspiratorial types. When the narrator compares Captain Wharton's trial explicitly to André's, the reference is only valid insofar as both cases were "stamped with greater notoriety than the ordinary events of the war. But spies were frequently arrested; and the instances that occurred of summary punishment for this crime were numerous" (S 299). André was one unlucky spy in a world full of spies, just as Captain Wharton was but one spy in a novel full of them. The unimpeachable George Washington was, once again, acting no different from Wharton. For that matter, neither were the novel's domestic spies. Caesar, the Wharton's house slave, keeps himself and his staff in the information loop through a "regular system of espionage" (S 49). Isabella Singleton confesses on her death bed that a woman's "life is one of concealed emotions" and inscribed with multiple hypocrisies (S 285). Near the end of the novel, when Captain Wharton is on the run, his sister, Frances, directly disobeys her military order of house arrest and comes to his aid. Treachery and disobedience are also afoot in Captain Wellmere, who courts Sarah Wharton, all the while keeping an English wife back home. Even the upright Captain Lawton becomes an accidental spy when he startles the parlor embrace of Wellmere and "the blushing Sarah" (S 236). Like the other characters in the novel who survive, Captain Lawton is a careful reader of spies and not to be fooled. "Certain significant signs, which were embraced at a glance by the prying gaze of the trooper, at once made him a master of their secret" (S 236). Even though the title suggests there is only one spy, the work is replete with double agents.

Such was the political indeterminacy in the Neutral Ground, a place where Wharton could well attest "the law was momentarily extinct." Indeed, "great numbers . . . wore masks, *which even to this day have not been thrown aside;* and many an individual has gone down to the tomb, stigmatized as a foe to the rights of his countrymen, while, in secret, he has been the useful agent of the leaders of the revolution; and, on the other hand, could the hidden repositories of divers flaming Patriots have been opened to the light of day, royal protections would have been discovered concealed under piles of British gold" (S 10; emphasis added). The novel insists we all wore the mask during the rebellion and continued to wear it as late as 1821 when *The Spy* was written. Veterans were thus cast into two molds in the early decades of the nineteenth century. In some ways, it was a tale of two soldiers—of Major John André, whose cautionary tale redeemed the nation from the fragility of its origins, and of Private Joseph Plumb Martin, whose tale of unrequited obligations sought to shake the uneasy bonds of American citizenship rather than stabilize them.

Joseph Letter has positioned *The Spy* at the intersection of what he calls "vernacular memories" of the war—represented by the personal accounts and testimonies of Americans who lived through the war—and the larger "historical discourse of the new nation" that presumably was influenced by second-generation Americans.[17] The messy result of these forces was *The Spy*, widely considered the first historical novel written in and about the United States, and the text is certainly at the intersection of competing memories of the Revolutionary War. Yet the interchange that Letter begins to map has even more on-ramps and off-ramps that must complicate our understanding of how war memory functioned in the early Republic and what the role of veterans was in forming that memory. Rather than "vernacular," I prefer the term "living" memory, by which I mean the individualized and embodied knowledge of lived experience.

Although there are points to be made about the unreliability of personal memory and how eyewitness accounts are prone to suggestion and misremembering, living memory differs from other "operations of memory" (to borrow Carol Gluck's term) such as generational memory and collective memory.[18] Generational memory of the Revolutionary War might further be split along the unstable subcategories of "civilian" and "veteran" memory—just as it was for Cooper, who served with the United States Navy before the War of 1812 (veteran) but who was born in 1789 after the events of the Revolution had concluded (civilian). For Cooper, a man who had no memories of the war and whose family really did not play any substantial role in the Revolution, the figure of André and the questions he raised about civil-military relations weighed heavily.

Thus *The Spy* is a second-generation war story (yet told by a veteran of the military) that masquerades as the collective and official memory of the Revolutionary War. First-generation veteran memoirists, such as Joseph Plumb Martin, wrote against these memories of authors who were not there yet who nonetheless controlled the representation of war as an André story of conflicting loyalties (and in the process created a sense of shared sacrifice that ultimately united disparate Americans in search of a common identity). The counternarrative that Revolutionary prisoners of war began, and which aging veteran memoirists continued into the 1820s and 1830s, often emphasized an antitheical memory of the nation's disloyalty and the surprising lack of sympathy among early Americans, especially for veterans and their rhetorical appeals of suffering, loss, and displacement. What is at stake in this generational contest between civilian memory and veteran memoir is the question of who controls the curation of early Republic literary culture. Who does the nation authorize to remember and tell its war stories, and for what ends?

Sarah Purcell has argued that as the early decades of the nineteenth century unfolded, civic memory of the Revolutionary War expanded and became more inclusive. Plans for public memorials of the prison ship *Jersey*, for instance, were crafted in the years leading up to the War of 1812, but only then because hawkish Democratic Republicans wanted to raise support for the war by recasting Revolutionary heroism as a popular uprising instead of something relegated to a few "great men." Federalist ideology, in contrast, insisted the looming war with England was a war of choice rather than the populist war of necessity the Revolution had been. At the heart of the struggle over the meaning of the Revolutionary War in the early decades of the century was a debate over the nature of civic sacrifice, and for Purcell at least, these overlapping memories of the Revolutionary War "created national identity by allowing early Americans to imagine a shared history of common sacrifice, at first by great war heroes and then increasingly by average people as well."[19] Whichever way it was cut, the glorification of the common soldier's military service was a retroactive halo inaugurated in large part by an upswing of patriotism after the War of 1812. Alfred Fabian Young has noted that Boston waited until the fiftieth anniversaries to commemorate the Boston Massacre (1820) and the Tea Party (1823). "The 'jubilees' of local military events, on the other hand, were observed in the mid-1820s on a scale without precedent, dwarfing the annual Independence Day celebration." Throughout the 1820s and 1830s, politicians commonly exploited veteran celebrations on the campaign trail.[20]

Similar to Purcell, John Resch has suggested that the nation's lip service for veterans after the war was likewise a result of the widespread political belief that the Revolution had been "a people's war won by a virtuous citizenry."[21] Since everyone was assumed to have sacrificed and served, no one could claim special status as having sacrificed more. It followed that no soldier would have any claims to the public welfare. Folk heroes such as George Washington and Israel Putnam certainly needed no community assistance, nor did they seem to need constant reminders of their country's gratitude. In particular, the popular mythology surrounding Putnam, rumored to have laid down his plough in the field and walked to the front line after hearing about the Battle of Lexington, advanced the normative ideals of a citizenry averse to the belief that war produced separate classes.

Putnam squarely personified American republicanism: he was the Cincinnatus of old, self-regulated by his civic virtue and sacrifice, and loath to covet political power. One of the Hartford Wits, David Humphreys, was the first to celebrate Putnam's life story in an address before the Connecticut Society of the Cincinnati in 1788.[22] His publishers reissued the biography in 1794, and it would enjoy numerous runs thereafter: New York in 1796, 1810, and 1815; Philadelphia in 1798 and 1811; Vermont in 1812; Delaware in 1814 (in a volume alongside the life of John Paul Jones); and Boston in 1818. In 1825, Cooper was still celebrating Putnam in his novel *Lionel Lincoln*. In the 1830s, privates would rely on Putnam's celebrity in their pension applications.[23]

In contrast, Joseph Plumb Martin in his 1830 memoir, *A Narrative of Some of the Adventures, Dangers and Sufferings of a Revolutionary Soldier,* remembered Putnam and the officer class as exploitative and as symbols of the political inequalities and legal injustices that befell veterans. The end of Martin's military service in 1783 coincided with the near disbandment of the entire Continental Army, a dissolution that came not a moment too soon. Many soldiers had not been paid for several years, and the tone of the army was growing more and more mutinous by the day.[24] Martin recalls during his service receiving only one month's wage, in specie, "the first that could be called money . . . since the year '76, or that we ever did receive till the close of the war, or indeed, ever after" (*N* 191).[25] Throughout the 1770s and early 1780s, many soldiers resigned or deserted as a result of not being paid.

Shortly after Arnold's treason and André's execution in 1780, Congress had promised officers half pension for life, but the government commuted its contract in March of 1783 to half-pay for only five years.

General Henry Knox, a "soldier-bookseller" from Boston who would eventually serve as the nation's first secretary of war, conceived of a lobbying organization to protest delinquent payments as early as 1776. Along with General Jedediah Huntington, Knox founded the Society of the Cincinnati in 1783 as a fraternal organization open to everyone who had served in the officer corps (notably, infantrymen were uninvited).[26] The society came into being at the same time financial promises were being broken and the collective bargaining position of the military was weakening; it would be devoted as much to shoring up the officer bonds of friendship and elite fraternity in a postwar America as it would be to creating a pressure group on Congress to support its veteran officers.[27]

The same General Knox of the Society of the Cincinnati controlled the Waldo Patent territory in Maine where Martin lived following the war. Knox ran his lands there as a virtual fiefdom, caring little for the veterans he had formerly led in battle and who were now living under his care.[28] No one seemed to notice the general's exploitation of them. Praising the "hard and fatiguing" work of his fellow infantrymen in the *Narrative,* Martin rhetorically shakes his head at "the apathy of our people at this time" (*N* 78)—a comment as much about the 1830s as it was the 1770s. He reflects on one nameless but nonetheless hard-fought skirmish that receives no notice back on the home front, "the reason of which is, there was no Washington, Putnam, or Wayne there . . . Great men get great praise, little men, nothing" (*N* 82–83). Martin and other veteran memoirists in part wrote to correct the Revolutionary memory of the officer class, about which Martin saw little to cheer.

In an episode early in the war, Martin and his company are scavenging for food and come across a cellar full of Madeira wine. As the soldiers feast on their good fortune, the owner of the cellar goes in protest to find General Putnam. "The General immediately repaired in person to the field of action; the soldiers getting wind of his approach hurried out into the street, when he, mounting himself upon the doorsteps of my quarters, began 'harangueing the multitude,' threatening to hang every mother's son of them" (*N* 20). In response to Putnam's scolding, Martin waits patiently for him to finish speaking and then returns back inside to finish his wine. "I never heard any thing further about the wine or being hanged about it; he doubtless forgot it" (*N* 21).

Putnam does not understand the needs of the men under him, and furthermore, his protests are only a perfunctory ceremony for the sake of the owner.

Martin's sketch of Putnam as clueless is a sardonic challenge to the official war memory of great men, but as is often the case, Martin is quick to modulate his voice and grow suddenly serious. Besides getting Putnam wrong, the current generation of the 1820s and 1830s had completely ignored the real casualties of the war. "We were soon ordered to our regimental parade, from which, as soon as the regiment formed, we were marched off for the ferry . . . We soon landed at Brooklyn, upon the Island, marched up the ascent from the ferry, to the plain. We now began to meet the wounded men, another sight I was unacquainted with, some with broken arms, some with broken legs, and some with broken heads" (*N* 21–22). Here the stakes of war memory are no longer a rhetorical game about reputation but an uncomfortable reminder of the nation's responsibilities to the facts they are "unacquainted with," namely, veterans and their wounds that presumably have not healed. Martin's memoir repeatedly asks what is owed veterans, not only by the narrator's imagined civilian readers but also by Martin as a veteran addressing other veterans. Indeed the vocal switch in pronoun from "I" to "we" points to a recurring problem over exactly whose story the *Narrative* is telling. Is it one veteran's autobiography describing his individual disenchantment with his officers, his pay, and his suffering, or is it a collective reflection of the common experiences of Continental Army veterans?

Martin is aware of the overlap in his reluctant roles as veteran and author, both of which were tied to his moment of military induction. "Soldiers were at this time enlisting for a year's service; I did not like that, it was too long a time for me at the first trial; I wished only to take a priming before I took upon me the whole coat of paint for a soldier" (*N* 16). In the course of his vacillation, he comes to realize the agreement he would enter into to become a soldier would actually be fixed and immutable—"If I once undertake, thought I, I must stick to it, there will be no receding" (*N* 16)—and when at last he arrives at the recruiting station, the scene is written as an uncanny and out-of-body assent. "So seating myself at the table, enlisting orders were immediately presented to me; I took up the pen, loaded it with the fatal charge, made several mimic imitations of writing my name, but took especial care not to touch the paper with the pen until an unlucky wight who was leaning over my shoulder gave my hand a stroke, which caused the pen to make a woful scratch on the paper. 'O, he has enlisted,' said he, 'he has made his mark, he is fast enough now'" (*N* 16–17). Martin's first oaths are mere simulation. The pen does not meet the paper until "an unlucky wight" takes control of his hand, and the unsure transaction of the signature occurs concomitant with a transformation in his character. Both are described as irresistible spiritual changes. "And now I was a *soldier*, in name at least, if not in practice" (*N* 17). The soldier's life begins for Martin with the giving up and giving over of his name.

Immediately the "I" disappears and the problematic "we" that will take control of the narrative speaks for the first time. For the remainder of this particular chapter in the memoir, paragraphs begin with this new identity: "We continued here some days to guard the flour" (*N* 28); "We went on a little distance, when we overtook another man belonging to our company" (*N* 36); "We now returned to camp, if camp it was;—Our tent held the whole regiment and might have held ten millions more" (*N* 38); "We had eight or ten of our regiment killed in the action, and a number wounded, but none of them belonged to our company" (*N* 39). His veteran community sets the cadence of his thoughts. "We were marching on as usual, when, about ten or eleven o'clock, we were ordered to halt and then to face to the right about. As this order was given by the officers in rather a different way than usual, we began to think something was out of joint somewhere, but what or where, our united wisdom could not explain; the general opinion of the soldiers was, that some part of the enemy had by some means got into our rear" (*N* 109). Making sense of the variety of voices and identities of the early American veteran was a task that few canonical authors before the Civil War would take on, yet Martin tried, even though the community he entered into was "out of joint somewhere."

Alternatively self-assured and alienated, proud then broken, the *Narrative* stands as one of the earliest and most unsettling testimonials of military experience in the United States. What makes Martin's *Narrative* so important in the long history of veteran authorship is its self-awareness in trying to account for the overlapping categories of veteran communities—officer, militia, Continental—as well as its struggle to pit these competing and at times incoherent veteran memories against the shifting civilian memory of the war as a spy's game between gentlemen. Veterans had become an American underclass in the shuffle.

Joseph Plumb Martin was born in Berkshire County, Massachusetts, on November 21, 1760, a day "I have been told . . . [which] was a thanksgiving day" (*N* 6). His father, Ebenezer Martin, was intelligent and ambitious, a graduate of Yale, though he was also prone to extravagance. Notoriously bad with the family finances, Ebenezer eventually failed as the Congregational minister in the frontier town of Becket. His bankruptcy forced him to send Joseph at the age of seven to live with his grandfather in Milford, Connecticut, where, Joseph recalls, life was even and pleasant enough for him up until around 1775. Against his grandfather's wishes, Martin joined the Continental Army in June 1776 at the age of fifteen and stayed for the duration of the war, being mustered out in 1783 at the age of twenty-two.[29]

During his service, Martin fought in several major engagements, including the defense of New York City and the Battle of White Plains in 1776, the Battle of Germantown in 1777, the Battle of Monmouth in 1778, the near mutiny at Morristown in 1780, and the siege of Yorktown in 1781. He was as seasoned as they came, a soldier who had served longer than most and lived to tell about it. After the war, Martin married and relocated with his wife, Lucy, and their four children to the town of Prospect, near the Maine coast, where he would serve as the town's clerk for most of his adult life. In 1830, a Hallowell, Maine, printer published his *Narrative* to "virtually no public notice." He died in 1850 poor but not quite destitute, having fought for and finally received an eight-dollar-a-month pension from the federal government that allowed him and his aging wife barely to get by.[30]

The belated writing of Martin's wartime memory raises important questions about the repressed emergence of veteran memoir and its relationship to larger traditions of nineteenth-century literature, specifically life writing. Before the age of Frederick Douglass, Henry David Thoreau, and Ralph Waldo Emerson, autobiographical writing was a much-maligned category often associated with hoaxes and self-promotion; the serious person had to be clever in order to avoid recriminations of vanity and licentiousness. Thomas Jefferson, for one, did not begin writing

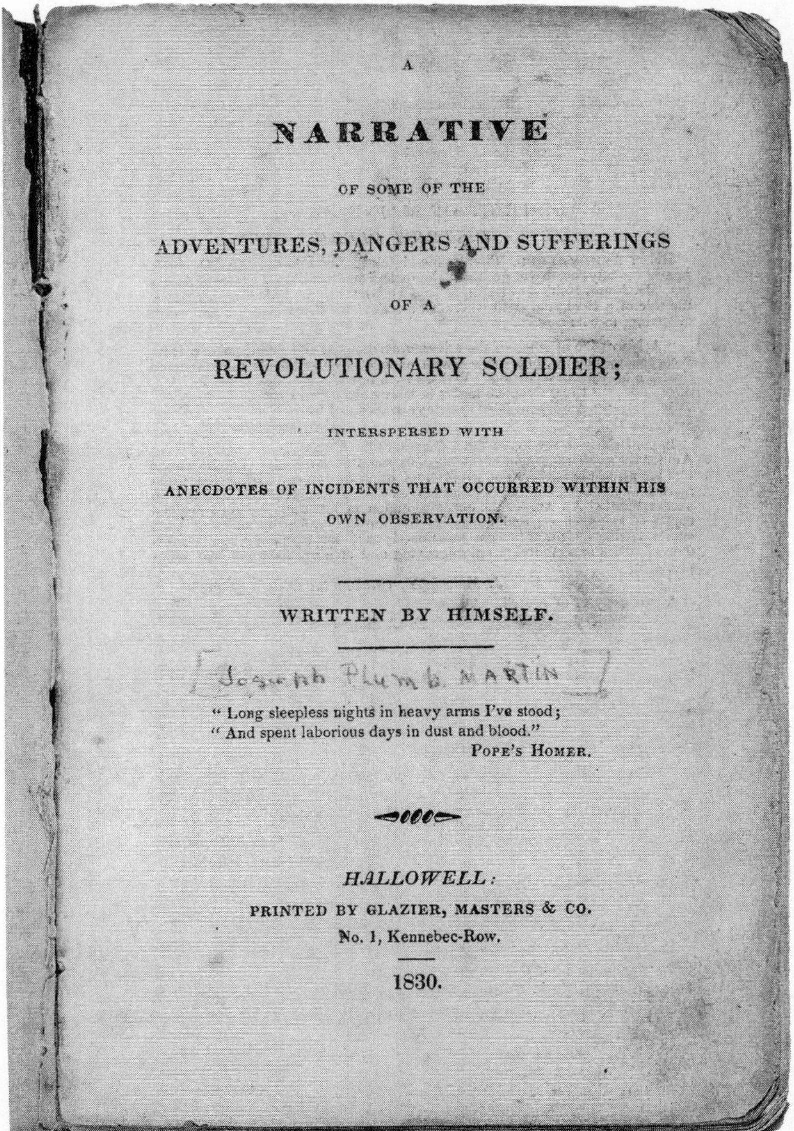

A

NARRATIVE

OF SOME OF THE

ADVENTURES, DANGERS AND SUFFERINGS

OF A

REVOLUTIONARY SOLDIER;

INTERSPERSED WITH

ANECDOTES OF INCIDENTS THAT OCCURRED WITHIN HIS
OWN OBSERVATION.

WRITTEN BY HIMSELF.

Joseph Plumb MARTIN

"Long sleepless nights in heavy arms I've stood;
"And spent laborious days in dust and blood."
POPE'S HOMER.

⸺ₑₑₑ⸺

HALLOWELL:
PRINTED BY GLAZIER, MASTERS & CO.
No. 1, Kennebec-Row.

1830.

FIGURE 4. Joseph Plumb Martin, *A Narrative of Some of the Adventures, Dangers and Sufferings of a Revolutionary Soldier*. Courtesy, American Antiquarian Society.

his autobiography until very late in life and did not publish it until 1821. Although composed between 1771 and 1790, *The Autobiography of Benjamin Franklin* was not published as a complete volume for English readers until 1818. Both these texts embody what Sacvan Bercovitch meant by auto-American-biography, a text that converts "a social mode of personal fulfillment into a personal mode of social fulfillment."[31] They document the public events their authors helped shape and are less a reflection of the statesmen's inner lives than of the nation they helped mold.

The very opposite is typically said of veteran memoirs. Daniel Shea has suggested "the autobiographical writings of veterans of the War for Independence, such as Joseph Plumb Martin's . . . are the military memoirs of the common soldier rather than perspectives on the transformation from a colonial to a national identity."[32] Neither during his life nor in the centuries since has Martin been recognized as a national actor—he certainly was no Jefferson or Franklin—and yet the course of his writing career followed a parallel path to these national figures. Almost fifty years after his military service had ended, having had no formal schooling or inclination to write, and while still mired at the age of seventy in a cycle of poverty that required most of his time and energy to overcome, Martin decided, with little hope of financial return, to record his memories of the Revolution in print. Why so late after the war? Why, for that matter, at all?

The folklorist Richard Dorson has attributed the distinct latency of early veteran memoir production to a national disinterest in war in the early decades of the nineteenth century. Most Revolutionary War memoirs like Martin's were published between 1820 and 1840 because by that time a certain "historic glamour" had been attached to the Revolution and to the individual soldier's experience. Grandchildren of aging veterans wanted to hear about their family's predisposition for valor and courage. Demand was also spurred following the War of 1812 by a postwar and largely nonmilitary generation of readers who looked back more and more nostalgically on the Revolution because by then it was becoming increasingly apparent that the nation was going to "take."[33] Such arguments are convincing, yet they overlook the political needs of early American veterans to be recognized as agents of their own lives and to influence the legacy of the war. Consider that when Daniel Webster dedicated the Bunker Hill monument in June 1825, he paid particular homage to the dead ("We are among the sepulchres of our fathers") and when Lafayette returned to the United States in 1824, his grand tour revived the heroic glamour attached to extraordinary men like himself.[34] Yet the "ordinary" living veteran had no champion.

The 1820s was a transitional decade insofar as Jefferson, Franklin, Lafayette, and other "exceptional" citizens of the Revolutionary generation were fading and new guardians of Revolutionary memory, such as Cooper and Webster, were fashioning a second generation of representation that imaged the past as a closed prologue to the promising future of the United States. Lost amid this memory shuffle were such aging veterans as Martin who worried well into the 1840s about the value and role of their living memories within their imagined communities. Early veteran memoir was thus a literary appeal in protest of the changing tides of generational memory that were seen as threats to the meaning of veterans' living memories.

Even before *The Spy,* most representations of the Revolutionary War rendered military experience at the service of nationalist mythmaking. William Huntting Howell reads Martin's *Narrative* as "offering a corrective to the endlessly circulating stories of soldering that center on elite virtue," in particular David Ramsay's *History of the American Revolution* (1789), Mason Locke Weems's *A History of the Life and Death, Virtues and Exploits of General George Washington* (1800), and Mercy Otis Warren's *History of the Rise, Progress, and Termination of the American Revolution* (1805).[35] Another round of histories would surface in the 1820s with such figures as Salma Hale, Charles Goodrich, Emma Willard, and Noah Webster—the same decade that Lafayette would return to the United States and the cornerstone of the Bunker Hill monument would be laid. Such normative works were prone to remembering the Revolution as a coherent narrative with pitch-perfect development and led by extraordinary men. There was a clear beginning to the war with the "shot heard round the world" at the Battle of Lexington, then the requisite setbacks as at Bunker Hill, only to be followed by increasing successes such as Saratoga, and ultimately an unambiguous ending at Yorktown when Cornwallis surrendered. In contrast, Martin's *Narrative* is relentlessly episodic, and Howell suggests the author's writing scheme is a careful attempt to urge "his readers to think of war as a state absolutely incommensurable with coherent storytelling."[36]

That Martin is experimenting with memory as well as literary craft is apparent from the opening lines that dryly disavow the autobiographical conventions of the time. "The heroes of all Histories, Narratives, Adventures, Novels and Romances, have, or are supposed to have ancestors, or some root from which they sprang. I conclude, then, that it is not altogether inconsistent to suppose that I had parents too" (*N* 5). From captivity narratives to Benjamin Franklin's *Autobiography,* the tradition of life writing at the time (those histories and narratives Martin declares he is not writing) often compelled the text to justify its authorial voice by foregrounding the writer's heritage. Thus established, the writer could go on to extricate himself from his forebears (be they Franklin's "obscure family" of scriveners, dyers, and priests, or Frederick Douglass's mixed-race parentage) to become a self-made success story.[37] But war for Martin was not a success story, and he feels as little allegiance to autobiographical narrative schemes as he does his civilian parents, whom he only subversively acknowledges and quickly disavows.

Howell picks up on what is largely unexplored in the scholarship, namely, how the *Narrative*'s political protest is partnered with Martin's repeated acts of narratological protest—Martin is an artist as much as he is a veteran. The relatively scant treatment Martin has received in recent decades has mainly come not from literary historians but from social historians in the tradition of Jesse Lemisch and Howard Zinn, all of whom bypass Martin's political and aesthetic crisis.[38] Instead, Martin serves as the spokesman for the "common man" in Alfred Fabian Young's introduction to *Liberty Tree: Ordinary People and the American Revolution* (2006), in large part because Martin was for Young exactly the type of neglected figure whose present-day recovery represented "history from the bottom up."[39] For Young as for Lemisch, Ray Raphael, and Charles Royster, Revolutionary veterans have been imagined as a dispossessed group in similar ways as African Americans, women, and Native Americans, each of whose influence in early national society, they would argue, has not been studied enough.[40]

Charles Patrick Neimeyer takes the matter one step further in *America Goes to War: A Social History of the Continental Army* (1996), wherein he carves his soldier study into respective chapters on Irish, German, African American, and Native American troops. Neimeyer cites Martin as the marginalized heroic everyman—the "'G.I. Joe' of the American Revolution."[41] Each of these previous studies has insisted on a new historical calculus that includes "outsiders" and those on the "bottom" of social and political hierarchies. To that end, Martin has been read as an index of the "common man" to the detriment of how he actually saw himself. He looked for commonalities with other veterans as well as with the nation but found very few. Martin and his fellow veteran memoirists were not simply silenced victims whose injustices were interchangeable but rather wry and inventive literary practitioners whose craft was an appeal to preserve veteran memory of the Revolutionary War.

The critic James Kirby Martin estimates that in addition to Revolutionary prisoner-of-war captivity narratives, there are extant today more than five hundred Revolutionary veteran texts, ranging from ephemera such as autobiographical sketches and diaries to polished prose in public memoirs, "but Martin's *Narrative* represents [by far] the most complete memoir by a common soldier."[42] By most complete, Kirby Martin suggests Plumb Martin's was the most detailed and most contemplative memoir, and indeed the *Narrative* does exhibit many of the political and affective concerns common to aging Revolutionary veteran authors of the time. Protest undergirded second-generation veteran writing, which helps to explain why mostly only Revolutionary veterans were writing and publishing during this time. Largely absent were veterans of the Barbary and Indian Wars and the War of 1812, primarily because those conflicts were fought by militiamen and mercenaries who were not as troubled as Martin was with what it meant to be a veteran who did not get his due.

Martin wrote the *Narrative* in 1830 in large part to right a grievance, specifically in regard to his military pension. In 1832, Congress would pass a new Pension Act removing the poverty test and opening up eligibility to all veterans regardless of need, but by then it was too late for Martin. The last page to the *Narrative* underscores how the government was just waiting for veterans like him to die. "But if the old Revolutionary Pensioners are really an eyesore, a grief of mind, to any man, or set of men, (and I know they are,) let me tell them that if they will exercise a very little patience, a few years longer will put all of them beyond the power of troubling them; for they will soon be 'where the wicked cease from troubling, and the weary are at rest'" (*N* 252). Other soldiers lodged similar complaints.[43] Martin had applied for a federal pension before a judge in Hancock County, Maine, in July 1820. Years before he wrote the *Narrative,* he had testified there that "I have no real nor personal estate nor any income whatever[,] my necessary bedding and wearing apparel excepted—except two cows, six sheep, [and] one pig"; that he was "by reason of age and infirmity . . . unable to work"; and that his wife was "sickly and rheumatic."[44] Martin was most likely overstating his case, but then again, most applicants embellished their suffering lest they risk having their pension denied.[45]

In his petition, Martin requested ninety-six dollars a month and was awarded only eight. He would publish his *Narrative* almost a decade after the court had decided his case, and his memoir reads as an appeal of the court's decision. As Catherine Kaplan puts it, the text is "less a conventional war memoir than it is a bill—figurative and literal—for services rendered." Martin had endured war for seven years. As subsequent years passed, Martin felt veterans like him were increasingly unrewarded for their service and sacrifice.[46] As I noted in chapter 1, Congress passed the original 1818 bill but did not fund it, and the groundswell of needy veterans met empty coffers. By the end of 1818, some 20,000 soldiers had already applied. Subsequent amendments in 1820 and 1823 created harsher standards that were more discriminating. Over the course of the various pension programs, the government would receive more than 80,000 applications.[47] Considering that at least 200,000 men had served in the Revolutionary military, and "some fifty thousand of them were still alive in the 1820s and 1830s," the percentage of soldiers demanding recognition and reparation was extremely high.[48] The Pension Acts directly contributed to the occasion of Martin's literary appeal. And yet even more than restitution, Martin wrote in an effort to expose and correct the distortions of what a Revolutionary veteran was—both the misperceptions of the self-sacrificing officer as well as the volunteer infantrymen who asked for nothing in return. Neither image was an accurate reflection of the average fighting man.

Throughout the early days of the war, volunteer minutemen and local militias were quick to organize, but for many, revolutionary zeal quickly ran up against the reality of responsibilities back home. Plain farmers felt compelled to return to their harvests. Slave owners in the

South protested they could not stay at the front lines because they were needed on the plantation to prevent potential slave insurrections. Social historian Ray Raphael has pointed out that by the fall of 1775, the first wave of what Thomas Paine in *The Crisis* called "summer soldiers and sunshine patriots" had "packed up to go home."[49] Faced with a rising tide of desertion and the need for a reliable source of replacements, Washington proposed a system of incentives to attract a more trust-worthy corps. A reluctant Continental Congress authorized modest bounties of ten and then twenty dollars for all soldiers who enlisted in the newly created Continental Army. Recruitment, however, continued to suffer, and the newfound conscription system imposed quotas on each state. States in turn ordered towns to raise set numbers of compa-nies. These companies formed the Continental Army, composed mostly of poor, young, and unmarried boys eager to make some money. For-mer militiamen paid apprentices and drifters to be their substitutes. Military recruiters widely targeted the indigent.

In contrast to the militia soldier who typically owned property and benefited from the extensive social and political networks of marriage and commerce, the Continental soldier represented an underclass amalgamation of already marginalized peoples. Some estimates suggest Irish immigrants and African Americans were, respectively, 30 percent and 15 percent of the Continental Army by 1780 (*N* x). What united the various backgrounds initially was the promise of employment. Martin enrolled for the first time in the Continental Army at fifteen because there was a one-dollar bounty, not because he felt a patriotic calling (*N* 8). As one historian phrases his sentiment, "in Martin's portrayal of the Revolution, self-sacrifice becomes self-sale."[50] Martin reenlists after six months once "the men gave me what they agreed to, I forget the sum" (*N* 54), and then again in 1783 only after another man offers a substitu-tion fee of sixteen dollars (*N* 242).

Martin takes exception to the militia as he did to the officers because both types of men exploited his labor while taking all the credit. "It has been said by some that ought to have been better employed; that the Revolutionary army was needless; that the Militia were competent for all that the crisis required . . . I hope the citizen soldiers will be as ready to allow, who are not so good as regulars; and I affirm that the Militia would not have answered so well as standing troops, for the following

reason, among many others. They would not have endured the sufferings the army did" (*N* 249). Martin imagined the separation between
his living memory of the regular army and the popular impression "said
by some" of a grassroots militia to be the qualitative differences in their
suffering. Prone as they were to early retreats and shaky resolve, militia
soldiers—like officers—did not suffer in the same manner as Martin.

For him, the designation "soldier" was not an honorific given to anyone who picked up a rifle at some point during the course of the war
but a political and psychological mark of difference that Martin still
feels even decades after the war was over. "That the Militia did good and
great service in that war, as well as in the last, on particular occasions,
I well know, for I have fought by their side; but still I insist that they
would not have answered the end so well as regular soldiers . . . The
regulars were there, and there obliged to be" (*N* 249–50). The regulars
served by virtue of a contractual oath, widely regretted but freely given,
that compelled them to stay until the war's end. André had reminded
early Americans about their collective treachery in rebelling against the
British Crown, but Martin positioned veterans like him as the cure to
their countrymen's disloyalty. They stayed even when they had suffered
so much and had reason to leave.

Martin represents veteran suffering as a trope that is unique and
incomprehensible to his fellow Americans—both of his own generation
and of the subsequent generation. This sense of being exceptional most
often comes from his hunger, and one of the more famous passages
from the *Narrative* details a Thanksgiving meal in 1777 while Martin is
stationed in defense outside Philadelphia.

> While we lay here there was a Continental thanksgiving ordered by
> Congress; and as the army had all the cause in the world to be particu-
> larly thankful, if not for being well off, at least, that it was no worse, we
> were ordered to participate in it. We had nothing to eat for two or three
> days previous, except what the trees of the fields and forests afforded
> us. But we must now have what Congress said—a sumptuous thanks-
> giving to close the year of high living, we had now nearly seen brought
> to a close. Well—to add something extraordinary to our present stock
> of provisions, our country, ever mindful of its suffering army, opened
> her sympathizing heart so wide, upon this occasion, as to give us some-
> thing to make the world stare. And what do you think it was, reader?—

Guess.—You cannot guess, be you as much a Yankee as you will. I will tell you: it gave each and every man *half a gill* of rice, and a *table spoon full* of vinegar!! After we had made sure of this extraordinary super-abundant donation, we were ordered to attend a meeting, and hear a sermon delivered upon the happy occasion. (*N* 87; emphasis in original)

Martin's sarcasm is contemptuous not only of the paltry meal he received but also of his reader's expectations. As he builds the passage, anticipation grows over what this "extraordinary superabundant" meal could possibly be, but just as Martin's hunger was not satisfied with his half a gill of rice, so the reader is left unsatisfied. Martin quite carefully "recreates in miniature the experience of privation" by denying the reader's growing appetite.[51] Martin's text often presents itself as "a kind of brief in an imagined lawsuit over a broken social contract," and in response, Martin retaliates with his own broken narrative contract.[52] Less satirical than disdainful, the tone connects Martin's memory of disappointment with his current attitude toward his readers in 1830 who actually believed the country's "sympathizing heart" had been "so wide" that starving soldiers were lavished with food and drink.

The longevity of his famine and sense of deprivation separates Martin from the civilian readers he imagines because he understood what Elaine Scarry articulated in a different context, that "to have great pain is to have certainty; to hear that another person has pain is to have doubt."[53] The body's pain manifests itself at times psychologically, such as following Martin's indecisiveness over whether or not to enlist. Martin fears his readers will consider his dithering to be cowardly or, worse, unrepresentative of the ambivalence and doubt of the freshly inducted soldier. He turns on the reader quickly. "One thing I am certain of, and that is, reader, if you had been me you would have done just as I did. What reason have you then to cavil?" (*N* 14). More frequently, Martin's anguish manifests itself in his relentless need to eat (as the Thanksgiving passage suggests).

Passages detailing his extreme hunger and thirst dominate the book, occurring no less than twenty-five times. He is "literally starved" (*N* 148) during much of his military service, reduced at times to scavenge for dead cats and livestock (*N* 72).[54] When "the worm of hunger" was so bad it "kept us from being entirely quiet, we therefore still kept upon the parade in groups, venting our spleen at our country and government, then at our officers, and then at ourselves for our imbecility, in staying there and starving in detail for an ungrateful people, who did not care what became of us, so they could enjoy themselves while we were keeping a cruel enemy from them" (*N* 160). Memories of hunger like these are rhetorical opportunities to snipe at his countrymen's full bellies.

In contrast to his readers' contentment, substandard nutrition often triggers violent disease and disorder in Martin's body.[55] Severe indigestion follows a meal of "an old ox's liver" that he comes upon, and so the regimental doctor gives Martin "a large dose of tartar-emetic, the usual remedy in the army for all disorders": "I had not strolled a half or three fourths a mile from camp, when it took hold of my gizzard; I then sat down upon a log, or stone, or something else, and discharged the hard junks of liver like grapeshot from a fieldpiece. I had no water or any other thing to ease my retchings. O, I thought I *must* die in good earnest. The liver still kept coming, and I looked at every heave for my own liver to come next, but that happened to be too well fastened to part from its moorings" (*N* 164–65). The unpleasantness of this scene could perhaps be but a moment for the reader, but Martin refuses to let it pass. As he often will, Martin lingers in his discomfort to emphasize the magnitude of his suffering. "Perhaps the reader will think this a trifling matter, happening in the ordinary course of things, but I think it a 'suffering,' and not a small one neither, 'of a revolutionary soldier'" (*N* 165). Martin's voice demands that the vomiting be recognized as a "suffering," which for him is a political category of entitlement. Later a bunch of rotten apples "caused me to discharge the contents of my stomach . . . I never before thought myself so near death, and it was all occasioned by eating a few apples . . . This was one 'suffering' of a Revolutionary Soldier" (*N* 174–75). Near starvation at the end of the war, Martin jokes with a fellow soldier that he would eat his friend if only he had the proper tools. "But, truly, this was one among the 'sufferings' I had to undergo, for I was hungry and impatient enough to have eaten the fellow had he been well cooked and peppered" (*N* 196). By the end of Martin's *Narrative*, his appeal has transformed into an angry affidavit claiming quite clearly that this hunger is the property of himself and veterans like him—civilians should neither compete with nor claim veteran experience. But that, of course, is exactly what generational memory had done over the past half century.

* * *

Thomas Jefferson wrote George Washington in 1784 that the "institution of the Cincinnati," and in particular Washington's involvement in it (he was selected the first President-General of the society in 1783 and would remain in the position until his death in 1799), "has been [a] matter of anxiety to me." Jefferson's protests spoke to a larger distrust of the ruling classes. "The objections of those opposed to the institution shall be briefly sketched . . . They urge that it is against the Confederation; against the letter of some of our constitutions; against the spirit of them all, that the foundation, on which all these are built, is the natural equality of man, the denial of every preeminence but that annexed to legal office, and particularly the denial of a preeminence by birth."[56] In its charter, the Society of the Cincinnati limited membership to those officers who had served in the Revolutionary War and their male descendants. Jefferson worried about the precedent such a closed class system would establish: too much prestige and the officer class would gain an unfair political advantage. Keenly aware of the unease surrounding a perceived consolidation of military privilege and power, the society deployed a rhetoric of deference to civil authority.[57]

Congressman and Revolutionary historian David Ramsay tried to settle the matter of trust in civil-military relations by downplaying the extent of sacrifice and therefore the credit the "average" veteran deserved. In a speech before the South Carolina Society of the Cincinnati in 1794, he dismissed the notion that a separate military class was even necessary. "In these states there is a vigorous execution of the laws . . . these blessings are secured to us without the intervention of a standing army. Our government resting on the affections of the people, needs no other support than that of citizen soldiers. How unlike this to foreign countries, where enormous taxes are necessary to pay standing armies, and where standing armies are necessary to secure the payment of enormous taxes."[58] That they might ward off allegations of elitism, wartime officers of the society chose an image of themselves as a volunteer band of citizen-soldiers rather than as a permanent army with professional ranks.

"Every citizen, is perfectly free of the will of every other citizen, while all are equally subject to the laws," Ramsay continued. "Among us no one can exercise any authority by virtue of birth. All start equal in the race of life. No man is born a legislator. We are not bound by any laws but those to which we have consented."[59] Such talk of civil-military parity by the officers did no favor to the Revolutionary infantrymen, who quite strongly believed they actually were a different type of citizen crippled by a chronic inability to get their voices heard. So frustrated, one veteran memoirist named Josiah Priest in 1839 lamented that "the pen of the writer cannot describe [the full truth]; for the *truth* of such disasters and sufferings are not to be depicted by the pen of any man, so as to give the reader an idea of the same kind of feeling the sufferer endured."[60] With officers portraying themselves as the common citizen-soldier, there was no rhetorical room for the more typical Continental veteran to translate his suffering for his reader. In the race to the populist bottom, soldiers such as Priest and Martin could not compete with officers in the national discussion of the war.

Narrative divisions reflect political divisions for other veteran memoirists as well. Revolutionary veteran Christopher Hawkins prefaced his memoir by highlighting the class divisions he felt in early American society.

> No literary ambition has prompted its publication. I am an unlettered man, and cannot possibly have a desire to be ranked among the *literati* of my own or any other conntry [*sic*]. The literary critics of course will not notice my work, for in it, there can be no food wherewith to feast their refined and delicate appetites. To refined and classical writing I offer no claim. It is my desire to leave behind me a faithful and unvarnished narrative of my early sufferings, in which I was not alone. My intention in publishing this narrative is confined to the attention of my children, grandchildren, and their descendants, with the hope that they will duly appreciate not only my own sufferings, but those of my contemporaries in the arduous struggle of my country for independence, in which, success crowned the efforts of those who embarked in the American cause.[61]

Early veteran memoir often debased itself as unworthy and meek ("I am an unlettered man") and nothing more than a family affair. Hawkins wrote a private war "confined to the attention" of his family, one that was quite different from the one being remembered publicly (furthermore, "my early sufferings" might remain as foreign to his descendants as they were to readers in the post-Revolutionary generation). This posture is insincere insofar as a text not meant for publication outside its proclaimed "family" would not need a defense of its literary merits. Yet veteran memoir repeatedly insisted on a civilian audience it also shunned. It made strong yet caged demands of its imagined civilian readers as a way to self-protect.

Martin was no exception. "The critical grammarian may find enough to feed his spleen upon, if he peruses the following pages; but I can inform him beforehand, I do not regard his sneers; if I cannot write grammatically, I can think, talk and feel like other men" (*N* 2). Whenever Martin evokes similar self-reflexive defenses of himself, an address to his imagined civilian reader is soon to follow. When Martin is promoted as a noncommissioned officer (NCO), he welcomes the reader's judgment *of his writing* as proof of his ability to be an NCO. "How far [the Major who promoted him] was to be justified in his choice the reader may, per-haps, be enabled to judge by the construction of this present work; I give him my free consent to exercise his judgment upon it" (*N* 167–68). When Martin suspects he may be coming off as too self-congratulatory, "the reader may take my word if he pleases" (*N* 129). The degree depends on the context, but such deference is always in some measure feigned if not avoided entirely. "All things considered, the army was not to be blamed [for deserters]. Reader, suffer what we did and you will say so too" (*N* 157). The prose wants to convince a skeptical civilian public and at the same time is preemptively dismissive of audience members should they fail to be convinced.

A similar fear of civilian rejection prefaces the journal of Charles Herbert, a Revolutionary War captive of Old Mill Prison whose fam-ily waited until 1847 to publish his work. "In presenting the following pages to the reader, the publisher has no ambition to aspire to the char-acter of an author, and what is perhaps more rare, he has no private interest to serve; he does not seek to gratify the fastidious part of the community, who would have more respect for the dress, or appear-ance, than for the subject matter. He is perfectly aware that the Journal is not without some imperfections; but it must be kept in mind that it was not written for the public, with an eye to publication, or to make a book—but simply as a memorandum of the events of each day." As with Hawkins, the question must be asked: If there was never an eye to publication, why address the reader in such a public way? The editor tells us clearly because Herbert and his family were hopeful that civilian readers would come around and finally pay up. "It is to be regretted that Mrs. Herbert has not been able to obtain either the pension allowed by the law of our land to widows of Revolutionary soldiers and sailors, or the prize money due to her husband from government. How slow are we to reward those who struggled hard for our liberties."[62] There is a sense throughout antebellum veteran literature of subtle (and sometimes not so subtle) confrontation with the civilian readers it needs—not only financially (someone has to buy these memoirs) but also affectively.

Ignorant civilian readers were the perpetual irritant of nineteenth-century veteran literature because they always need to be persuaded and cajoled and yet never appear persuaded or cajoled. The result was a frustrating ambivalence that bordered at times on despondence. Revolutionary captive Ebenezer Fletcher ends his 1813 narrative by avoiding his anger directly. "And now, kind reader, wishing that you may forever remain ignorant of the real sufferings of the veteran soldier, from hunger and cold, from sickness and captivity, I bid you a cordial adieu."[63] Just as with Herbert and Hawkins, one must question why Fletcher would describe his "real sufferings" if he was earnest in wanting to protect his readers from them. Martin did not suffer from this strain of veteran passive aggression in his memoir. Rather, he states clearly that he is addressing civilians. "Mr. Reader, every one can tell what he has done in his lifetime, but every one has not been a soldier, and consequently can know but little or nothing of the sufferings and fatigues incident to an army" (N 2). After Martin, civilian readers could not plead ignorance or hide behind the cover of supplicant veterans who walked the line between wanting to be paid and wanting to be respected. In short, veteran memoir demanded that veterans be read on their own terms and in their own words, even if that desire was imperfectly met.

Martin is at his most desperate when describing the suffering of his fellow veterans. "No one who has never been upon such duty as those advanced [scouting] parties have to perform, can form any adequate idea of the trouble, fatigue and dangers which they have to encounter" (N 59). Describing soldiers like himself is the only time when words seem to fail him.

I leave to my reader to judge. It is fatiguing, almost beyond belief, to those that never experienced it, to be obliged to march twenty-four or forty-eight hours (as very many times I had to) . . . Fighting the enemy is the great scarecrow to people unacquainted with the duties of an army. To see the fire and smoke, to hear the din of cannon and musketry, and the whistling of shot; they cannot bear the sight or hearing of this . . . I never was killed in the army; I never was wounded but once; I never was a prisoner with the enemy; but I have seen many that have undergone all these; and I have many times run the risk of all of them myself; but, reader, believe me, for I tell a solemn truth, that I have felt more anxiety, undergone more fatigue and hardships, suffered more every way, in performing one of those tedious marches, than ever I did in fighting the hottest battle I was ever engaged in, with the anticipation of all the other calamities I have mentioned added to it. (*N* 248–49)

The civilian reader's deficit of experience was the limit of the narrative's ability to represent the veteran story. For those soldiers unlike Martin who were the fatalities of combat, even less could be communicated. One soldier obsessed with foretelling his own death soon falls lifeless on the battlefield. "'Now I am going out to the field to be killed'; and he said more than once afterwards, that he should be killed; and he was—he was shot dead on the field. I never saw a man so prepossessed with the idea of any mishap as he was" (*N* 47). An anonymous sergeant "was cut in two by a cannon shot" (*N* 79). Martin has no more to say about him. Of all the faceless men, "I saw Artillerists belonging to one gun, cut down by a single shot, and I saw men who were stooping to be protected by the works, but not stooping low enough, split like fish to be broiled" (*N* 80). Descriptions of violence seem to reassure Martin rather than traumatize him insofar as they confirmed his own incredulity. "At that instant a shot from the enemy . . . passed just by [a sergeant's] face without touching him at all; he fell dead into the trench; I put my hand on his forehead and found his skull was shattered all in pieces, and the blood flowing from his nose and mouth, but not a particle of skin was broken. I never saw an instance like this among all the men I saw killed during the whole war" (*N* 206). Appearances ("not a particle of skin was broken" because the bullet "passed just by his face") did not describe reality ("his skull was shattered all in pieces" because a bullet had, in fact, entered his body).

Earlier veteran authors likewise were numbed by the physical effects of violence. John Blatchford felt nothing in his 1788 captivity after being wounded by a British guard's bayonet, "it came near my navel; but the wound was not very deep."[64] He does not have much else to say, even after enduring eight hundred lashes for trying to escape. David Perry, who fought in the French and Indian War as well as the Revolution, described a similar remoteness in the witnessing of violence. "While a squad of regulars sat eating their breakfast in a tent, a cannon ball passed through it, and killed one man instantly; and another by the name of David Foster, belonging to Capt. Cain's company, was struck on the temple bone by a grape shot, which passed under his forehead, rolled his eyes out, and left a little piece of the lower part of his nose standing."[65] Veteran memoirs offer no comfort to the soldier's sufferings, dangers, and deaths, because in the end their authors suspected there might be none.

Unlike veteran authors, such civilian memory activists as Cooper believed in the possibility of redemption. *The Spy* never describes suffering soldiers as veteran memoirs do, but throughout the novel's action they are wounded and dying offstage. A surgeon by the name of Sitgreaves treats them even though we do not see their pain, and his reaction to their traumatized bodies is a useful comparison to Perry's description of combat. According to Sitgreaves, the real problem with war was that it killed people, when really "[death-blows] are useless in a battle, for disabling your foe is all that is required" (*S* 102). War was bad for his everyday business as a healer, and as Sitgreaves explains to Miss Peyton, "'All trades, madam, ought to be allowed to live; but what is to become of a surgeon, if his patients are dead before he sees them!'" (*S* 118). It would be too easy to dismiss Sitgreaves as comic relief or caricature as some critics have.[66] He is, in fact, quite representative of the civilian desire for a bloodless war devoid of casualties.

Everyone knows a soldier's body cut in two is dead—the corpse cannot be reunited. Yet Sitgreaves refuses to address the soldier's suffering. "'Occasionally a body must have been left in two pieces, to puzzle the ingenuity of [ancient medical researchers such as Galen] to unite. Yet, venerable and learned as they were, I doubt not they did it'" (*S* 235). Biological fact gives ground in noncombatant desire to forlorn hope. Was it truly possible to "unite two parts of the human body, that have been severed by an edged instrument"? The doctor truly believes it is, and even internalizes the fantasy on his own body. "I once broke my little finger intentionally, in order that I might reduce the fracture and watch the cure: it was only on a small scale, you know, dear John; still the thrilling sensation excited by the knitting of the bone, aided by the contemplation of the art of man thus acting in unison with nature, exceeded any other enjoyment that I have ever experienced. Now, had it been one of the more important members, such as the leg or arm, how much greater must the pleasure have been!" (S 236). The greater the likelihood of pain and death, "how much greater" the pleasure grew for the doctor who, like Cooper, saw his intervention in the war as a healer rather than as a witness.

As with Cooper and his second-generation audience, Sitgreaves reshaped Revolutionary memory to meet his inner therapeutic needs. The doctor's response to the unseen traces of war was a bizarre distortion of the fragility of veteran life, and Sitgreaves's fantasy is at once earnest yet also plainly aware of its own delusion. "'When it is only a bullet, I have always some hopes; there is a chance that it hits nothing vital; but, bless me, Captain Lawton's men cut so at random—generally sever the jugular or the carotid artery, or let out the brains, and all are so difficult to remedy—the patient mostly dying before one can get at him. I never had success but once in replacing a man's brains, although I have tried three this very day'" (S 101). This is the enduring image of civilian denial in relation to veterans of the early Republic: somewhere on a battlefield, a civilian is still hunched over a soldier's corpse, frantically cupping, pushing, and kneading a young man's brains into his open head in the hopes that it is not as bad as it looks.

The paucity of scholarly textual analysis of Joseph Plumb Martin caused Kaplan to remark that his "*Narrative* has gone entirely unnoticed by literary scholars." In contrast to Martin's neglect, Cooper has been well studied. John Cawelti and Bruce Rosenberg have already laid out a case for how *The Spy* became the urtext for the modern spy novel tradition.[67] Other critics have focused on the artistic indecision of *The Spy*, caught as it is between competing ideological and nationalistic demands of the American domestic romance and the British historical adventure, each requiring different attentions to genre and form.[68] Cooper complained to his editor that "the task of making American Manner and American scenes interesting to an American reader is an arduous one," yet he was nonetheless committed to doing so. "I take more pains with [*The Spy*]—as it is to be an American novel professedly."[69] Making *The Spy* American meant also making the British André American, a contradiction of character not unlike Natty Bumppo in *The Leatherstocking Tales* whose civilized savagery would make Cooper famous.

Indeed, Cooper has always been primarily known for his tales of the frontier. The first of the Leatherstocking tales, *The Pioneers,* followed *The Spy* in 1823. Cooper would subsequently give the United States the adventure novel of the sea, populated with military heroes his audience could easily recognize. In the same year as *The Pioneers,* Cooper also published *The Pilot,* a work loosely based on the swashbuckling life of John Paul Jones and a conscious attempt to emulate and improve upon the popularity of Walter Scott's recent historical novel, *The Pirate* (1822). Cooper returned to land next in *Lionel Lincoln* (1825), the story of a British major in pre-Independence Boston. Robert S. Levine has concluded about Cooper's sailors and soldiers in *The Pilot* and *Lionel Lincoln* what can likewise be claimed about the double agents in *The Spy*: these men bear "little resemblance to the bold Roman profiles of America's Revolutionary heroes."[70] They were soldiers and sailors the romanticized way Cooper wanted to write them, and contemporary audiences took notice.

A reader complained in 1823 about Cooper's tendency for idealization, "Neither poetry nor prose can ever make a spy an heroic character."[71] Decades later, Cooper's two-volume *Lives of Distinguished American Naval Officers* (1846) selected the biographies of ten American officers much to the dismay of many others of "heroic character" who were left out. The *History of the Navy of the United States of America* (1839) brought on a libel suit from Captain Jesse D. Elliott, upset over Cooper's cowardly depiction of him at the Battle of Lake Erie during the War of 1812.[72] Cooper won the lawsuit, but the controversies surrounding his military representations only attest to his proprietary and partisan eye. In 1843, Cooper published one more military biography, *A Life before the Mast,* detailing the maritime experiences of a former acquaintance of his from the navy named Ned Myers. Though the two had not seen each other between 1809 and 1833, Cooper insisted his biography was a facsimile of the former sailor's life. *Before the Mast* claimed to capture the "language, deportment, habits and consistency of this well-meaning tar," without any "cant or exaggeration." At the same time the text claimed to be authentic, it also came with the following disclaimer: "In this book, the writer has endeavoured to adhere as closely to the very language of his subject, *as circumstances will at all allow.*"[73] Cooper gives himself permission, as he had in *The Spy,* to ventriloquize military experience. This disturbance of authorship is significant because years earlier he had grown angry when another author had taken the same liberty with *The Spy.*[74]

Following the success of *The Spy* in 1821, the relatively unknown H. L. Barnum came out in 1828 with his own revisionary text, *The Spy Unmasked.* Describing the piece as an exposé, Barnum claimed that by virtue of his own good fortune and investigative skill he had fashioned at long last the "*Authentic Account*" of the real-life spy behind Cooper's Revolutionary War novel. *The Spy Unmasked,* subtitled *Memoirs of Enoch Crosby, Alias Harvey Birch, the Hero of Mr. Cooper's Tale of the Neutral Ground,* authorizes itself as a sensationalistic addendum to Cooper's work because "it seemed to be generally admitted, that [Cooper's] Spy was not a fictitious personage, but a real character, drawn from life." Barnum breezily pens an "unauthorized dedication" to Cooper in the prefatory pages, then an introduction that begins to make a case for its authenticity and legitimacy as a useful and necessary supplement to the novel.[75]

Crucial to this task was the chain of custody of the veteran's story, from the actual events in the Neutral Ground three decades past to the current version of the narrative now offered. "A gentleman of good standing and respectability, who has filled honourable official stations in the county of Westchester, and who has long enjoyed the friendship and confidence of Mr. Cooper, informed the writer of this article, on the authority of Mr. Cooper himself, that the *outline* of the character of Harvey Birch, was actually sketched from that of Enoch Crosby; but filled up, partly from imagination, and partly from similar features in the lives of two or three others, who were also engaged in *secret services,* during the revolutionary war."[76] What was to be the true-to-life story of a true-to-life spy was instead a composite of hearsay, innuendo, and fabrication—an ironic narrative subterfuge within a novel built on subterfuge and spies, "filled up, partly from imagination."

A clear problem of methodology and authority presents itself. Enoch Crosby was one of three models for the novel's Harvey Birch. The reliability of Barnum's representation, therefore, was only as good as the distortions of his story that were rendered through the anonymous "gentleman of good standing and respectability" (if such a man could even be said to exist). But, like Albert Greene editing Thomas Dring at the end of chapter 1, Barnum did not see a problem. He wagered he was making Cooper's fiction better by improving the novel with his particular brand of "correction." Whether his source and its history were any good is another matter altogether, as is whether or not Cooper did indeed rely on the model of Enoch Crosby as he wrote *The Spy*.[77] But if we allow for the moment that some truth exists to Barnum's claims, then what is startling is that even though Cooper believed the opposite—that his novel was made worse by Barnum's intervention—the impulse in both men was to mediate the memory of Revolutionary War veterans. Underwriting both texts was the urge common to antebellum literature to modify veteran representation without concern for the proprietary nature of military experience that veteran memoirists were asserting.

The real-life Enoch Crosby was entirely unaware that a novel had been written about "his" Revolutionary service. Even though Cooper's novel had been widely read and circulated for several years by the time of *The Spy Unmasked,* Crosby had never heard of, let alone read, *The Spy,* "as novels were not included in his present course of reading." Barnum arrogantly assumes veterans did not read novels. It necessarily follows that they did not write them. That was for others to do, others like Barnum and Cooper. Even though Cooper had never met Crosby and Barnum had never met Cooper, Barnum insists, "Enoch Crosby was certainly the *original* which [Cooper] had in his 'mind's eye.'"[78] Whether Barnum really had his finger on what drove Cooper cannot be proven; however, these questions of accuracy and authenticity point us to more wide-ranging questions surrounding veteran silencing in the decades leading up to the Civil War. One cannot help but ask, in addition to whether Barnum (or Cooper) wrote Crosby as he really was, whether he wrote Crosby as the veteran would have written himself.[79] The case of Joseph Plumb Martin and his fellow early veteran memoirists strongly suggests not. Moreover, as civilian memory worked to appropriate veteran representation, that precedent affected veteran literary culture for the generations that followed and effectively created a forgotten age of amateurish veteran literature that is the focus of chapter 3.

Civilian competition with veteran authors over the control of military experience in the decades following the Revolutionary War conflated the multiplicity of veteran experience into a single story—a stereotype of lawlessness and, at times, bitterness, which was met with civilian suspicion and, at times, pity. Such was the lasting image of the Revolutionary captives from chapter 1, of André from the beginning of this chapter, and of Harvey Birch and Enoch Crosby half a century after the war was over. New York humorist Asa Greene was still mesmerized by the character of Harvey Birch as late as 1834 in his social protest novel, *The Debtor's Prison*. His story begins when a traveler in need appears on a winter's night before a happy family's home.

> The countenance of the old man was not without interest: and my daughters, who had been reading tales of romance, and especially the historical novels of Cooper, declared from the first moment they saw him, that he could be no less than the hero of some tale which would no doubt be interesting, if known, and particularly if committed to paper. "But who knows," said Lucy, the eldest, "but what is committed to paper and published?" "Why, do you think," said Harriet, "that the hero of a written and published tale would be wandering abroad, without clothing and without shelter, this bitter cold night?" "Why not?" replied Lucy. "Now the thought strikes me, that he is no other than the hero of Cooper's Spy." "What, Harvey Birch?" "The same. You know, Harriet, that he is just about the age of Harvey Birch would be by this time. You know that Harvey was a real character of the revolution; that he passed through the many hair-breadth 'scapes, and wandered about in poverty and disgrace, exposed to cold, hunger, and thirst, in order to serve his country."[80]

When a beggar comes asking, his fellow countrymen assume he must be the romanticized veteran of civilian memory. Why? Because the story of "Harvey Birch" coincided with what had become by midcentury the ingrained expectations of the veteran story as a hard luck picaresque. Indeed, Greene's caricature welcomes those conventions when the character claims to be a Revolutionary veteran and leaves open the possibility that he very well may be Harvey Birch after all. Playing to type, the veteran needs to feed his family (like Joseph Plumb Martin) and thus the mysterious traveler soon gets in with criminals (like Henry Tufts and Stephen Burroughs), which lands him thirty days in jail. Then his family dies, he has no other option but to join the army again at age 60, and his poverty cycle is triggered again.

As in the cases of Charles Cummings and Israel Potter in chapter 3, the predicament of the veteran throughout the early Republic was always synonymous with all kinds of unsavory associations, including begging, debt, and crime. Well into the 1830s, to see a beggar meant you saw a veteran (indeed, a *fictionalized* one at that, if we recall that Harvey Birch was Cooper's character; Enoch Crosby was the supposed true-to-life veteran), and to see a veteran meant you saw a beggar. Was there even a meaningful distinction between the two identities? Whereas antebellum civilian representation assumed that military experience was the cause of the social ills attendant to veterans—that is, Harvey Birch would not have been in such a pinch if he had not enlisted—early veteran literature argued the opposite, that the social ills which surrounded veterans were the symptoms of their widespread social estrangement rather than the source.

This distinction of cause and effect matters insofar as what was ultimately at stake in this decades-long back-and-forth between veteran memoir and civilian memory was how, if at all, aging Revolutionary veterans would reintegrate into American society. The civilian strategies outlined in this chapter to commandeer and appropriate veteran voices complemented other civilian tendencies described in chapter 3 to characterize veteran authors as incompetent, amateurish, and unworthy not only of a space in literary marketplaces but in American society as well. These literary practices interfered with veteran reintegration into civilian society, and such Revolutionary veterans as Joseph Plumb Martin and Thomas Painter lamented as much.

Like Martin's invective, Thomas Painter's memoir reveals the intersection of many of the patterns in early veteran representation already discussed. In Painter, we see glimpses of the Prodigal Son and the criminalized stray who is largely invisible to civilian Americans, all of whom refuse to believe his story and provide him comfort. Painter, who wrote his memoir in 1836 when he was seventy-six years old (his family would publish it privately in 1910), enlisted in 1776 at the age of sixteen because he was an orphan and saw no other path in life (*ATP* 7–8, 100). When the war starts, he quickly grows tired of it: "I then returned back to West Haven, thoroughly sick of a Soldier's life . . . I then determined to try my fortune Privateering" (*ATP* 16). The pirate's life proved little better, as soon he was captured and imprisoned aboard the *Good Hope,* only to escape after getting the guards drunk and swimming to shore (*ATP* 23–26). Having returned home exhausted and naked, he could only find a place to sleep in the Bowery in New York amid the "Bushes and Brambles":

> Here I lay very quietly, till some time in the afternoon, when I heard some persons, in conversation, and it appeared by the noise, that they were approaching me. I soon discovered, that it was a Gentleman and Lady, who, it seems, had made choice of my retreat for their own amusement. They came and took a seat on the grass, close to my feet, and fell into conversation on various subjects which however for a person in my situation was not very interesting. Now my chance of Escape, as I thought, appeared to me to be very small because I thought it almost impossible for them to leave, and not discover me. But there was no other way but for me to lie still, keep my Eyes nearly closed, and wait the Event. At length the Gentleman happening to turn his Eye directly to where my feet lay, discovered them. After piquing (and peeking) a little closer, he says to the Lady, there is a Boy, lying in the Bushes. This seemed rather to discompose her Ladyship. But he still continued peeking and peeking, and finally sings out Yo ho—Yo ho—. But I lay motionless, making no answer. He then speaks to the Lady, and says by G-d, I believe he is dead,—upon which they both retired, and to my great Joy, I saw the last of them. (*ATP* 28–29; emphasis in original)

As I hope has been shown up until this point, veteran memoir repeatedly detailed the failures of veteran reintegration into a civilian world. Here, the veteran's homecoming is met not only with the humiliation of sleeping naked in the bushes but also with the indifference of his fellow countrymen, who notice him yet do not seem to see him. These two lovers deny Painter's presence when they turn away from what they supposed to be a dead body and continue their flirtation elsewhere.

Still seeking help, Painter manages his way to New Jersey where he comes across a mill. "So I walked along very slowly towards the house, and at the same time, heard a drum beat a little back, and keeping a steady look at the house. I observed, that the people would come to the door,—stand, and look apparently at me, for a moment, and then turn about, and run in" (*ATP* 36). Yet again, civilians see the veteran but refuse to witness his presence, let alone welcome him inside their home. Becoming desperate, Painter comes across a Dutchman and his two sons cutting grain. "[The Dutchman] immediately looked at me with a stern, and unfriendly look, and demanded to know where I came from. I at once told him, that I had been a prisoner in New York, and had run away from the prison Ship, from which I had Escaped by swimming ashore in New York, and then by swimming across the North River, by which, means I had got as far as here. He then hung his cradle [of the scythe] on his arm, and advanced towards me, and, as appeared to me, with a much more angry countenance than before, and said, 'he did not' 'believe a word that I said,' and then again demanded to know where I came from, with a severe caution to tell the truth" (*ATP* 39; emphasis in original). Eventually the Dutchman warms up and starts to believe Painter's incredible story of escape, even offering him food and clothing. "He then gave me two dollars in money, and offered me a horse and a boy, to carry me on to his son[']s house. This I refused, for strange as it m[a]y appear, after all this kindness, I could not get entirely clear of the fright he had first given me, and I felt very anxious to be on my way, so as to get a little farther from the Enemy's lines" (*ATP* 42). Even when his countrymen come around, Painter balks and becomes suspicious of "this kindness" as a result of the "fright" he could not settle after initially being refused. His shock results from surprise at his countrymen's skepticism and indifference from which he would never overcome.[81]

The promise of military service to incorporate veterans within configurations of early American citizenship was rarely met. Philosopher Nancy Sherman has theorized veteran resentment not as a plea for pity or sympathy but "at its most basic, [as] a bid for respect" to recognize the injustices of the past: "Although resentment cannot *demand* that the other undo the past, the retrospective fantasy is more than just a wishful imagining of an alternative past. Its focus is on an *alternative deliberation*—that someone had a reason to do the right thing and didn't. And that is future-oriented; it's about how one normatively expects to be acknowledged in another's deliberations, in general and in future dealings, where there is forward-looking responsibility."[82] For early veteran memoir, there was little sense of a future in which the past would be made right. In the words of Benjamin Frederick Browne upon his release from a military prison during the War of 1812, "I had not, that I knew of, a single friend in the wide world who had the ability to assist me. I was returning, feeble and penniless, and for awhile I almost wished myself in Dartmoor [Prison] again, to stave off, for a few months longer, that future which I dreaded to encounter."[83] The future for nineteenth-century veterans who served well after the Revolutionary War would prove to be just as uncertain.

CHAPTER 3

A Bunch of Veteran Amateurs

1830–1865: Charles Cummings, Israel Potter,
Herman Melville, Edgar Allan Poe, William Richardson

"Comrade, there is one of two things a good American will do when he
is busted, he will either write a book or take up a collection."
 —*Charles Cummings,* The Great War Relic *(1890)*

Ann Fabian organizes her *Unvarnished Truth: Personal Narratives in Nineteenth-Century America* into four main groups: beggars, convicts, slaves, and Civil War prisoners of war. Her book is deft at tracing out the different anxieties of each identity, yet what is nonetheless common across each group is their amateurish scope and desire to get paid by whatever means necessary. In short, personal narratives in nineteenth-century America were "local projects designed to make a little money." A beggar begs, but so does the convict—his printed confession makes a bid for sympathy and redemption from its reader. The slave also begs for freedom, often by stretching the truth in hopes of achieving such ends. Civil War prisoners of war appear in Fabian's account to be the most manipulative, going so far as to appropriate representational strategies from slave narratives to conflate their captivity with slavery.[1] Whatever their

100

THE
GREAT WAR RELIC

TOGETHER WITH

A Sketch of My Life,

Service in the Army,

AND HOW

I · Lost · My · Feet

Since the War,

ALSO

Many Interesting Incidents

Illustrative

of the

Life of a Soldier.

Respectfully dedicated to my Comrade George E. Reed, Post 58, G. A. R., Dept. Penn'a
Harrisburg. Pa., for his Valuable War Relic, "The Campaign of the Sixth
Army Corps," thereby assisting me to compile this work.

Valuable as a Curiosity of the Rebellion.

COMPILED AND SOLD BY

CHAS. L. CUMMINGS.

Late Private Co. E, Twenty-eighth Michigan Infantry Volunteers.

FIGURE 5. Charles Cummings, *The Great War Relic*. Courtesy, American
Antiquarian Society.

station, life writers of the nineteenth century would say anything to sell a book, and the accounts they offered of their experiences were therefore distorted and self-interested—hardly "the unvarnished truth" at all.

Fabian's analysis reserves one of its strongest rebukes for Civil War veteran Charles Cummings and his embellishment of his war injuries in *The Great War Relic,* which went through several reprintings in the late 1880s and 1890s.[2] I would not disagree that Cummings's tone throughout often comes off as disingenuous. The opening of his 1890 narrative reads like a carnival barker trying to market his new and improved product: "And now I have decided to answer all, as it will be found in this book, AND IN NO OTHER WAY; if the information is worth having, it is worth something, AND I CAN'T LIVE ON QUESTIONS, as they have been fired at me for so many years. I have lately revised and added new material to the work, thereby increasing its value, and making the book better than ever." There is also the frequent reminder that his enlistment supposedly cost him everything: "I had missed my chance to acquire an education and the other boys had secured the good situations, and there was nothing left me but the rough work, which I was not fit for, all on account of having been too patriotic." To be sure, Cummings hams up his military service by making it seem by his title, *The Great War Relic,* that he lost his leg in the war, when he actually lost his leg many years later in an accident while working on the trains.[3] At the same time all this self-promotion is going on, his narrative is also undeniably honest about the economic realities of veteran authors in the middle to late nineteenth century. Rather than being strictly a case of crude veteran opportunism as Fabian suggests, Cummings's text is also—like the amateur veterans in this chapter—an example of nineteenth-century veteran sincerity that was dismissed by contemporaries then and somewhat incompatible with much of current scholarship now.

Meredith McGill, Michael C. Cohen, and Lara Langer Cohen have emphasized how literary markets for much of the nineteenth century were often hostile to the concept of stable and reliable authorship, thus making the headwinds for veteran Americans such as Cummings and the veteran memoirists from chapter 2 all the stronger. At issue is when early Americans wrote, be they veteran or not, was what they wrote true, accurate, and their own? McGill ascribes the fever at which modern critics have debated what texts should properly be credited as Edgar Allan Poe's to the fact that our present culture cannot tolerate literary anonymity, which is at odds with an antebellum "culture of reprinting," wherein texts were not only reprinted but often anonymously or with unclear attribution.[4] As a result, editors, reviewers, and authors indulged in a widespread practice of "puffing" that Langer Cohen argues allowed them to shamelessly publicize and cross-promote one another. In concert with Langer Cohen, McGill suggests that "textual integrity and authorial identity were common casualties of the reprint process," which might seem a problem to us today, but antebellum anonymity provided comfortable cover within early American print culture.[5]

For example, Michael C. Cohen insinuates that Nathaniel Hawthorne actively avoided attaching his name to tales such as "Mr. Higginbotham's Catastrophe" because to declare authorship was to invite the reading public's "open scorn." Criticism from readers was frequent and significant in the early decades of the nineteenth century because the "decentralized circulation of cheap print" was facilitated by figures such as iterant peddlers who moved through private homes and also public country stores (a space that William J. Gilmore deemed the "most critical local agent of transatlantic commerce and culture"), thereby increasing readers' access but also their opinions.[6] As Cohen notes about the social function of poems in particular, such a local and fluid literary culture "lies outside the institutionally sanctioned, author-centered, national tradition" of how we often understand American literature.[7] Indeed, early Americans were stuck within the "double bind of circulation in the U.S. at the beginning of the market revolution: a country open to the free movement of people, products, and information was a country vulnerable to gossip, slander, sedition, libel, or lies."[8] To put your name on something was to put yourself at risk of being scorned, and my point here is not to disagree with these critics but to note that the antebellum market realities of distrust and anonymity conspired against the political aspirations of early veteran Americans who desired the opposite. To wit, veterans very much wanted their names on the cover so that that they might be known (what I mean by "sincerity"), in addition to being paid, and that they might correct the civilian scorn, gossip, and slander that so often shaped nineteenth-century veteran American identity.

Although it is possible he overstated his experience, given the war and his accident, we might ask: What else was Cummings supposed to do? He secured "a permit from the mayor of a small Western city, in the year 1879, to sell stationery on the street," but that venture was largely unsuccessful. "I very soon found I had friends" at a Grand Army of the Republic post in Harrisburg, Pennsylvania, where Cummings debates whether to enter a soldier's home and live on charity alone. When a fellow veteran tells him "Comrade, there is one of two things a good American will do when he is busted, he will either write a book or take up a collection," he decides he would rather work at writing than live on the dole. "The reason I don't go to a soldiers' home is that I consider my business [be it writing or selling knives on the street] as honorable as that of any other person, and that I have as much right as others to make a living—*if they have a better right, where did they get it?*"[9] Here, Cummings reacts against the presumption that nineteenth-century veterans were only fit for certain work (begging or charity) and consequently unfit for other work (authorship). Such is his right: if other Americans "have a better right [to engage in literary labor], where did they get it?" Whatever else might be said about Cummings, his question is an honest one. It reveals a veteran perception in the middle decades of the nineteenth century that civilian professional writers had a "better right" to literary markets, a privilege that excluded further the supposed amateurism of veteran literature—as late as Cummings in 1890 and as early as Israel Potter in 1824.[10]

Israel Ralph Potter was a Revolutionary minuteman born in Cranston, Rhode Island (the year is unclear, either 1744 or 1754), who left his home at a young age once a love affair forbidden by his father spoiled his chance at a family life, who fought and was injured at Bunker Hill, and who subsequently was captured by the British and brought to England as a prisoner of war only to escape and live on the streets of London for almost fifty years as a "chair-mender." Potter returned to the United States in 1823, destitute and without any known family, only to die soon after his memoir came out the following year. *The Life and Remarkable Adventures of Israel R. Potter* was published in Providence in 1824 and went through three editions in that year alone. The *Magazine of History* reprinted the tale in 1911, in part because the original version "awoke so much attention as to be hawked by peddlers throughout New England."[11] Street vendors in London did the same. Calling the book a "fugitive memoir," Walter Bezanson, along with others such as David Chacko and Alexander Kulcsa, has noted how Potter's text was in many ways a "characteristic document from American popular culture of the 1820's," by which they meant it was a lowbrow circus act like much of print culture at the time.[12] Potter's publisher in 1824 was Henry Trumbull, a known peddler of "obscene books and pamphlets" and a man whom one historian calls "one of our early and most prolific liars." In 1841, Trumbull would publish *History of the Indian Wars,* a so-called history, that, "in addition to its narrative deficiencies, was known to contain as many as twenty-two chronological errors on a single page." In the same year Potter's "memoir" came out, Trumbull also reissued John Filson's problematic "autobiography" of Daniel Boone, of which Boone wrote not one word.[13]

Given the swirling suspicions of historical accuracy and authorial coherence, the only safe bet is that both Trumbull and Potter wanted to sell books. The 108 pages of the *Life and Remarkable Adventures of Israel R. Potter* read in part as a document of exaggerated folklore in the vein of Boone and Davy Crockett (*The Life of Davy Crockett* came out in 1834 and was most likely ghostwritten by Richard Penn Smith), and whatever Israel Potter might have said "by himself" without his bending to the marketplace and the pressures of an unscrupulous editor can never be known. Just as unknown hands imprinted Thomas Dring and Enoch Crosby, questions arise as to how we are to read Potter's text as well as the remainder of antebellum veteran literature. Is Potter's *Life* a reliable document of a veteran's sufferings written by himself? Or if it is ghostwritten, was the editorial imprint in earnest? Or is it an opportunistic fabrication, a mere adventure yarn and nothing more? Furthermore, if Israel Potter could be said to have had any control over his own story in 1824, he surely had none by midcentury after yet another hand rewrote his life story.

Israel Potter (1855) is Herman Melville's only self-proclaimed "biography," and it takes as its primary source the original *Life and Remarkable Adventures of Israel R. Potter* (1824).[14] Why would Melville rewrite a veteran's memoir thirty years after it had arguably already been "retouched" by Potter's original editor? Partly for money. Saddled with the financial failure of *Pierre* (1852), Melville was in financial need. He had known about the poor peddler and owned a copy of *Life* as early as the 1840s. In a journal entry dated December 18, 1849, Melville found himself in a secluded London bookstore. "Looked over a lot of ancient maps of London. Bought one (A.D. 1766) for 3 & 6 pence. I want to use it in case I serve up the Revolutionary narrative of the beggar."[15] The "serving up" of Potter came into being after *Putnam's* opened in 1852 as a competitor to *Harper's,* which had passed on the initial chapters of *Israel Potter.* Melville subsequently sent the first sixty pages of the manuscript off to George Putnam with the following disclaimer: "I engage that the story shall contain nothing of any sort to shock the fastidious. There will be very little reflective writing in it; nothing weighty. It is adventure. As for its interest, I shall try to sustain that as well as I can."[16] Melville felt sympathy for Potter to the extent that Potter was an exiled veteran who "did not reap the benefits of the Revolution he helped to win" and who had "no one but himself to relate his history."[17] The historical distance between Potter's tragedy and Melville's imagination had blurred the veteran's life into mere "adventure," whose "interest" for midcentury readers was contingent on its possessing "very little reflective writing."

The novel ran in *Putnam's* from July 1854 through March 1855. When the book version came out soon thereafter, Melville added a dedication, "To His Highness The Bunker-Hill Monument," in which he asserted that his novel "preserves, almost as in a reprint, Israel Potter's autobiographical story." Trumbull's version was by then out of print, but, Melville tells us, "from a tattered copy, rescued by the merest chance from the rag-pickers," he had saved the story. The present volume, he insists, might "be not unfitly regarded something in the light of a dilapidated old tombstone retouched."[18] Melville presumes he is the authorized curator of Israel Potter's estate and the welcomed guardian of his monument and memory. Yet his version is a complete revision rather than a light retouch, and *Israel Potter* reflects the midcentury rhetorical arrogance toward veterans that is both widespread and, to nineteenth-century audiences, surprisingly unproblematic.

At first, Melville is fairly true to the language and the plot from the first half of Trumbull's *Life,* but after Melville's chapter six (there are twenty-six chapters total), *Israel Potter* becomes a bit unhinged.

As way of example, the 1824 *Life* mentions only briefly how Potter met
with Benjamin Franklin in Paris, but Melville capitalizes on the occasion and gives Franklin several of the more interesting chapters in
the book. Celebrity of this sort runs throughout the novel. Potter also
hobnobs with King George III, swashbuckles with John Paul Jones,
and rubs elbows with Ethan Allen—all historical encounters unsub-
stantiated by any historical record, but included, Joyce Sparer Adler
has argued, to caricaturize American excesses of character.[19] Trumbull's *Life* was Melville's primary source, but we also know he worked
from *A Narrative of Ethan Allen's Captivity* (1779), Robert C. Sands's
Life and Correspondence of John Paul Jones (1830), and James Fenimore
Cooper's *History of the Navy of the United States of America* (rev. ed.,
1840).[20] Israel Potter became in the 1850s what Major André and Enoch
Crosby were in the 1820s: a narrative opportunity rather than an actual
biographical subject. For Melville, Potter was more of a criminal
than he was an honest beggar, a confidence man before there was *The
Confidence-Man* (1857). Potter bemoans to Benjamin Franklin, "So,
I've got to stay in this room all the time. Somehow I'm bound to be
a prisoner, one way or another."[21] In the memory of the 1850s, Potter is indeed confined, restricted, and often forced to impersonate so
as to escape: he masquerades as a gardener in King George's court, a
cloistered monk, a pirate on a ship. Continuing the trend begun in the
1820s outlined in chapter 2, the 1850s similarly sensationalized veteran
adventure at the expense of veteran suffering.

Peter Bellis has noticed how the Revolutionary War in Potter's 1824
text is in the present tense, still open and alive, whereas in the 1850s
Melville situates the war in the past tense, where the war can be forever
gone—an object of historical regret to be petrified like the Bunker Hill
memorial (the image that opens his version and ends Potter's).[22] Writing of the Battle of Bunker Hill, where he was injured in both the hip
and the ankle, Potter suggests that his memory of the war was still a
constant companion in 1824, some forty years removed from his experience: "The conflict, which was a sharp and severe one, is still fresh
in my memory, and cannot be forgotten by me while the scars of the
wounds which I then received, remain to remind me of it!"[23] Melville,
however, does not look long at the scars. When he gives the best scenes
to Franklin, Jones, and Allen, as a consequence he must remove some

element of Potter's original autobiography. Similar to James Fenimore Cooper's removal of dying soldiers in *The Spy*, what gets cut is Potter's prolonged suffering, exile, and imprisonment in England. His poverty accounts for almost half of the 1824 text but only a few pages in Melville's 1855 retelling.[24]

In Potter's version, the streets of London are filled with con men, gypsies who "kidnap little children," and "Footpads"—men described as little more than armed robbers and murderers. Unassuming gentlemen are often killed in the street for money. Melville, however, does not examine the criminal undertones of Potter's life in exile, whereas Potter relates how he was sent to debtor's prison after defaulting on loans that he took out in order to feed his wife and ten children. Seven of his offspring would die in childhood and two more in their early twenties; after these devastating losses, his wife died soon thereafter. When Potter is finally able to return to the United States, he arrives with his lone surviving son and visits Bunker Hill for the duration of only one sentence. The narration ends with his return to his birthplace in Rhode Island in hopes of securing an inheritance of land from his deceased father. Potter's brothers, however, had already sold his share and moved out of the state.[25]

Within the competing versions of Potter's life—as adventure or as suffering—are echoes of the veteran memoirists from chapter 2 and the problems that generational change caused for veteran authors. History transferred Potter's living memory of suffering into Melville's nostalgic imagination. Indeed, Potter writing in 1824 was already several decades removed from the Revolutionary War, yet he still had a claim on it that Melville did not. Melville knew as much. After all, both Melville's grandfathers had served in the Revolutionary War. His paternal grandfather, Major Thomas Melvill, was reported to have been one of the painted Indians at the Boston Tea Party, but in his later days, Melvill became a relic and caricature of his former self. He was Oliver Wendell Holmes Sr.'s inspiration for "The Last Leaf" (1831), a poem alternatively tittering and penitent, in which Melvill, the obsolete old soldier, roams about the modern cityscape still dressed in his tattered uniform, as the elderly man was often reported to have done among the streets of Boston.

I know it is a sin
For me to sit and grin
At him here;
But the old three-corned hat,
And the breeches, and all that,
Are so queer!

Ridiculing the old soldier quickly unnerves Holmes's speaker, however, for no sooner does the poem have its fun than it quickly regrets its impertinence. The speaker imagines that there was a time, in the major's youth, when "not a better man was found":

But now he walks the streets,
And he looks at all he meets
Sad and wan,
And he shakes his feeble head,
That it seems as if he said,
"They are gone!"[26]

Among the coterie at Pittsfield as throughout the nation, the veteran was still the double image of Colonel Manly from *The Contrast* split between the nostalgia history had overlaid on him and the nervous discomfort his aging presence made for a nation no longer needing his services. "They are gone," Major Melvill mourns in 1831, presumably never to be seen or needed again. By and large, veterans *were* gone in the decades leading up to the Civil War, either an aged and dying population, as were Israel Potter and Major Melvill, or a new generation of displaced laborers stationed in far outposts on the frontier engaged in escalating skirmishes with Native American and Mexican populations. Indeed, early veteran erasure in the stretch from the 1820s through the 1850s was exacerbated by a new generation of veterans unconnected to the Revolutionary War.

In part, Israel Potter and Major Melvill disappear because of generational change, but the passing of time also brought with it an increasing friction between discourses related to amateurism and professionalism. Israel Potter could be revised and overwritten first by Trumbull and second by Melville because Israel Potter was, like all veterans, a hack, a charlatan, a beggar, a confidence man—in short, an amateur whom no one had to take seriously. This stratification took place both within print culture and also within competing institutional definitions of the military, such as (amateur) state militias versus (professional) soldiers trained at West Point and the Naval Academy, which was founded in 1845. Melville struggled with making a living from his writing in the 1850s, yet he was nonetheless a "professional" author in the sense that he had access to urban printing centers such as Putnam's and Harper's, and he had credibility with their editors. The veteran had neither access nor respect in literary spheres. And although Melville did work in the New York Custom House and could not support himself exclusively through his writing (surely a criterion for how we would define professional authorship today), his condition was undoubtedly more secure than the cultural headwinds Israel Potter and his fellow veteran authors faced in the decades preceding Melville and the Mexican War. Veteran identity at midcentury became an empty ideal—an authority lacking any status—which meant that it was a political and rhetorical opportunity for a growing civilian professional class to "varnish" as they themselves saw fit.

The middle point of the nineteenth century was a period of shifting identities in literary marketplaces. Sometime in the 1820s, Nathaniel Hathorne became Nathaniel Hawthorne. During the 1830s, Herman Melvill added the "e" to the end of his name and Frederick Bailey transformed into Frederick Douglass. In 1827, Edgar Allan Poe enlisted in the United States Army under the alias Edgar A. Perry. As the historians Paul Foos and Edward Coffman have noted, the antebellum peacetime army between 1830 and 1860 was mostly composed of the lower classes—largely immigrants and laborers—"groups viewed by most of the nation as riffraff and generally condemned for voluntarily giving up the rights that proper civilians enjoyed."[27] Consistent with a Jacksonian spirit of reinvention, the army was a crucial space for Poe to make it on his own without his father's purse strings to support him and among a mélange of disenfranchised people he had not known previously. In this new role, "Private Perry" served as a battery clerk for almost a year until he was promoted to artificer, the position responsible for crafting ordnance. Several months later on January 1, 1829, he was promoted once again, this time to sergeant major, the highest rank possible for an enlisted man.

As William F. Hecker has noted, Poe's rapid rise was remarkable because "the advancement from recruit to the army's highest enlisted rank typically took decades; Poe did it in less than two years." Promotion tended to be slow for enlisted men as well as for officers because the army faced constant cuts to personnel and, even worse for those who stayed, increased competition for the spots that did remain.[28] Colonel Sylvanus Thayer became superintendent of West Point in 1817 and instituted a series of educational reforms that would be his legacy after his departure in 1833, leaving the military academy with a growing reputation as a school of engineering. Thayer's leadership allowed subsequent West Point leaders, such as Dennis Hart Mahan and Henry Halleck, to inaugurate what Samuel P. Huntington termed a period of "Military Enlightenment" during the 1830s and 1840s, when even more parvenus like Poe came to West Point to make their mark.[29] These conditions made the military job market incredibly tight; soldiers had to hope for those above them either to resign or to die. Yet despite the odds, Poe's record suggests he was a rising star within the army and that he certainly thought of himself as one. By 1829, Poe had decided to end his infantry enlistment early and apply instead for an appointment at West Point; eventually Poe would enroll at West Point in July 1830 but only last seven months.

Private Perry had endured and advanced for almost two years, yet Cadet Poe did not make it through a full year—according to Hecker, because he wanted to be kicked out after his growing disillusionment with the officer corps. Their bureaucratic pettiness and jockeying for promotion did not meet his idealized image of professional "gentleman-soldiers" operating on a merit system as he had thought would be the case while Private Perry.[30] Poe's expectations of military manliness also fell short, just as they would years later in "The Man That Was Used Up" (1839), in which all the rumors and gossip surrounding the mysterious Brevet Brigadier General John A. B. C. Smith make him out to be a gorgeous specimen with "the handsomest pair of whiskers under the sun" and a "mouth utterly unequalled," containing "the most brilliantly white of all conceivable teeth." The man turns out be a grotesque and disassembled pile of misfit parts with a strange voice who is missing "seven-eighths of [his] tongue."[31] His celebrated war injuries have made him less of a man, not more, as the chatter of the story has suggested. Indeed, the military has "used up" the general—broken, exhausted, and depleted him—despite his swagger and bluster to the contrary.

Poe would certainly not be the only army man to be disappointed by the prospects and disillusioned by the closed and braggadocious system at West Point. Cadet Edmund Kirby Smith graduated from West Point in 1845 but was denied a commission because of his eyesight. His brother, Captain Ephraim Kirby Smith, wrote him with faint encouragement. "The army in our country is certainly not a desirable profession for any young man who has ability and perseverance [*sic*] to succeed in any other. With your talents and education, a few years of industry will most certainly place you in a position far in advance of your classmates, who will lead the enervating and indolent lives of subalterns, and I by no means desire that *my* sons should ever wear a sword. I would certainly prefer that they become honest, industrious mechanics." While he was West Point superintendent in 1853, Robert E. Lee was similarly morose: "I can advise no young man to enter the Army. The same application, the same self-denial, the same endurance, in any other profession will advance him faster and farther." Pay for officers was so far below that of counterpart civilian industries that officers often moonlighted or took sabbaticals from the military to work in banking (such as William Tecumseh Sherman in California during the 1850s), farming, and land speculation.[32]

Poe renounced his military life, which is to say he did not identify as a veteran. His work, therefore, does not lend itself to the same kind of analysis of someone such as Charles Cummings or Israel Potter. Indeed, "The Man That Was Used Up" is the only tale explicitly concerned with military life. As Private Perry, Poe produced his first book, *Tamerlane and Other Poems,* as well as his second book, *Al Aaraaf, Tamerlane and Minor Poems,* yet the subject of this early verse is not veteran life per se. Soon after his dismissal from West Point, the former Cadet Poe published *Poems* in 1831, "to the U.S. Corps of Cadets this volume is respectfully dedicated." The West Point *Poems* (as they are commonly called) also fail to address military life explicitly. This could be because Poe wanted to avoid an unpleasant and unfulfilling chapter of his life, either consciously or not, or because he found veteran identity uninter-esting or unimportant—I cannot speculate too far. But his absence of veteran concerns is important insofar as it is in the shadow of both Poe's own military experience and also that of veteran memoirists discussed in chapter 2. Rather than hold on to wartime memory and demand redemption as they had, Poe forsakes his peaceful if frustrating expe-rience in the military. I bring up Poe's biography not because it helps better explain his writing (again, the military is mostly missing in it) but because his turn away from his own time at West Point maps onto a larger midcentury rejection of the military as a desirable and prom-ising place. Poe quit and forgot the regular army because it was a dead end—a bunch of amateurs passing for a professional class.

In describing the military at midcentury, Coffman is quick to point out that "professionalism" might be an anachronistic twentieth-century concept that we overlay onto the economic life of nineteenth-century Americans; nonetheless, within the antebellum United States Army "there are discernible patterns . . . of professionalism: the training in and development of a special skill which has a responsible social appli-cation concomitant with the awareness of the practitioners." Laurence Buell assumes there was a parallel "great change" in authorship between 1830 and 1860 from "an amateur pastime" to "literary emergence" (that is, professionalism) in the opening to his seminal *New England Literary Culture.* More recently, Leon Jackson has argued that the terms "ama-teur" and "professional" are so vexed and anachronistic that we would do better not to use them at all because there were, in fact, many different markets and systems of exchange for literary production.[33] Throughout *The Business of Letters,* Jackson dismantles William Charvat's influential assumptions in *The Profession of Authorship* (1968) that the 1830s and 1840s constituted a period of growing separation between "profession-als" who could make a go of it (such as James Fenimore Cooper and Washington Irving) and "amateurs" who would tend to write here and there and then disappear from literary history (such as Charles Cum-mings and Israel Potter). For instance, Buell calculates that between 1800 and 1870, less than 10 percent of American life writing was done by "creative writers either by trade or avocation." Very few would pub-lish more than one book, and almost three-fourths of this literature was "topical narratives of extreme suffering," including "Indian captivities, slave narratives, and prisoner-of-war experiences," all generally considered at the time to be "plebeian," amateur, and lower class.[34]

According to Jackson, Charvat defined the difference in these terms: "The terms of professional writing . . . are these: that it provides a living for the author, like any other job; that it is a main and prolonged, rather than intermittent or sporadic, resource for the writer; that it is produced with the hope of extended sale in the open market, like any article of commerce; and that it is written with reference to buyers' tastes and reading habits." Within the context of my argument, it is important to note that veteran literature before the Civil War met none of these criteria. Though not writing specifically about veterans, Jackson's thoughts about the overlapping markets of minor antebellum writers closely apply to veteran authors, and especially in magazines and periodicals (as we shall see): "Authors wrote to raise charity, to receive charity, to compete for prizes, to pay ransoms, to raise bail, to leave legacies, and to please patrons. They were supported by publishers, by subscribers, by institutions, even by public lottery. And printed material was written for a salary, written for spending money, and written, sometimes, as a last resort: survival." The difference between first-generation veteran authors such as Israel Potter and later-generation veterans such as Edgar Allan Poe was that Potter was crushed by these economic realities of literary marketplaces and Poe and others adapted and conformed to them.[35]

The curious case of Poe's brief military career suggests the dual challenges of being both a military man and a literary professional. And while I am still mindful of Leon Jackson's objections to the rigidity of the terms "amateur" and "professional," they remain useful (as they were for Buell and Charvat) and useful specifically within the context of veteran literature because they also describe a hierarchy of antebellum American citizenship that relates to veterans. Poe wanted to be neither a veteran nor an amateur, in part because each term implied the other. In the conception of nineteenth-century veteran literary amateurism that I am advancing here, such a writing practice is hackneyed, untrained, and unschooled, undoubtedly unaware of its relationship to the "tradition" of literature that has come before it. Veteran amateurism is piecemeal rather than deliberate, ultimately unserious, a lark, a hobby, and a distraction from more deserving literature. It is also a literary system predicated on fraudulence in the way Lara Langer Cohen understands the term to mean a second-class textuality that is defined by such terms as "*fraud, imposture, puffing, sham, hoax, plagiarism, quackery, humbug, and counterfeit.*"[36]

As Poe complains in his opening "Letter to Mr.—" in the West Point *Poems,* professional writing, on the other hand, has cultural value, is the result of inherited literary forms and customs, and can be known by its signs of education and support by pedigreed people (namely, editors, amanuenses, and printers) who authenticate and vouch for the bona fides of not only the work but also that the person behind the work is a worthy American, which is to say, a valued citizen.[37] Such is the realm of Langer Cohen's notion of an antebellum "core" literature that is "largely northeastern, urban, white, and middle- to upper-class"—as opposed to an amateur "periphery" composed of "women, people of color, and rural populations," and, I want to add here, veterans.[38] The emergence of a core professional American literature was neither a linear nor a coherent path, just as the emergence of military professionalism—from militia to regular—was not linear. Indeed, amateur discourses surrounding the antebellum militia directly engage with the pitiful representations of Revolutionary regulars we have seen up to this point. Israel Potter the sympathetic beggar and Edgar Allan Poe the apostate veteran would intermingle with Colonel Pluck the militia buffoon.

In his discussion of militias in Philadelphia from 1775 to 1840, Albrecht Koschnik notes that as the regular army was small but growing modestly in stature during this time, "in contrast, the regular state militia remained an 'ill-trained, ill-equipped, and ill-organized rabble' that did not enjoy full support from elected officials, the public, or most militiamen." Such disenchantment had festered since at least the Federal Militia Act of 1792, which declared that while Congress had the power to deploy state militias, the states were nonetheless in charge of choosing officers and training. "The 1792 act required all white male citizens aged eighteen through forty-five to enroll in the militia (about half a million men at that point), but made no attempt to distinguish between them in terms of training, readiness, or how they would be called into service." Class divisions soon arose between the regular militia and the richer volunteer companies who could afford nicer accoutrements and serve in "cavalry, artillery, and rifle companies," which carried with them "a host of economic and social distinctions." Increasingly as the first half of the nineteenth century unfolded, tensions grew. "Militiamen did not turn out for the required musters, or appeared without the arms and equipment stipulated in the militia law. Poorer men resisted militia service as an expensive, burdensome, and unnecessary obligation . . . They also pointed to exemptions that allowed certain classes of men, such as ministers, to avoid service altogether. The militia of the early 1800s, characterized by numerous partisan volunteer units, had given way to a system in which a comparatively small number of volunteers coexisted with a much larger number of men who resisted and ridiculed militia duty in numerous ways . . . Neither the commanding officers nor the militiamen hid their dissatisfaction." The militia as Koschnik describes it was a kind of chronically dysfunctional tax system that levied no clear benefit for the poor masses who paid it and instead benefited those already with means to increase their social and economic stature by appearing to be noble volunteers.[39]

This image would be the one that found its way into many antebellum periodicals and newspapers. As a way to mock the absurdities of militia "duty," one regiment in May 1825 parodied the system. "[They] took the 'legalized misrule' one step further and mocked their superiors and the militia system by choosing John Pluck, a stable cleaner and 'poor, ignorant, stupid fellow,' as their colonel. Pluck, elected for seven years, personified popular opposition to the militia system: an unskilled laborer with a particularly unsavory occupation, possibly mentally handicapped, was put on the same level with the merchants and lawyers among the other military officers. Pluck appeared intoxicated at musters and parades, barely comprehending the proceedings and certainly not in command. His superiors eventually declared him unfit for office."[40]

In this David Claypoole Johnston lithograph from 1826, Colonel Pluck dons a hat that maintains its large shape despite the excessive weight of feathers and epaulette ornamentation. The oversized sword he holds only adds to Pluck's emasculation. Even the quotation on the bottom from *Henry IV*, Part I, mocks the soldier's lack of refinement in comparison with Shakespeare. The image is not of a suffering veteran or an earnest beggar but of an oblivious and amateurish fool concerned only with the

FIGURE 6. David Claypoole Johnston, "Col. Pluck." Courtesy, American Antiquarian Society.

pageantry of parade (indeed, that sword would be an unwieldy handicap during a skirmish). At the same time as military identity was undoubtedly fragmented between "regular" veterans, such as Joseph Plumb Martin and Israel Potter, and "militia" veterans, such as Colonel Pluck, the one constant between them was that each veteran group was easily ridiculed and consequently marginalized. In the first case, they were lying beggars; in the second, they were transparent charlatans.

Militia derision was both produced and reflected in amateur literary periodicals such as the *Champagne Club,* published in Washington, DC, in the 1830s, which described itself as "A Chronicle and Critic of Military and Fashionable Events and Things, and Criminal Record of Literary and other Misdoings." An issue from December 1834 describes a pretentious "frolick" in the nation's capital that is "interesting to the man of pleasure, the philosopher, the sage, and the soldier."[41] The editors lump together libertines, fashionable man of leisure, and the militia—each a category of idleness and each guilty of "misdoings" that deserved the playful critique of a publication such as the *Champagne Club.* Other magazine editors were more pointed in their indictments of militia fraud and excess.

The affectations of self-important military men were strongly excoriated in the *Literary Harvester,* published in Hartford, Connecticut, which singled out the militia in particular for their frivolity. "Tributes for the Brave" (1843) was a mock heroic following Dorr's Rebellion, a brief insurrection in 1841–42 that was fought over suffrage being tied to property restrictions. "We are informed that Gov. King of Rhode Island, has ordered three thousand two hundred and five *Leather Medals,* to be constructed immediately, and distributed among the gallant troops who captured the evacuated Fort at Chepachet, and who voluntarily left their wives and little ones for the long space of two days and eight hours, and returned crowned with garlands of whortlebury [*sic*] bush and fire-red scoke berries!"[42] Such sarcasm for militiamen who "worked" only so that they might be praised with medals and seen on parade—and as late as the 1840s and the eve of the Mexican War—underscores the longevity of antebellum veteran ridicule that targeted prisoners of war, veteran memoirists, and periodical writers alike.

In counterpoint, some magazines and periodicals celebrated veteran culture rather than upbraid it. Self-identified military newspapers and periodicals were usually structured around a series of short sketches and letters—most of them reprinted material, but occasionally never-before-seen copy—and these publications were for amusement and distraction rather than mockery. A great number were also conscious of the need to defend military (and especially militia) character against the negative attacks personified in someone such as Colonel Pluck. Moreover, many papers sought to correct the cultural image of the militia by representing veteran identity as a craft and a profession rather than as a hobby and performance. The *U.S. Military Magazine and Record of the Volunteers of the United States,* which was published in Philadelphia beginning in 1839, was openly critical of the hypocrisy that "the genius of American institutions, opposed as it is to that restless spirit of conquest which actuated and convulsed so many nations of antiquity, the middle ages, and even a later day, would seem to be unfriendly to the development of military talents. Neither the requirements of a super-abundant population, nor any of the usual incentives to an increase of territory, always flagrant in aged and despotic countries, have yet arisen to counteract the anti-military tendencies of our form of government and social polity."[43] The nation was similarly ungrateful according to *The Citizen Soldier,* published in Windsor, Vermont, from 1840 to 1841, which put forth the complaint that the militia was being unfairly vilified as unnecessary for the country; the paper expressed the fear the militia would soon be replaced completely by a standing army.[44] These partisan and defensive militia papers defended their veteran audience on the grounds that the militias were performing the kind of public labor—like fire departments—that no one else wanted to do (a point that Paul Foos convincingly makes).[45]

Published in Tivoli, New York, the *Eclaireur* ran from 1853 to 1856 and was sympathetic to the same anxieties latent in *The Citizen Soldier* over militia veterans' sense of estrangement and imminent extinction from cultural relevancy. An early issue of the *Eclaireur* is dedicated to "To The Militia" . . . When every body thinks himself a soldier, no one really is so," and also "To the Firemen," who are laudable for their "ORDER," "PRESENCE OF MIND," and "SILENCE." The first dedication illustrates how militia papers sought to demarcate and protect veteran identity; the second dedication describes the principles of poise and professionalism that supposedly define such an identity. Indeed, the

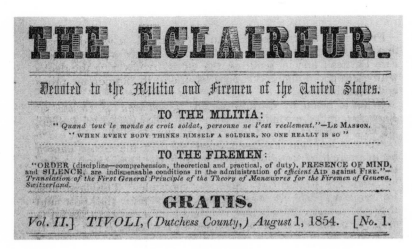

FIGURE 7. *The Eclaireur.* Courtesy, American Antiquarian Society.

Eclaireur presented itself as a type of instructional trade manual, discussing the daily practice of the militia, such as fire prevention, and how to control and negate street fighting. Furthermore, there were common complaints about turf wars, such as over how the armories were being replaced with civilian superintendents rather than military men.[46] A military periodical such as the *Eclaireur* reads as a kind of guild publication intent on protecting veterans from hostile competitors hell-bent on taking their jobs.

Periodical culture at the time was a fragile capitalistic enterprise threatened with the constant risk of failure. Veteran literary culture was no exception. The *Military Gazette,* published by Charles G. Stone in New York in 1859, describes the challenges inherent with all military newspapers, namely, that they were all what we might call "amateur startups" today. Added to the regular unsure prospects of print culture were the difficulties in attracting and retaining veteran readers when so many of these papers were a flash in the pan: "We have had to struggle with the usual embarrassments incident to the commencement of any new undertaking, and especially, it seems to us, with many difficulties which were peculiar to a military newspaper. Other military papers had failed to be issued with regularity and permanency, and it was natural that this should be feared of our enterprise, and that it should be looked upon with somewhat of distrust. Knowing now, more fully than we could at the outset, what of prejudice and of reasonable doubt was to be overcome before we could gain the confidence of our military friends, we look upon the results of the year with very great gratification."[47] Despite the high hopes of that last line, the *Military Gazette* would run for only two years, although it closed presumably because of the advent of the Civil War rather than by a failure to overcome "distrust," "prejudice," and "reasonable doubt." Nevertheless, it, along with other military papers, underscored the relative incoherence of veteran periodical literature. They were quick to appear and quick to disband, aimed mostly at militia veterans but occasionally for regular troops as well, and edited by businessmen who were motivated as much by economic opportunity in getting veterans to buy papers as they were in providing a service for veterans to be incorporated into civilian life.

Indeed, who was doing the writing and the publishing was not usually clear. Very few newspapers explicitly claimed a veteran editor, which suggests that these publications were often written to soldiers and veterans but not necessarily by them, which is to say they were for their supposed benefit but not necessarily by their own effort. One of the few visible veteran editors was Colonel William Ward Tompkins, publisher of the *New York Military Magazine,* the *United Service Journal,* the *Military Journal,* and the *Army and Navy Journal.* According to his 1882 obituary in the *New York Times,* Tompkins joined the army at the outbreak of the War of 1812 and afterward "took a very active interest in the local Militia," which led to the creation in 1826 of his own company, "Tompkins Blues." Tompkins's military interests extended to the regular army as well. After stints in Jefferson Barracks, Missouri, and campaigns in Florida during the Seminole Wars, Tompkins fought under Zachary Taylor in Mexico.[48]

Here was a veteran who had served across the nation and yet remained strongly provincial. The first page of the *Military Journal* from 1845 declared its aim to be solely for "this city [New York] and city of Brooklyn," yet it also imagined itself at the same time to be representative of a national military. "The Military Journal will be devoted principally to the military institutions of the country, especially to the militia thereof. It will sustain the Army and Navy, and stand by the Military Academy at West Point." Furthermore, this labor would not be part-time, as so many other newspaper editors were. "The undersigned has abstracted himself from all other engagements, for the purpose of devoting his entire attention to this work."[49] Tompkins's military and literary vocations are significant because they stand at the intersection of several problems that contribute to the fragmentation of nineteenth-century veteran literary culture. His careers call attention to the fault lines that existed between civilian readers and veteran writers, between civilian writers and veteran readers, between state militias and the regular army, and, as we will see in the troop newspapers and subsequent veteran literature of the Mexican War, between isolated urban publishing centers, such as Philadelphia and New York, and the rudimentary presses on the frontier. Indeed, after the Mexican War, Tompkins would become "the first editor of the *Army and Navy Journal* and the *Military Magazine*," which would go on to become two of the larger military magazines of the nineteenth century.[50]

Midcentury veteran periodicals and magazines tended to be vernacular, local, and isolated, and they struggled against one another to garner national credibility and cachet. Tompkins aspired to make veteran concerns a professional and respectable enterprise by combining militia and regular readers rather than separate them as had been common, yet veteran literary culture was incredibly diffuse insofar as it had to be to survive the competition. As has been seen, different military periodicals catered to different market tastes, such as wanting to mock veterans, wanting to defend veterans, and wanting to defend the militia specifically (and unapologetically). Different publications also largely sidestepped the issues related to inclusive citizenship and veteran authorship until the arrival of the Mexican War and the veteran literature that resulted.[51] Ultimately, there were two stories being told midcentury about veteran life. The first story took place in the peacetime military newspapers and periodicals and concerned veterans but was not necessarily written by them. The second took place during the Mexican War, when soldiers were suddenly present again in ways they had not been since the Revolutionary War. Active duty and recently discharged soldiers wrote in such new forms as troop newspapers, confidential memoirs, and penny press novels—literary forms that often allowed veterans to resist (and at times conform to) a midcentury exploitation of their amateurism.

* * *

Veteran literary culture during the Mexican War often was divided by contradictory impulses to manufacture consent for the imperialist justification for the war and to critique American expansionism and the U.S. occupation of Mexico. As Alfred Cornebise has noted, troop newspapers were established in every conquered Mexican city during the war: some twenty-five different newspapers in sixteen occupied cities. The image of a patriotic soldier writing from the front lines was tempting to appropriate in the political rationalization of the war, and undoubtedly troop newspapers did function as an instrument of American imperialism. Their dispatches often found their way into newspapers back east, and politicians and military leaders leaned on them as proof of Manifest Destiny. "Speaking at the University of North Carolina, Polk's Secretary of the Navy, John Y. Mason, stated that nothing was more remarkable, 'or more indicative of the intelligence and education of our people than the fact that newspapers have been established in every town of importance which has been captured from the enemy.'" Literate soldiers were proof of national intelligence. "The *Washington Union* concurred, observing that wherever the armies had penetrated, the printing press soon made its appearance, becoming the 'herald of information and the pioneer of civilization.'"[52]

Other troop newspapers, however, were more limited affairs that did not necessarily become co-opted by the war machine, such as the *Republic of the Rio Grande and Friend of the People* that began publishing on June 1, 1846. The *Republic* bucked the trend of pulp periodicals and troop papers by publishing bilingually (implicitly inviting Mexican and nonmilitary readers to participate in veteran literary culture) and by having "a column in which the soldiers could air their complaints. Its purpose was suggested by its title: to urge the establishment of an independent republic composed of the four northern states of Mexico."[53] One would imagine President Polk would not have been too happy with his soldiers advocating for a two-state solution. A similar dissent was found across the country and within civilian literature, for example, James Russell Lowell's antiwar *Biglow Papers*.

There should be little surprise that veteran literary practices were still as fractured during the Mexican War as they had been in the military periodicals in the decades preceding it. The regular army of the United States was still small and untested when the war on the frontier erupted in the mid-1840s. After Zachary Taylor's unexpected victories at Palo Alto and Resaca de la Palma in February 1846, young men could not sign up fast enough for Polk's call for fifty thousand volunteers. For the first time since the Revolutionary War, the Mexican War became, in the words of Robert Johannsen, a war for the young and the adventurous, "a civilian war from the outset, clothed with all the romance of a conflict that touched the popular imagination."[54] The reality of camp life for the regular soldier was more dismal and less heroic than the press represented, and the incredible influx of volunteers put the militia system into a state of crisis over whether states or the federal government would fund the troops.

Paul Foos has documented how the United States Army "explicitly prohibited officers from publishing their own accounts of battles," yet many officers and infantrymen nevertheless did publish their personal accounts in troop papers and in memoirs that "as much as possible . . . offer commentary that eschews the heroic mode so common in personal and public accounts of the 1840s."[55] George Ballantine wrote his *Autobiography of an English Soldier in the United States Army* (1853) to correct the civilian public's misperceptions of military gallantry: "What has hitherto appeared on the subject, beyond the official despatches [*sic*], has more resembled romance than history, being in the main confined to dashing narratives of the personal adventures of roving or belligerent Hotspurs, who knew little and cared less about the discipline and routine of the every-day life of the regular soldier." He describes his style as "nervous yet chaste, and free from the coarseness which too often disfigures a soldier's narrative."[56] Some thirty years after Israel Potter's memoir—one that similarly resembled a "coarse romance" rather than history—Mexican War veterans were also relegated authors who nonetheless took on more and more professional risk by publishing their military experience and in ways that resisted the strong undertow of American romanticism.

Both Johannsen (a modern scholar) and Ballantine (a contemporary veteran) critique the bulk of Mexican War literature for its tendency toward romance. Indeed, American literary romanticism lurks as an unindicted coconspirator against veteran authorship. Take, for instance, romanticism's emphasis on the uncanny or that sense of dislocation produced when texts render familiar experiences strange. After West Point, Poe indulged in this practice often, such as in "The Fall of the House of Usher" (1839), in which the narrator enters his childhood friend's home after a long time away. "While the objects around me—while the carvings of the ceilings, the somber tapestries of the walls, the ebon blackness of the floors, and the phantasmagoric armorial trophies which rattled as I strode, were but matters to which, or to such as which, I had been accustomed from my infancy—while I hesitated not to acknowledge how familiar was all this—I still wondered to find how unfamiliar were the fancies which ordinary images were stirring up."[57] In such a moment, readers presumably identify with the negative capability of being both comforted and disoriented, just as they would in a similar situation Hawthorne describes in his Custom House introduction to *The Scarlet Letter* (1850).

Hawthorne prescribes the romance writer's purpose as defamiliarizing what we take as ordinary, much like when a strange light recasts objects we see every day. "Moonlight, in a familiar room, falling so white upon the carpet, and showing all its figures so distinctly,—making every object so minutely visible, yet so unlike a morning or noontide visibility,—is a medium the most suitable for a romance-writer to get acquainted with his illusive guests."[58] While romanticism is well-charted critical territory, what I want to underscore for a moment is how the mature aesthetic of writers from Melville to Poe and Hawthorne assumed that a community of experience existed between author and audience, one that would subsequently be disturbed by the uncanny in the text, yet still, there was the presumption of a shared experience. That is to say, we have all returned to places from our past and felt estranged from them and from ourselves, just as we have all felt shame about our behavior. And even if readers never committed adultery per se as did Hester Prynne or set foot on a whaling ship such as the *Pequod*, the allegories of sin, obsession, and revenge resonate with romantic readers and entangle them with their romantic texts.

Amateur veteran literature of the Mexican War rejected the very premises of shared community and experience that romanticism extolled because veterans of the frontier frequently perceived their experience to be insular and nontransferable to nonveterans back east. Mexican War veteran George Furber prefaces his 1848 memoir by calling attention to his multiple and incompatible audiences. "To his numerous fellow-soldiers, who, at Victoria, Mex., Tampico, Vera Cruz, Plan del Rio and Jalapa, subscribed to the work, upon hearing the details of

the manuscripts and examining the drawings of places,—on the promise, too, on his part, that it should be issued from the press by the 1st
of November, 1847,—the author owes an apology, for his failure to produce it in that specified time." Furber feels guilt for not publishing his
experience fast enough for his comrades. To his putative civilian readers, however, he feels no such responsibility. "To the general reader, the
author would remark, that in this work there has not been the slightest
opportunity, even had he been so disposed, for the flight of imagination, or any departure from truth: for thousands witnessed the scenes
here described. The errors would have been instantly detected by them;
and especially condemned by those whose aid and support has been
freely given to the work only on account of its faithful details, whether
of important operations, or of lighter scenes in camp."[59] The leap of faith
for civilian romantic readers would be to take amateur veteran literature
as true, yet it was also ultimately unverifiable because the experience
represented was so alien and remote. Veterans such as Furber attested
again and again at midcentury: you'll just have to take our word for it.

Amateur veteran claims for credibility were not that they had made
the familiar unfamiliar, as with romanticism, but rather that they had
made the unfamiliar familiar, that they had preserved veteran experience and transcribed it unembellished. "The author has aimed at no
excellence of style; he has endeavored to use the more familiar words
and every day expressions of life, conscious that the relation of facts
would be the main object with the reader, rather than the language in
which they might be dressed," Furber would go on to say. War of 1812
veteran Samuel White similarly described himself and his style as transparent: "A plain man himself, he has not attempted to embellish his narrative with high-flown language, nor to impose upon the credulous, a
string of fictitious adventures, but has been content with offering them
a plain statement of facts, and as such he hopes it will be acceptable
to the American reader." So too would Mexican War veteran Benjamin Franklin Scribner characterize his straight talk in the preface to *A
Campaign in Mexico, by "One Who Was Thar"* (1850): "In thus bringing
myself before the public as an author, I offer no apology. I make no
pretensions to literary merit. The following pages were written in the
confusion and inconvenience of camp, with limited sources of information, and without any expectation of future publication. I offer nothing

but a faithful description of my own feelings, and of incidents in the life of a volunteer. To such as may be interested in an unvarnished relation of facts, connected with the duties, fatigues and perils of a soldier's life, I respectfully submit this volume."[60] Like so many amateur veteran authors, Scribner marks himself as "unvarnished," an attribute that Ann Fabian suggested was self-serving and disingenuous at the beginning of this chapter. Yet the claim of being unvarnished was also a veteran rejection of contemporary literature that *was* varnished, of a pretentious literary culture that romanticized, embellished, and assumed authority when it had no basis—in short, of all things professional. The result was a sort of renegade or confidential veteran literature that straddled the line between public and private, amateur and professional.

Much of the amateur veteran literature of the Mexican War perhaps protested too much, especially when it came to its repeated assertions of meager skill and (some might say false) modesty. In response, what I label "confidential veteran literature" sought to drop the pretense and operate as if author and audience had both dropped the veteran mask. This type of narrative policed the countertendency toward exaggerated timidity. For example, *The "High Private," with a Full and Exciting History of the New York Volunteers* (1848, author unattributed) critiqued how "too many letters have been written by the officers of the volunteer corps, as well as by 'regulars,' to ever arrive at real facts as they actually occurred. The officer is inclined to false pride and self adulation; of course, their actions are predominent [*sic*] over all the best germ of manly feeling for the poor hard-working and suffering soldier." Too many of the wrong soldiers (the "regulars") were writing romanticized fictions of the Mexican War. The result was widespread skepticism that required so-called real veterans to correct the representation of the war. Veteran Corydon Donnavan prefaces his *Adventures in Mexico* (1847) by lambasting the "numerous publications, already scattered over the States, purporting to describe the people, country, and institutions of a land to whose destiny all eyes seem now eagerly turned" that have caused a "spirit of distrust in which a new production [his own] may be received."[61] What was needed was an audacious correction to the drivel that spoke truth to power.

One such publication was Private William Richardson's journal. As had been true for earlier generations of veteran Americans, Richardson's literacy was select—for himself and other veterans—as opposed to being explicitly targeted for larger markets. Published by the author in New York in 1848, Richardson's journal continues in the veteran tradition of bitterness and despondency. He was less combative than his forebears, however, and appears more resigned to the fact that his words would likely be unread. He was also quite funny. Describing the scene aboard a ship headed to Mexico in January 1847, Richardson notes: "Some were occupied in washing their faces, others talking in groups, while many stood moody and alone—some looking with a wishful eye towards the shore, and some sat in different parts of the deck engaged at the *beautiful* occupation of picking *lice* from their persons!" (*J* 41). Sarcastic italics also color the descriptions of meals and how officers received preferential rations.

> Oct 28th:
>   We are now living in the midst of the greatest abundance of life's luxuries. As an evidence of our high living, I will transcribe our bill of fare for the week. It is as follows:
>   Monday.—Bread, beef, (tough as leather), bean soup.
>   Tuesday.—Tough beef, bread, and bean soup.
>   Wednesday.—Bean soup, bread, and tough beef, and so on to the end of the week.
>   The greatest *harmony* prevails in camp, especially among the officers; the Captain and first Lieutenant are the greatest *friends* imaginable; they do every thing in their power for the good of the company. They are the *bravest* and most *patriotic* officers in the regiment. In this lovely and fertile valley, encamped on the banks of the Rio Charma, we are enjoying all the *blessings* of life. We are charmed by the surpassing beauty of the Spanish ladies, and living in so much *harmony* with each other, that we almost imagine the "garden of Eden to have been again raised for our enjoyment; and then, Oh! heavens, what a luxury, amid these joys, to feel the delightful sensations produced by the gently and graceful movements of a Spanish *louse,* as he journeys over one's body! The very thought of it makes me poetic, and I cannot resist the temptation of dedicating a line to the memory of moments so exquisite. (*J* 27–28)

Richardson's disdain is reminiscent of Joseph Plumb Martin's scorn for his meager rations during his own "thanksgiving day" from chapter 2, and although it appears that Richardson is just another in a long line of disgruntled veterans, alone by himself complaining within the secluded pages of his diary, the author soon reveals that he had not written the lines we just read. An anonymous soldier—or soldiers—had taken up his diary and done the writing for him.

> When I took up my Journal to add a few items, I found the above had been written by some wag, in my absence. He was disposed to ridicule my description of the felicity of which I boasted. Our boys are rather mischievous, and I must confess that I felt rather waggish myself, when I made the boast of our possessing Eden-like pleasures. The continuation of my narrative pleased me so well that I consented to let it remain as it was written. Our mischievous feeling and manner of expression is the most innocent way in which we can relieve ourselves, for we privates are suffering many privations, while some of our officers refuse to speak to each other. I am glad, however, that our troubles are so merrily turned into ridicule; the best way sometimes to treat them. (*J* 29)

Not surprisingly, writing became a way to blow off steam and pass the time; moreover, it existed as a communal veteran practice of literary mischief that was unconcerned and unattached to the vagaries of larger markets and civilian taste.

Richardson's journal was not alone in its authorship by committee.[62] The cover of anonymity allows the veteran multitude in *The "High Private"* to accuse the officers of the 2nd Regiment New York Infantry (and one Colonel Ward B. Burnett in particular) of outright deception. "I boldly pronounce, that the whole Regiment was got up by fraud—a fraud on the soldier, a fraud on the City of New-York, and a fraud on the Government of the United States." Much of the alleged dishonesty stems from questions surrounding suspected embezzlement. In a chapter entitled "Who Got That Money?," an unidentified "I" is defiant and unafraid in his accusations: "I may *dare* to speak, and I intend to speak and write what I think, and what a few richly deserve—that it may hereafter be a warning to treat *men* like *men*—not like common slaves—and that there may be as good men in the ranks as any who ever wore a gold epaulet. I promised men on their dying beds 'I *would* do *it*,' and as Gen. Shields says, 'I believe my life was preserved for some good[.]' It was formerly a frequent remark 'who struck Billy Patterson?' At present it's 'who got that money?' I can tell where a *small* part of it went, and perhaps Col. Burnett and his officers can tell what became of the *larger part?*" The slogan "Who Got That Money?" is folksy yet direct, both a light-hearted jibe and a serious allegation. Its tone aspires to dismantle conventional wisdom about military experience by asking pointed questions. Were camp sutlers honorable? "The poor soldier is actually *robbed* of one half of his pay by these *leeches,* who charge about five hundred per cent for everything they sell." Did good moral soldiers read their Bibles? "I never saw but one man read them, and he was *crazy;*—men only *abuse* and commit *sacrilege* at such times—for I pledge my honor, many were thrown *over-board*—others used for *waste* paper—the balance were left upon the sand-hills of Vera Cruz, as it was impossible to carry them on a *tramp,* besides thousands of dollars worth of clothing that were thrown away."[63] Confidential moments such as these revealed a different kind of unvarnished truth that sought to shock and unsettle rather than beg and groan.

Richardson in particular is surprised at the writing mania in camp. On November 3, "I found our boys writing down a vocabulary of Spanish words. They have become very erudite of late" (*J* 31). On the fourth, "all this day we did nothing but write down words from the language spoken by the people, who, from their complexion, appear to be a mixture of the Spanish and Indian races. We made a pretty good dictionary among us" (*J* 31). This frenzy over writing ultimately led to the production of a troop newspaper (another cowritten document) that soon overshadowed the recording of Richardson's own private thoughts and experiences. "During the past week I have had no time to write in my journal. I have been busy writing letters for others, and assisting in writing out requisitions, &c. I received to-night the first number of the 'Anglo Saxon,' a paper printed by our boys, and the first American newspaper ever published in Chihuahua" (*J* 66–67). The soldiers' appetite for reading and writing eventually extended beyond the physical boundaries of their own community. On September 16, "I took my seat quietly in the tent this morning, and thought I would rest, as we were to stay a day or two at this place. I was presently surrounded by soldiers begging me to write a few lines for them 'to father, mother, wives, friends and homes.' I wrote *seven* letters without removing from a kneeling posture, and was kept busy almost the whole day" (*J* 16).

On October 23, "the country here is bare and sterile to a great degree, but there is improvement with regard to fuel, which is so necessary at this season, in this mountainous country . . . I was kept busy all day writing letters for the soldiers, many of whom very gladly do my washing and mending in return for this slight service. I had rather at any time write than cook and wash and mend clothes" (J 26). Reading and writing provided a sense of purpose for Mexican War soldiers beyond the capriciousness of the war. Moreover, writing became a side profession for Richardson, just as it would for a whole host of veteran memoirists and novelists after the war. He imagined himself to be a clerk and a letter writer as well as a diarist and newspaper reporter.

Richardson's versatility reflects a larger problem endemic to troop newspapers and self-published memoirs but also amateur veteran literature more broadly, namely, that the praxis is intrinsically disposable because its sites are so scattered, like the Bibles described in *The "High Private"*. Indeed, what happened to the copy of the Bible and of the "Anglo Saxon" that Richardson read to the troops? What happened to the letters he wrote on behalf on his fellow soldiers? Some are lodged in archives to be sure, yet the historical activity of nineteenth-century veterans reading and writing has left very little trace. Indeed, many of the texts here described were published as pamphlets with cheap bindings and occasionally with flimsy wood covers—signs of evanescent thrift rather than permanence. An association exists between what we cannot see (veterans reading and writing) and what we believe (Were veterans really reading and writing?), and so it follows that because the Mexican War was embedded within a kind of disposable veteran literacy far off on the frontier, not just in texts produced from the front lines but also in the cheap pamphlets and dime novels that circulated in population centers in the East, much of this literature has been erased.

To exacerbate matters, many civilian writers of autobiography and nonfiction sensationalized Mexican War veteran stories, thereby reinscribing veteran identity as a romanticized form of amateurism, speculation, and light-hearted criminality and adventure.[64] For example, the *Life and Adventures of the Accomplished Forger and Swindler, Colonel Monroe Edwards* (1848) describes the "colonel's" counterfeiting and slave-smuggling activities throughout Mexico and the United States. Reputed to be Herman Melville's inspiration for the shifty veteran in *The Confidence-Man*

(1857), Edwards never actually served, but in January 1838, he assumed "for the first time the redoubtable title of Colonel, which he subsequently sounded to so much account," because the title gave him a certain "air and figure" that he liked.[65] Beginning as early as Major John André's trial, military character had contributed to what David S. Reynolds termed the "likeable criminal" of American culture, a tantalizing yet finally inscrutable and incoherent opposition of moral identities. In the words of Ned Buntline's confidence novel *The G'hals of New York* (1850), an American "'must make up his mind whether he will cheat or be cheated, whether he will dupe or be duped, whether he will pluck or be plucked.'"[66]

Melville began this chapter and so he will help to end it, in part because his interest in veteran identity stretched from the Revolutionary War in *Israel Potter* through to the Civil War in *Battle-Pieces and Aspects of the War*. As a documenter of the Mexican War in *The Confidence-Man*, Melville mixes veteran identity into his eponymous avatar of the American multitude. The steamship *Fidèle* includes "United States soldiers in full regimentals" alongside "Broadway bucks in cravats of cloth and gold." This confidence man takes on many disguises and personalities, including a crippled black beggar, a Methodist preacher, a captain of industry, and an herb doctor. None is more forthcoming than the next. Only one character ever admits his deception. He is the "soldier" Thomas Fry, described at the beginning of the chapter entitled "A Soldier of Fortune," as possessing "a grimy old regimental coat, a countenance at once grim and wizened, interwoven paralyzed legs, stiff as icicles, suspended between rude crutches." Fry's military appearance at first dupes the herb doctor, who comes upon him on the main deck—"'Mexico? Molino del Rey? Resaca de la Palma?'"—to which Fry responds, "'Resaca de la *Tombs!*'" Not a veteran of the late war in Mexico as his appearance would suggest, Fry is in fact a veteran of the penitentiary (specifically Manhattan's Hall of Justice, commonly referred to as "the Tombs"). As Fry tells the story, his suffering started when he was wrongly imprisoned for a rich man's murder. During this confinement, Fry's legs supposedly atrophied and he became the crippled beggar the herb doctor encounters. When Fry finishes his Tombs story, the herb doctor (himself a confidence man) responds simply, "'I cannot believe it.'"[67]

With the Civil War about to descend on the United States, veterans and their stories were still spurious affairs. Doubt proves prudent in

Fry's case because he only pretends to be a veteran and readily admits, "'Hardly anybody believes my story, and so to most I tell a different one,'" namely, that he served and was disabled in the late war (a situation similar to Charles Cummings following the Civil War). After confessing to his military deceit, Fry wanders about the deck begging the passengers, "'Sir, a shilling for Happy Tom, who fought at Buena Vista. Lady, something for General Scott's soldier, crippled in both pins at glorious Contreras.'"[68] Fry's veteran masquerade gathers some alms from the crowd, after which he disappears from the novel's surface altogether. Still, his presence underscores a typical civilian characterization of the veteran as a version of a confidence man rather than as an experience-based political identity and literary tradition in need of a proper hearing.

The confidence man was an appropriate image of the Mexican War veteran for Melville because the conflict was largely communicated to the reading public through propagandistic civilian novelists and newspaper correspondents. Reynolds contextualizes the figure of the confidence man within the late 1840s and the "sensational journalism and popular fiction of radical democrats" such as John Neal (*The Down-Eaters* [1831]) and George Lippard (*The Quaker City* [1845]), which exposed the hypocrisies of American capitalism and political life.[69] Lippard, for one, advocated not only for urban reform but also very strongly in support of the expansionist Mexican War in which Fry claimed to have fought. Lippard's two war novels, *Legends of Mexico* (1847) and *'Bel of Prairie Eden: A Romance of Mexico* (1848), figure prominently in what Shelley Streeby calls "the print revolution of the late 1830s and 1840s [that] directly preceded the war."[70] During that period of "revolution," readers came to know of the problems in the West mainly through newspapers and the new and popular penny press, often in the form of "novelettes" written in haste by civilian hacks and professional writers.[71] Streeby has argued that "the penny press and other forms of popular culture helped to produce feelings of intimacy, immediacy, and involvement in the war as papers reported, for the first time on an almost daily basis, the details of battles in Mexico."[72] At this time, various newspapers formed the Associated Press to help streamline delivery routes, and the telegraph made dispatches to large population centers an almost constant stream of information that helped fuel a "war mood that approached hysteria."[73]

"Mood" is an apt category through which we should consider amateur veteran literature between the Revolutionary and Civil Wars insofar as the mood surrounding former soldiers, sailors, and prisoners of
war and what they were writing was never neutral. What we are left
with on the eve of the Civil War is a constellation of emotional associations surrounding veteran authorship—hysterical, fraudulent, malin-
gering, buffoonish, opportunistic, unlearned. All these terms belong in
the same discursive set as amateurism, which in light of veteran literature should not be viewed as simply nonprofessional but moreover as
noncitizen in that veterans, like amateurs, could never garner sufficient
authority to be trusted, let alone read.

Melville certainly had difficulty reading the newspaper accounts
of unbridled heroism in Mexico. In a letter from May 12, 1846, to his
brother, Gansevoort, Melville was amazed by the war fever enveloping
the nation. "People here are all in a state of delirium about the Mexican
War. A military arder [sic] pervades all ranks—Militia Colonels wax red
in their coat facings—and 'prentice boys are running off to the wars by
scores.—Nothing is talked of but the 'Halls of the Montezumas.' And
to hear folks prate about those purely figurative apartments one would
suppose that they were another Versailles where our democratic rabble meant to 'make a night of it' ere long . . . But seriously something
great is impending. The Mexican War (tho' our troops have behaved
right well) is nothing of itself—but a 'little spark kindleth a great fire' as
the well known author of the Proverbs very justly remarks—and who
knows what all this may lead to."[74] During the Civil War, similar dispatches from the front lines would once again fuel the zeal of young
soldiers and worry Melville about how "seriously something great is
impending" in the faraway war zones he could only read about. But
Melville was never confident about what he heard. In the short-lived
humor magazine *Yankee Doodle,* he anonymously satirized the reliability of both the military's leadership and the news coming from
the Mexican front. Through a series of fabricated dispatches from the
front lines, "Reported for Yankee Doodle by His Special Correspon-
dent at the Seat of War," Melville lampooned the "simplicity and unaf-
fectedness of old Zach's habits" in contrast to his own "authentic and
reliable particulars."[75] The imperial interests of Manifest Destiny and
Polk's war machine guaranteed that all war writing from the front

lines—including veteran writing—should never be taken too seriously. There were no "authentic and reliable particulars" even (or perhaps especially) in the words of soldiers. Be they the militia dandies in the periodicals or the supposedly sensitive auteurs in camp writings or the con men in pamphlets and dime novels, such veteran characters could be easily dismissed as on the fringes of not only American citizenship but also print culture. It would take the Civil War to bring in veterans from the margins.

During the Civil War, most of what Melville learned of the front was mediated through the local dispatches as well as the immense and unofficial periodical of the war, *The Rebellion Record*. When the fighting started, Melville was forty-two years old, "an onlooker," Hennig Cohen tells us, "sensitive and compassionate, but personally remote" (*BP* 13). In 1861, Melville had joined the Pittsfield militia and even did exercises with the squad through much of 1863, but nothing close to active duty came his way. As in the case of *Israel Potter*, all Melville knew of the experience of war derived from secondhand accounts, except now Melville was living through a war instead of imagining an old one. Only after the fall of Richmond would he begin to write what became *Battle-Pieces and Aspects of the War* (1866). The novelist-turned-poet waited until after hostilities had stopped because he needed time and distance from the events to smooth out the "excesses of grief, anxiety, anger, and exultation"; his purpose was to calm the nation by means of a "coherent literary entity . . . Studied, symbolic, and encyclopedically allusive, [*Battle-Pieces*] understands events as increments of a larger, unified experience of the nation in which the war was a product of the American past and an anticipation of the nation's future."[76] Varying forms and speakers within *Battle-Pieces* inaugurate the distinct rhythms and moods of different battles in an attempt to prove wrong Walt Whitman's famous declaration in *Specimen Days* that "the real war will never get into the books."[77] More so than prose, verse allowed Melville to abstract the war as an epic national trauma. At the same time, the war poetry was mediated by Melville's difficulty in seeing the events of war clearly.

The poem "Donelson," for example, underscores Melville's dissatisfaction with his ability to properly visualize the distant battle. "Donelson" is a significantly longer poem than most in *Battle-Pieces*, its pace much slower and more deliberate. Whereas many of the verses in the collection are quick synopses of skirmishes, "Donelson" aims to mimic in real time the actions and chronology of the decisive three-day battle at Fort Donelson in February 1862. At "Saturday morning at 3 A.M.," the poem tells us, the rebels stir (*BP* 58). The "STORY OF SATURDAY AFTERNOON" is broken down by "an order given" at 1:00 p.m. and "the work" that "begins" at 3:00 p.m. (*BP* 60–61). At the same time combat is happening, the poem aims to re-create the reactions and anxiety of civilians at home who must read about the battle in disjointed dispatches broken up over multiple days. An unnamed town's "bulletin-board" organizes the poem's form. Every day "a band / Of eager, anxious people met" (*BP* 52) to read news of the battle for Donelson. They learn of the battle at the same time and alongside the external readers of the poem. These temporal complexities create two speakers, representative respectively of combatant and civilian perspectives of the war. Melville alternates between the italicized speech of the frontline dispatches and the roman type of the reading crowd, and in this back and forth the distance between war participant and war observer is formally rendered.

In "Donelson," as in each of Melville's poems, no soldier gets to be his own first-person speaker. As a result there were no clear protagonists of the war, and soldiers existed mostly as metaphors that had the effect of displacing their individuality. "Our heedless boys / Were nipped like blossoms," cries one dispatch (*BP* 57). "Three columns of infantry rolled on, / Vomited out of Donelson—" compares another (*BP* 59). Yet another describes the rebels' "glare like savages" (*BP* 61). Men whom "the College Colonel" (another poem) commands are "like castaway sailors" (*BP* 113). In "Gettysburg," "our lines it seemed a beach," over which "three waves in flashed advance / Surged, but were met" (*BP* 88). "The March to the Sea" focuses less on General Sherman than on the swelling sea of men. "The columns streamed like rivers / Which in their course agree, / And they streamed until their flashing / Met the flashing of the sea" (*BP* 120). In *Battle-Pieces,* Melville imagined the soldiers of the Civil War no longer as antebellum confidence men but rather as an inscrutable force of nature. Soldiers flood the landscape of "The Muster": "The Abrahamic river— / Patriarch of floods, / Calls the roll of all his streams / And watery multitudes" (*BP* 134); young men pool into a waterfall above a "Gorge so grim" in "A Canticle": "Multitudinously thronging / The waters all converge" (*BP* 128). *Battle-Pieces* conceives of human beings in combat as a fluid and undifferentiated mass, in part because, as with many of his contemporaries, Melville could not cognitively make sense of the unheralded volume of soldiers the Civil War produced.

After 1865, the United States suddenly had more veterans than ever before. The War of 1812 had mustered approximately twenty-five thousand Americans into military service, and the Mexican War produced between fifty thousand and ninety thousand troops, though only about forty thousand were active at any one time. By the time the Civil War was over, a staggering 2.5 million Americans had exchanged blows.[78] Oliver Wendell Holmes Sr. realized while the Civil War was unfolding how the culture's sensitivity to war was unlike any that had come before. "War is a very old story, but it is a new one to this generation of Americans," he lamented. If Americans ever thought of war before 1861, they looked back to 1776. "As for the brush of 1812, 'we did not think much about that'; and everybody knows that the Mexican business did not concern us much, except in its political relation . . . No! War is a new thing to all of us who are not in the last quarter of their century. We are learning many strange matters from our fresh experience. And besides, there are new conditions of existence which make war as it is with us very different from war as it has been."[79]

Holmes describes some of the "new conditions of existence" in an 1862 article in the *Atlantic Monthly* detailing his journey to the front lines after hearing his son had been gravely wounded. Upon nearing the front line, Holmes comes upon a seemingly infinite "caravan of maimed pilgrims. The companionship of so many seemed to make a joint-stock of their suffering; it was next to impossible to individualize it, and so bring it home as one can do with a single broken limb or aching wound."[80] In the decades preceding the Civil War, there had never been a serious acknowledgment of the "aching wound" of veteran suffering. Only the startling numbers of Civil War veterans would cause them to be amateurs no more. As the following chapter demonstrates, the nation began to notice veterans but not necessarily recognize them as many were beginning to recognize themselves, namely, as artists and as citizens estranged from American society yet still struggling through print to negotiate the gulf between their military experience and their fellow Americans.

CHAPTER 4

The Real and Written War

1865–1880: William Oland Bourne,
John William De Forest

The actual soldier of 1862–65, North and South, with all his ways, his incredible dauntlessness, habits, practices, tastes, language, his fierce friendship, his appetite, rankness, his superb strength and animality, lawless gait, and a hundred unnamed lights and shades of camp, I say, will never be written—perhaps must not and should not be.

—*Walt Whitman,* Specimen Days in America *(1882)*

V eteran literature was colored by two cultural tendencies before the Civil War. The first extended through the 1840s and 1850s and alternated between mocking veterans and exploiting them. The living memories of aging Revolutionary War veterans gave way to later generations of veterans who had to struggle with the lingering associations between veterans and amateurism. In tension with these headwinds was a later inclination toward supposedly heartfelt charity because veterans often became easy targets for sympathy during the 1850s and 1860s. As more Americans had served after the Mexican War and especially after the Civil War, newspaper and periodical printers increasingly realized that veterans were both a population deserving of charity and also an increasingly lucrative opportunity for their own business speculation. Even before the nation witnessed the unprecedented slaughter of the Civil

War, newspapers such as the *Citizen Soldier* and the *Eclaireur* advertised themselves as veteran charities. "Devoted to the Military, and the Fire Department," the *New York Pioneer* in 1840 advertised a ball to benefit the militia and fire department. Furthermore, "every citizen has, or ought to have a deep and abiding interest in . . . the purity and hallowedness of true charity."[1]

"True charity" seems a noble requirement of "every citizen" that is imperfectly met, yet the question of veteran charity raises further issues about veteran authorship and its audience. One could logically conclude that militiamen and firefighters themselves were not the readers expected to attend the ball described in the *Pioneer*. That was the responsibility of the civilian public who "ought to have a deep and abiding interest" in veterans, including the New York Ladies Educational Union, which published the *Volunteer* in 1862 and imagined its editorial voice to be a kind of "honorary" soldier. The inaugural issue proclaims: "*The Volunteer* herewith presents himself for inspection and review . . . *The Volunteer* will be on hand at 'roll-call,' 'armed and equipped as the law directs,' in every regiment, in every company where *ordered*. He will, in full dress, accompany the staff and line officers, on all occasions where his services or advice may be desired. He will also mess with the private; skirmish, forage, or stand sentry with him; will sit with him by the camp-fire, amuse his leisure hour, cheer him when sad, and bring him each month, in rich variety, the choicest offerings of friendships from loved ones left behind, in whose hearts he lives, and in whose prayers he has continued remembrance."[2] Here is a troop paper not written by the troops but a charitable offering meant to amuse and distract them during the war. Similarly, the inaugural issue from 1864 of the *Soldier's Casket,* published in Philadelphia, solicited soldiers to write for the paper, although it is unclear to what degree veterans wrote for them or if they even read the serial. But at least the offer was made. The *Springfield Musket* was the result of the "Fair for the Soldiers' Rest" in similar fashion to other charity events and societies, such as the *Soldier's Aid* from 1865 published in Rochester, New York, by the Soldier's Aid Society, and the *Cleveland Sanitary Fair Gazette* in 1864.[3]

The great outpouring of civilian charity after 1865 has its roots in antebellum literary periodicals. Moreover, such charity also carried with it altruism's opposite—abuse. The *American Volunteer,* published in Boston by Cheney and Frost at the end of 1865, proclaims it is "dedicated to the Interests of Returned Soldiers," which means, among other things, paying in advance for a subscription: "$2.50 a Year, in Advance. Single Copies Six Cents." Speculating for subscriptions was a common practice across print culture, yet the uncommon uptick in the volume of veteran papers and periodicals after the Civil War suggests that veterans became a niche market for civilian publishers. *Home Mail* out of Phelps, New York, which ran from 1874 to 1875 and was renamed *Neighbor's Home Mail* from 1876 to 1882, relied on cheap amusement pieces and advertisements soliciting veterans to pay pension agents just as *Bennett's Reporter* (1857) had done before the Civil War.

Such a practice was not unique to New England. After the Civil War, Washington, DC, supported at least two newspapers marketed to veterans, *Claim Agent* in 1871 and *United States Record and Gazette* begun in 1875. Poet and lawyer C. Augustus Haviland edited the cheap pamphlet *Gem of the West and Soldier's Friend* in Chicago, which, despite the implication of its title, avoided veterans directly and instead marketed itself to women (through fashion articles and advertisements) and children (through didactic and adventure stories).[4] These charity periodicals made the veteran into an absent presence—an empty sleeve who was unable to read and write and therefore needed someone else who would do the work for him. Importantly, however, the Civil War signaled a new impulse within veteran literary culture insofar as it largely rejected charity from others and assumed instead a new authority in the form of literary realism. This chapter and the conclusion that follows it argue not only that realism at the end of the nineteenth century was rooted in veteran experience but also that civilian realist authors quickly took over what veteran literary culture had started. Such a gesture was "charitable" in its proclamations of sympathy and generosity for veterans, yet it was also oblivious to how the arrogant and paternalistic appropriation of Civil War military experience worked to marginalize nineteenth-century veteran Americans yet again.

In late July 1865, *Harper's Weekly* announced an open call for essay submissions from veterans of the recent war. The soldiers' firsthand accounts of wartime experience were to be the materials for "Left-Handed Penmanship," a writing competition thought up by William Oland Bourne,

who had been a sporadic producer of poetry, moralistic children's literature, and religious tracts since the early 1850s.[5] He also began publishing
a short monthly newspaper in the last years of the war while serving as
chaplain of Central Park Hospital, during which time he had veterans
inscribe their thoughts in autograph books. "Left-Handed Penmanship"
was advertised in that paper, *Soldier's Friend,* as well as in *Harper's, Frank
Leslie's Illustrated Newspaper,* and several regional newspapers in the
Northeast and Midwest.[6] And though he was himself no soldier, Bourne
was "always devising some fresh pleasure or benefit for the soldiers" and
sought to award five hundred dollars to "the best four specimens of penmanship by 'left-armed soldiers of the Union.'" The phrasing was vague
and crude, but then so was the condition of the audience *Harper's* was
seeking—those walking wounded who had lost their right hand to combat and were now forced to write with their left.

> Any man who has lost his right arm in the service may compete. He
> may write an original or selected article upon a patriotic theme, and
> he must write not less than two nor more than seven pages upon fine
> letter paper of ordinary size, leaving an inch margin at the sides, top and
> bottom of the paper. The writer must also give his name in full; his reg-
> iment, company, and rank; the list of battles in which he was engaged;
> the place where he lost his arm, and his post-office address.[7]

Little more than three months after Appomattox and the end of the war,
"Left-Handed Penmanship" was one of the first public spaces that made
literate and gave validation to the stories Civil War soldiers had to tell.
Not only soldiers, but specifically mutilated soldiers, were directed to
apply. Whereas this restriction might stem in part from a morbid and
kitschy curiosity about amputees and how they functioned with their dis-
abilities, it seems more likely that for Bourne, *Harper's,* and the general
passersby on the street, the visible effects of war demanded some form of
immediate public expression.[8] Indeed, the ubiquity of soldiers was unlike anything the nation had seen before. Their presence was the real and
undeniable reminder of how human experience was in fact irreversible—
that men are born with two arms, and that some thing, some event, had
happened during the war that took away those arms forever.

Absent limbs were unsettling not merely because they deformed
bodies but also because there was an experiential finality inherent in

their loss with which the culture was uncomfortable.[9] Arms, legs, and lives could never be replaced, yet Americans at the war's end were not entirely willing to concede the fact. "Left-Handed Penmanship" can be seen as symptomatic of a larger cultural tendency immediately following the war that symbolically wanted to undo the trauma of the conflict through a mnemonic sleight of hand. If the almost infinitely various experiences of individual soldiers could be quickly condensed and normalized into the collective memory of an uninjured nationalism—if a right arm actually *could* be replaced by a left arm as the contest suggested—then it was the larger, healthier narrative of marching forward together that mattered, not the acutely personal and painful circumstances of the individual's past. As had been true in the Revolutionary and Mexican Wars, the emotional property of the individual soldier was taken from him and made anonymous and interchangeable. This transaction was often willingly made because Bourne's contest provided much-needed hope for both the veteran contestants and their civilian readers that nothing had changed.

Initially, Bourne was skeptical if any soldiers would even bother to reply. He was soon overwhelmed by the response. Eventually, "there were some two hundred and seventy manuscripts collected from nearly every State in the Union."[10] Submissions kept coming in over an entire year, even after the contest was over, and public updates were made in *Harper's* every three months. Announcements in the *Soldier's Friend* were almost monthly. By November 1865, Bourne had read the first round of nearly illegible entries and pronounced them "back-handed," and yet he was nonetheless encouraged by the effort. "It is really astonishing," he notes, "how rapidly a man may learn to write admirably with his left hand."[11] The soldier's process of learning how to express himself again was as difficult as it was relentless. "The loss of two arms, indeed, did not daunt one competitor, who sent a specimen of writing with the mouth, which was remarkable and honorably mentioned" (see fig. 8).[12] The contest ended on April 7, 1866, with an elaborate description of the awards ceremony held at the *Harper's* offices in New York.[13]

The panel of judges included then governor of New York Reuben Fenton, president of the Sanitary Commission Henry Bellows, William Cullen Bryant, and Theodore Roosevelt Sr., among others. Ulysses S. Grant and the head of the Freedmen's Bureau, General Oliver O.

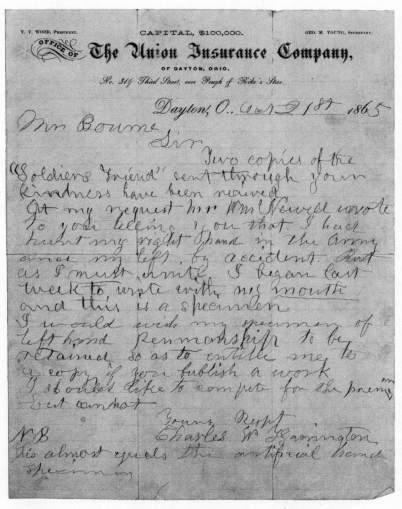

Dayton, O., Oct 21st 1865

Mr Bourne
          Sir,
                    Two copies of the
"Soldiers Friend" sent through your
kindness have been received
     At my request Mr Wm Newell wrote
to you telling you that I had
hurt my right hand in the army
and my left by accident. But
as I must write, I began last
week to write with my mouth
and this is a specimen
     I would wish my specimen of
left hand penmanship to be
retained so as to entitle me to
a copy if you publish a work
I should like to compete for the premium
But cannot
                    Yours Respt
N B   Charles W Harrington
this almost equals the artificial hand
specimen

FIGURE 8. Charles Harrington, submission to "Left-Handed Penmanship."
Wm. Oland Bourne Papers, Manuscript Division, Library of Congress.

Howard, himself an amputee from the war, were in the crowd. Standing in stark relief to the litany of distinguished public figures was the
unknown name of the winning soldier. "The first prize of the first class
was awarded to FRANKLIN H. DURRAH, private in the Thirty-first
Pennsylvania Infantry. There were twenty-eight prizes altogether, and
we wish we had room for the names of the recipients, who were from
every part of the country, from Maine to Dacotah [*sic*]."[14] These personal impressions represented, as Bourne suggested, the diverse wartime experiences of hundreds of veterans from multiple regions across
the Union, yet their full significance within the literary history of Civil
War narrative will remain forever obscure and incomplete. It is worthwhile to ask why, after having gone to the trouble of a year-long competition, both *Harper's* and the *Soldier's Friend* thought it unnecessary
in the end to publish any of the soldiers' stories.[15] When the contest
was first announced, the intention was clearly the opposite. "If enough
specimens are forwarded they will be exhibited, and the proceeds, if
sufficient, will be devoted to the publication of a memorial volume containing the essays, with a list of contributors; and a copy will be sent to
each contributor."[16]

What happened in the first year after the war that caused these stories
to be suppressed? These missing "brief sketch[es]" of "personal experience" strike a modern audience as peculiar, yet their absence makes
sense within the larger context of the literate Union's almost unanimous and immediate suppression of veteran personality following the
war.[17] Language, flair, and style—those very things that distinguish us as
humans—were editorially overlooked by a traumatized literary impulse
eager to avoid the faces of the men who fought. The last word Bourne
gives on the contest was that he had selected from the bunch a "representative left-handed soldier," who would stand in for a public tour culminating at the "exhibition at the Great Fair in Paris."[18] That anonymous
soldier's voice, like those of the others in the competition, was never
heard from publicly again.[19]

Modern historians such as David Blight have argued that the decades
following the Civil War were characterized by a national "politics of forgetting" wherein the collective sympathy of the North for the South created
a laxity in Reconstruction oversight that allowed for the establishment of
Jim Crow laws and rampant lynchings, among other sociopolitical ills.

Nina Silber in *The Romance of Reunion* (1993) paved the way for Blight's argument when she suggested that the nation's guilt during Reconstruction made it quick to forgive, forget, and by consequence authorize the social errors we were soon to make by the end of the nineteenth century.[20] Seemingly all commentators on Civil War memory operate under the assumption that the war was like a break in an important national bone and that the fracture was never set quite right. Looking back on the war on its hundredth anniversary, Robert Penn Warren wrote in *The Legacy of the Civil War* (1961) that the Northerner had over the years healed himself improperly along the lines of a self-proclaimed "Treasury of Virtue," wherein he gave himself a free pass on all sins past and present since he had freed the slaves and saved the Union.[21]

The Southerner had done no better in setting his cast. He settled for what Warren termed the "Great Alibi," wherein the South displaced responsibility for its own arrested social and economic development onto Northern indifference to the "Lost Cause." Neither memory of the nation struck Warren as particularly accurate, and yet he understood why both had persevered. "The Great Alibi and the Treasury of Virtue both serve deep needs of poor human nature; and if, without historical realism and self-criticism, we look back on the War, we are merely compounding the old inherited delusions which our weakness craves. We fear, in other words, to lose the comforting automatism of the Great Alibi or the Treasury of Virtue, for if we lose them we may, at last, find ourselves nakedly alone with the problems of our time and with ourselves."[22] I want to take seriously the perennial problem across American time of "the old inherited delusions" which by and large have constituted our collective memory of the Civil War in 1865, 1961, and into the contemporary moment. The conversations we have about nineteenth-century war and the urge to forget (or at least to remember selectively) generally fail to notice how memory has laid, like Bourne at the war's end, its "comforting automatism" over the diverse written experiences of veterans. Since there is no war without the actual fighting first, and no subsequent memory of war without first the actual experience of that fight, the personal knowledge of war, which the long tradition of nineteenth-century veteran writing argues can only be located in the men who served, is the starting point for the meaning we apply to the Civil War.

Put another way, I am making a necessary critical distinction between memory and experience that looks back to the wars of earlier chapters as well as forward to memory studies scholarship of the twentieth century. To paraphrase the work of Maurice Halbwachs and Pierre Nora, as soon as collective memory situates the sites of a national trauma, the clarity and significance of those sites quickly becomes unclear. Time unfolds and meaning is revised. Kirk Savage was concerned in part with this ameliorative process in *Standing Soldiers, Kneeling Slaves,* wherein he suggests that Civil War battlefields and public memorials became distorted and heroic *lieux de memoire* in the twentieth century.[23] Given the widespread critical consensus that nations conciliate and gloss pain and suffering over time, what remains largely undetected in the twentieth and twenty-first centuries (and even in the late nineteenth century when the Civil War was much closer to the lives of Americans) is not the grand and ossified memories of nineteenth-century war which we have long known but the individualized voices of veterans at war's end.

The 1880s and 1890s witnessed what David Blight termed a "burgeoning reminiscence industry" brought on by Union veterans who were publishing their personal tales in magazines such as *Century* at a surprising rate.[24] How should we consider these autobiographies, among which must be included the memoirs of Ulysses S. Grant (1885) and William Tecumseh Sherman (1875)? Like the delayed memoirs of Revolutionary War veterans, such writings undoubtedly have their own significance within the brotherhood of aging veterans and American life writing, yet this outpouring some ten or twenty years after the fact is absolutely not the same type of document as the immediate impressions transcribed by Franklin H. Durrah and the 270 others directly following the end of the war. In a similar vein, *The Red Badge of Courage* (1895) by Stephen Crane, who was not even born until after the Civil War, lacks the bona fides of a novel written by someone contemporaneous with the events. Walt Whitman was already making this same distinction of retroactive recovery when he famously wrote in *Specimen Days* (1882) that "the real war will never get into the books. In the mushy influence of current times, too, the fervid atmosphere and typical events of those years are in danger of being totally forgotten."[25] Whitman's comments make clear that though there was a distinct incubation period, it did not take long for public and private memory to start petrifying into the ideologies that Blight, Silber, Savage, and Warren, among many others, have described.

Experience, on the other hand, is the closest word we have to describe the absence of memory. It is that immediate and authentic sense of the war veterans throughout the nineteenth century claimed to have written and Whitman wished for in the 1880s but suspected had already missed its chance. These categories are not meant to be fixed or permanent, but within the context of nineteenth-century war, official memory is more a historical debate meant to persuade us as to the collective mood and lessons of the era, whereas individual experience, specifically here the experience of the veteran, remains an understudied literary and representational problem. Unlike during the Revolutionary and Mexican Wars, veterans in the Civil War were no longer an invisible population. Commentators such as Bourne were charitable and somewhat interested in what veterans had to say, but this development made civilians wrestle with questions that veterans had been asking themselves since the Revolution.

Where does the veteran's story begin? Where does it end? How are veteran narratives different from civilian accounts of war (narratives that we know are always subject to suggestion and revision)? How, finally, are we to reconcile the long history of nineteenth-century silencing of veterans before the Civil War with the multiplicity of veteran voices Bourne's contest indicates existed right after the fighting stopped? One of the lasting cultural gains from the Civil War was the rise of veteran authors who, despite difficulties in forging their stories and finding audiences, expanded on the precedent of nineteenth-century veteran political protest to consider further the aesthetic forms of their military experience. Bourne in part recognized this shift when he solicited his nameless veterans to tell their stories, not their historical or political commentaries. And while those solicited military accounts were once again forever withheld from contemporary audiences, one prominent and visible veteran narrative was not.

John William De Forest, who was a captain in the 12th Connecticut Regimental Volunteers and a veteran of the Louisiana campaign that withstood sieges on Port Hudson and Georgia Landing, began writing while still in the war what would become *Miss Ravenel's Conversion from Secession to Loyalty,* published in New York by Harper and Brothers in

1867. Unlike Bourne's contest, *Miss Ravenel's Conversion* was a commercial failure. The public did not respond to it, which in retrospect is quite surprising given that De Forest had, at his editor's insistence, reluctantly ratcheted up the novel's sentimental plot to attract the dominant market share of female readers. *Miss Ravenel's Conversion* even had the critical endorsement of both William Dean Howells and Henry James. The easy explanation for the novel's disappointing reception would be to say, as have many twentieth-century critics, that the novel simply is not any good. Even De Forest's perennial champion Howells would later remark that women readers were turned off by his misogynistic and unflattering portrayals of female characters.[26] Admittedly, neither his characters nor his melodramas seem entirely well executed; yet for all his heavy-handed and swollen prose, De Forest's infrequent descriptions of battle stood out at the time as nothing less than revolutionary for Howells. For Henry James, Stephen Crane, and other writers of his generation, they were a significant signpost of realist technique.

Most criticism of *Miss Ravenel's Conversion* can be delineated into two camps. There are those who want to imagine its domestic story line as a metaphor of familial and national rejuvenation and those who want to imagine its realism as a metaphor for the objective reality of the war—the "war as it actually was" to borrow De Forest's own words from his 1879 *Atlantic Monthly* article, "Our Military Past and Future."[27] Wade Newhouse has argued that the novel "turns the epistemology of war into a domestic commodity" of middle-class renewal and that within the bloody exchange of battle for peace, "individuality becomes an illusion, surrendered to an imaginary political collective in the service of postwar American nationalism."[28] Following Whitman, Michael Schaefer has aligned the combat and triage scenes in the novel with what Stephen Crane called "the real thing" of war, made more transparent for the reader by De Forest's journalistic sense of obligation to the "real thing" of his lived wartime experience.[29]

All these approaches have overstated the psychological function of metaphor and nationalism within De Forest's understanding of soldiering. Rather than making individuality an illusion or war an objective thing, *Miss Ravenel's Conversion* suggests individuality (in the subjective sense, that war and nation existed within and for each individual,

not the other way around) to be the only representational voice available for the Civil War veteran. Nineteenth-century war had always been
a personal matter for veterans, but whereas Revolutionary and Mexican
War soldiers had often fantasized that their suffering constituted an
alternate society, De Forest was less assured of the political implications
of his military service. More so than memoir, the novel suited De Forest because the form allowed him to document the individual soldier's
experience of estrangement against sentimental conventions of reunion
and community.

Having known the private, raw, and subtle experiences of the soldier that Bourne's contest and the later memory industry would overlook, De Forest could not even imagine the war in terms of metaphor
or nation existing somewhere outside individual consciousness and
experience—though he surely tried. Gregory S. Jackson has argued that
De Forest's fiction in the 1880s was informed by an affective desire for
"heartfelt" national reconciliation predicated on personal consent, yet
it should be noted that the sensibility and tendency of De Forest in *The
Bloody Chasm* (1881) and *Kate Beaumont* (1872) to write romances of
national reconciliation are quite different from the postdated sentimentality within the world of *Miss Ravenel's Conversion*.[30]

The novel's rough-hewn edges of ideological and domestic rejuvenation easily identified in Dr. Ravenel's and his daughter Lillie's exile
and return to the North are the remnants of a pressure to conform to
genre. It was how De Forest thought he should write, and his failure
to pull off the national story is one of the reasons why the novel often
reads as tedious editorial report instead of compelling fiction. Military
experiences do not conform well to the genre requirements of reunion
romance. In *Patriotic Gore* (1962), Edmund Wilson put the basic problem of De Forest fairly. Though he is "often boring and though his novels never quite come off, he is an honest and an informative writer . . .
He is the first of our writers of fiction to deal seriously with the events
of the Civil War."[31] That De Forest was in fact the first writer to deal
seriously with the events of the war was a result of his time as a soldier.
Furthermore, his wartime experiences provoked a realist aesthetic that
refused the affective potential of suffering for national ends.

De Forest's pragmatic insight into stark representation was largely a
frustrated reaction against a civilian imagination he felt was licensing

the ubiquitous mythologies of reunion and uninjured nationalism. Writings later in his career indicate how upset he was in the late 1860s with the way civilians were imagining soldiers instead of writing them as they were.[32] When Wilson distinguished De Forest as the first serious veteran author of the war, he surely was not unaware of these other writers, themselves not veterans, who were, like De Forest, writing about the Civil War as it was happening, albeit in different genres. Whitman published *Drum-Taps* in 1865, and Melville, *Battle-Pieces* in 1866. Louisa May Alcott put out *Hospital Sketches* in 1863 as a series of regular dispatches from the front lines in the magazine *Commonwealth*, and although she repeatedly insisted to her audience that this was the war as it actually was, that "these Sketches are not romance," the optimism of the prose undercuts her claims to verisimilitude. One soldier "lay on a bed, with one leg gone, and the right arm so shattered that it must evidently follow; yet the little Sergeant was as merry as if his afflictions were not worth lamenting over, and when a drop or two of salt water mingled with my suds at the sight of his strong body, so marred and maimed, the boy looked up, with a brave smile." Elsewhere, Alcott describes "the patient endurance of these men, under trials of the flesh, [that] was truly wonderful; their fortitude seemed contagious, and scarcely a cry escaped them, though I often longed to groan for them." One magnanimous soldier was "unsubdued by pain" and "uttered no complaint, asked no sympathy" while dying in the hospital. He was "earnest, brave, and faithful," one of the exemplary "true soldiers of the Lord" the war needed more of if the Union was to win.[33]

De Forest's description of the field hospital in *Miss Ravenel's Conversion* is markedly less grandiose: "The place resounded with groans . . . One man, whose leg was amputated close to his body, uttered an inarticulate jabber of broken screams, and rolled, or rather bounced from side to side of a pile of loose cotton, with such violence that two hospital attendants were fully occupied in holding him. Another, shot through the body, lay speechless and dying, but quivering from head to foot with a prolonged though probably unconscious agony" (*MR* 260). In contrast to the problems *Miss Ravenel's Conversion* had finding an audience, *Hospital Sketches* was a bestseller back on the Union home front. De Forest was in large part rejected by his reading public because that public wanted accounts such as Bourne's and Alcott's that put the humanity of war into the comfortable and recognizable forms of pleasant national memory—the valiant uncomplaining soldier who makes do, who gets wounded but suffers silently, who if he dies, dies stoic and confident that it was all worthwhile—as opposed to the gruesome and chaotic reality of De Forest's dying soldiers. De Forest showed just how alone the experience of the soldier really was, and he was the only writer who confronted that unspoken horror when the dust of the battlefield was settling in 1865. Other Union veterans would write their own fiction, poetry, and memoirs, but not until well after a decade had passed since *Miss Ravenel's Conversion*.[34]

De Forest wrote the fragmented and disillusioned experience he knew, not the national memory that others quickly condensed, bought, and sold in the popular romantic fiction of national reconciliation. The anxiety De Forest feels over what exactly a veteran is, what he should look like, and how he could relate to the peaceful world only reifies the anxieties of genre that surround *Miss Ravenel's Conversion*.[35] Is it even, in the final analysis, a novel? Travelogue? Memoir? *Miss Ravenel's Conversion* is aware of itself as a narrative written by an actual soldier about other imaginary soldiers. These two realities within the narrative structure rely on and authenticate each other. Their intermingling produces for De Forest, on the one hand, the sense of an autobiographical injunction of honesty and, on the other, a license and a space for literary experimentation that tended in his writing to celebrate the plurality of wartime experiences.

De Forest had always wanted to be taken as a serious writer of fiction, and indeed modest recognition had come before the war with the publication of two travel books—*Oriental Acquaintance* (1856) and *European Acquaintance* (1858)—both of which were excerpted, reviewed, and praised by *Putnam's Monthly, Harper's,* and the *New York Times*.[36] The young persona imbedded in these pages is a self-conscious man of letters, eager and ambitious to make his mark in the world. De Forest's purpose in going to Turkey and Europe had been to rejuvenate his mind and body. At the time, while living in Connecticut, he was having difficulty focusing on his writing and hoped that the experience of Italian, German, and Near East culture firsthand would sharpen his concentration. Childhood typhoid had also made

him weak, too weak for him to attend Yale as his father had hoped. He
went abroad an empty vessel, in search of artistic enlightenment as
well as physical cures. It is noteworthy for his sensibilities later in life
that neither hope lasted long.

A visit to the baths at Graefenberg, Austria, on a cold day to treat his
"monotonous invalidism" only made his condition worse. A trip to Ven-
ice left him emotionally drained: "Into Italy, therefore, I entered as into
a Valley of Vision, where I should behold glories little less than unut-
terable. Memorable and humiliating was my disappointment. Despite
of strong effort to realize the historic value of the scenes around me,
despite of dutiful pilgrimages to countless classic shrines, I remained
the same being that I had been in America, the spirit equally clogged
by the body, the wings of the imagination as easily wearied as ever, and
the terrestrial nature which they have to upbear as ponderous."[37] De
Forest had left America before the Civil War eager to find a release from
his physical and creative infirmities. He had wanted to be transformed
from an aimless amateur into a man of definite and strong purpose, yet
he soon learned that inspiration was not so easy. In Florence, he forced
himself once again. Setting out to translate Hawthorne's *The House of
the Seven Gables* into Italian, he found himself once more distracted
by the undisciplined rhythm of his mind. The volume never came out.

Once back in the United States, De Forest's psychological pattern
of shame, helplessness, and inability to produce continued. A novel of
modest acclaim, *Seacliff,* was published in 1859, but the outbreak of the
war quickly redefined the terms of De Forest's budding literary career
and artistic insecurities. As had Europe, the military promised a transformation in his character. On January 1, 1862, he was commissioned
out of his sedentary life near New Haven to recruit troops for the 12th
Connecticut Volunteers. A month later, De Forest and his company
were shipped to the Gulf of Mexico, where he began his official life as
a soldier. In a letter to his wife dated April 30, 1862, he describes the
typical cadence of his routine: "We smoked and read novels; we yawned
often and slept a great deal; in short, we behaved as people do in the
tediums of peace; anything to kill time."[38] De Forest's letters to his wife
often highlight how unspectacular and mundane were his experiences
in the military. As he had come to know civilian leisure abroad, he
similarly experienced his life as a soldier, which is to say in waste and

anxious waiting. His first recorded letter back home while stationed off Ship Island underscores De Forest's familiar sense of guilt that he was not being the type of serious soldier he thought he should be. "I am as indolent as passengers usually are; I cannot even study my drill book and the regulations. I smoke like a Turk; I walk the deck till the broiling sun sends me up to the breezy top of the wheelhouse; I load my revolver and shoot at gulls or floating tufts of seaweed; in my best estate I play at checkers on the quarter-deck . . . The general indifference to our future is curious and makes me wonder if we are beginning to be heroes. Nobody knows where we are ultimately going, and nobody appears to care."[39] Like many soldiers, De Forest would come to question his faith in the wisdom of his superiors at the same time he would resign himself to the dangerous and indifferent atmosphere of war. Amid the dearth of leadership in his life as a soldier, the drill books and regulations reminded De Forest that he should be ordered and attentive and that, as a reward for following discipline, he would be granted health and heroism. It was an idealism that would become one more disappointment in his balance as a novelist and a soldier.

Military manuals of the sort De Forest referred to in his letters home were nationalistic tools similar to Bourne's essay contest, and they tended to mechanize soldiers to encourage their anonymity. Regulations were there to sanitize the corrosive effects of individual personality within the group. In a representative Union manual from 1861, soldiers were subject to a litany of dietary and sumptuary restrictions. "12. Wear stout woolen drawers and shirts, winter and summer, day and night, and when too warm, or during active exercise, throw off your upper garments . . . Change your underclothing frequently . . . 13. Keep your body dry and warm; take off damp clothing as soon as possible." Much of what was expected from this behavioral code may simply be considered common sense, designed to protect the soldier's body from the noxious environs of camp life and combat. Be reasonable. Eat sensibly. Layer your clothing to regulate your body temperature. Even then, apparent paternalism quickly gave way to an almost paranoid restlessness. Do not even sit down, the manual warns, without adequate covering such as "thick cloths, blankets, dry straw, grass, leaves, wood, or something of the kind under you as a protection."[40] De Forest read his military manuals as he had Hawthorne in his youth, but in his life as a soldier, the twin promises of discipline and romanticism proved equally false.

In a letter dated September 2, 1862, to his wife, De Forest documents how military alertness quickly transformed into physical suffering. "The never-ceasing rain streams at will through numerous rents and holes in the mouldy, rotten canvas. Nearly every night half the men are wet through while asleep unless they wake up, stack their clothing in the darkness, and sit on it with their rubber blankets over their heads, something not easy to do when they are so crowded that they can hardly move."[41] Luxuries such as assembling grass before sitting down and switching out clean socks were not a genuine possibility, especially when peace gave way to violence. As had been true in his experience in Europe, the reality was not like how the books described it at all. In the attack on Port Hudson in *Miss Ravenel's Conversion,* the narrator similarly notes how by all predictions the engagement should have been ordered yet was anything but. "To keep the ranks closed and aligned in any tolerable fighting shape while struggling through that mile of tangled forest and broken ground was a task of terrible difficulty" (*MR* 249), and as the terrain deteriorated around the battalion's charging line into terrible noise, "heavy guns, bursting shells, falling trees, and flying splinters" (*MR* 250), the protagonist Captain Colburne inexplicably recalls his army regulations from basic training: "Soldiers must not be permitted to leave the ranks to strip or rob the dead, nor even to assist the wounded, unless by express permission, which is only to be given after the action is decided" (*MR* 254). De Forest's learning curve in the military traced (and trained) the development of his own characters. In both worlds, the state-sponsored stories of authority, preparation, and discipline finally did nothing to save lives in combat. Two short paragraphs later, an anonymous soldier becomes "pierced through the lungs by a rifle-ball" and quickly dies (*MR* 254).

De Forest's expectations of military life may have been illusory, but the literary effects of those disappointments were not. His time as a soldier was both like and unlike the peaceful world he had known in which he had already experienced failure; now, of course, failure meant he could die. As a way to counteract his anxiety over the arbitrary and brutal nature of the Civil War, De Forest documented again and again the discrete uniqueness of the ordinary and commonplace events of military life. The realism that resulted was a mode of writing that tried everything in the hopes of creating analogies between the varieties of his military experience and the civilian life he had known.[42] In search of a usable truth, De Forest relentlessly documented the individual habits and constitutions of the officers and soldiers around him. In a letter dated April 6, 1862, while stationed outside New Orleans, orders come in to stand down preparation for a skirmish, and De Forest takes the reprieve to cultivate his literary eye just as if he were in an everyday civilian setting. "You would perhaps like a sketch of General Butler," he writes to his wife, and so "in my character of novelist I made a study of him."[43] The sympathetic representation of the abolitionist General Benjamin Butler that follows in his remarks underscores a recurring concern in De Forest to celebrate the diversity of personality around him.

De Forest's impressions of General Butler show up in *Miss Ravenel's Conversion* as well. The narrator is quick to point out that the novel's descriptions of soldiers are influenced by his own subjectivity and by the subjectivity of the other characters. "I wish it to be understood that I do not endorse the above criticism on the celebrated proconsul on Louisiana. I am not sketching the life of General Butler, but of Colonel Carter—I am not trying to show how things really were, but only how the Colonel looked at them" (*MR* 98). The war as it really was mattered less to De Forest than the war as one soldier, whoever that may be, saw it. Privacy and perception controlled his craft. In *The Unwritten War* (1973), Daniel Aaron has noted De Forest's tendency for humble portraiture in his letters and diaries. What sets his account apart "from other competently written eyewitness chronicles is its conscious literary intention." There are in his private writings the impression of Butler, as well as "the abolitionist General John W. Phelps, grizzled, shambling, sarcastic, a splenetic disciplinarian laughed at and liked for his oddities," and lengthy sketches on the drunkard Sergeant Weber, among many others. In Aaron's analysis, De Forest "came to regard common soldiers with a kind of awe," and indeed his admiration for his fellow combatants should be seen as a political and aesthetic statement.[44] De Forest's translation of military life to the broader civilian world showed that men and women at war were recognized by a peaceful world, but only to a point. Once he entered the battlefield, sympathy broke down for De Forest, and the men who were once familiar and fraternal were now strange and unknowable. This failure was at the very heart of De Forest's understanding of realism.

The documentary impulse underlying De Forest's letters also animates *Miss Ravenel's Conversion*. Displaced by the impending war from his medical practice in Louisiana, the Northern-educated Dr. Ravenel relocates with his daughter, Lillie, to the fictional town of New Boston, whereupon they meet a fellow Southern transplant, Lieutenant Colonel Carter.[45] Carter turns out to be a womanizer and unscrupulous opportunist, but not before Lillie falls in love with him. Their marriage produces a child, much to the dismay of our true hero, the tight-lipped and dutiful Captain Colburne. Despite rhetorical clues that warn the reader he is no good, Carter is arguably the most intriguing and sympathetic character. He was the novel's greatest success for Henry James.[46] Colburne, on the other hand, is much more in line with the Union's expectations of its soldiers. He is a proper native of New England, and though he loves Lillie dearly, he must be tested by battle and the full term of their prolonged separation before events finally will bring the two together in the end. Although De Forest spends most of his pages detailing the elaborate story line of their personal reunion, it cannot be said that he cares much for Colburne and Lillie.

The tedium of their romance reads once again as a conciliation to convention, a long diversion, it is safe to say, from the twenty or so pages describing combat that could not be easily translated into popular literary taste. Because it was how a popular audience processed the world, De Forest had to make compromises with sentimentality, even though he recognized that "melodramatically considered, real life is frequently a failure" (*MR* 133). In an effort to find a new way of describing "real life," De Forest took some notable risks against sentimentality's better judgment that modern readers frequently have overlooked. In addition to the lecherous Carter, the reader is introduced to the scandalously explicit Mrs. Larue (who rivals Kate Chopin's Edna Pontellier in sexual immorality), the affable drunk Van Zandt, and the sympathetic former slave Major Scott, who, in an unusual display of interracial trust, fights and dies alongside Colburne and Dr. Ravenel at the siege on Fort Winthrop.

Is it fair to say that De Forest personally came to know personalities such as Carter, Larue, and Scott in his wartime interactions? Reflecting on the novel in 1898 some thirty years after its publication, De Forest acknowledged how his life as a soldier had taken its toll on his approach to writing narrative. While it still might be fair to weigh the merits of his artistic execution, for De Forest, at least, the restriction of his vision to the people and places he intimately knew was deliberate, and by design. "[*Miss Ravenel's Conversion* was] a book out of my own experience. Perhaps the book was out of the ordinary in some respects at that time. Certainly it was not of the same style as any of my previous work. In that book for the first time in my life I came to know the value of personal knowledge of one's subject and the art of drawing upon life for one's characters. In my younger days everything was romance."[47] De Forest renounces the "romance" of his youthful writings that can be clearly found, for example, in his Hawthornesque historical novel set during the Salem witch trials, *Witching Times* (1856). What was required in light of the Civil War was not romance, not melodrama, but an empirical realism. De Forest reads himself somewhat obliquely as a writer of novelized memoir, yet even more precisely as a writer of "personal knowledge," something to be garnered only through the people and actions he himself knew.

Personal knowledge of the war told De Forest that his daily experience as a soldier—that cross section of boredom and ambition, frustration and success, dilettante and artist—was only accessible to the civilian public through analogies to their own experience. Melodrama was one parallel. Mortality was another. Yet in those brief battlefield scenes that depict various states of death and dying, it is apparent that there was no narrative method sufficient to translate fully the horror and specificity of combat trauma. No previous veteran in the United States had even tried to this extent. Readers could concede the varieties of at-ease military life as civilian equivalences would allow, but the varieties of death and combat were a different affair altogether. They paralyzed both the author's and the reader's imagination alike. Personal knowledge told De Forest that when the war finally did happen in the very real flashes of battles, fear, and death, it happened to discrete soldiers like himself, not to monolithic nations and not to civilian readers. The soldier's consciousness often reads in the novel as a solipsistic impasse that had no bridge, and this stalemate helps explain why it is that as De Forest's gaze became more perceptive and realistic, it also became more internal and emotionally detached.

Following the Confederate attack on Port Hudson in *Miss Ravenel's Conversion,* the narrator describes the scene at a central army hospital behind the front lines. "It was simply an immense collection of wounded men *in every imaginable condition of mutilation,* every one stained more or less with his own blood . . . all lying in the open air on the bare ground, or on their own blankets, with no shelter except the friendly foliage of the oaks and beeches" (*MR* 260; emphasis added). The wounds the narrator sees importantly exist completely within the restrictions of his own imagination. They survive only in the mind of one witness, locked in for him alone to make sense of. The act of reading De Forest's battle scenes was not sympathetic for a contemporary audience but rather aggressively voyeuristic. What these images were not was the idealized soldier that readers found in cultural mitigators such as Alcott and Bourne.

Instead, the novel's sequences of war subtly implied that the possibilities for representing gore and destruction were at once infinite but also short lived. This was for De Forest the phenomenological payoff from the soldier's personal knowledge, that the commonalities of his experience could only be read and written one soldier, and one sentence, at a time. Each particular one is identified biologically "with his own blood" amid the "immense collection" of suffering bodies. The preoccupation with such fine demarcation in this scene is meant to show that no two wounds were the same, thus no two representations could be the same. Every wound, like every experience of soldiering, signaled a different need of expression. "In the centre of this mass of suffering stood several operating tables, each burdened by a grievously wounded man and surrounded by surgeons and their assistants. Underneath were great pools of clotted blood, amidst which lay amputated fingers, hands, arms, feet and legs" (*MR* 260). Much like the photographs from the workshops of Mathew Brady and Alexander Gardner, De Forest's stagnant pile of body parts underscores the plurality of discursive sites of experience that will never get to speak for themselves. And while some soldiers do get names in the novel—Colburne, Carter, Major Gazaway, Van Zandt—most do not, and their appellative absence carries over into the hollowness we read in the main characters themselves.

Echoing Whitman's sentiment, De Forest in the act of writing war is among "the infinite dead," those who in their obscurity speak "on monuments and gravestones, singly or in masses, to tens of thousands, the significant word, UNKNOWN."[48] When Colburne retreats at Port Hudson with his own wounds, he comes across his commanding Lieutenant Colonel "with a bullet-wound in his thigh which the surgeon whispered was mortal" (MR 261–62). The officer dismisses the pronouncement on the grounds that he was the best interpreter of his wound. "'It's a lie!' exclaimed the sufferer. 'It's all nonsense, Doctor. You don't know your business. I won't die. I sha'n't die. It's all nonsense to say that a little hole in the leg like that can kill a great strong man like me. I tell you I sha'n't and won't die'" (MR 262). What the soldier believes and what he had experienced and come to imagine were finally independent of how the war exacted itself. "In an hour more he was a corpse, and before night he was black with putrefaction, so rapid was that shocking change under the heat of a Louisiana May" (MR 262). The mortal change happens fast despite personal and symbolic protest, imagined not as a denial—I choose not to believe—but rather, to use the soldier's own words, nonsense—I *cannot* understand that death and defeat come, because this hole does not trigger the knowledge of death.

Looming death was the limit point of personal knowledge for Civil War soldiers, and De Forest refuses to portray it as redemptive. What was that limit for those who made it through alive? Amid the diversity of wounds, genders, races, and regions is the novel's modest realization that what we believe depends on what we have experienced. In the aftermath of the North's defeat at the battle of First Bull Run early in the novel, Union soldiers return dejected, much to the surprise of the Ravenels and Colburne. "Stragglers arrived, and then the regiments. People were not angry with the beaten soldiers, but treated them with tenderness" (MR 61). The war turns in this scene suddenly from a safe ideological debate set in the distance into the actual "beaten soldiers" who had fought and brought their loss back with them from the front lines. Inscribed in the tatters of their "ragged shoddy uniforms" is the denial of the Union narrative of quick victory. It was not at all the way the story was supposed to go, and the unexpectedness of the defeat is only made worse by the unforeseen capture of Carter by the Confederates. This moment in the novel is one of the rare instances when the disillusionment from the war feels intimately personal to the main characters. The scene is a surprising twist in a novel of mostly predictable outcomes, and it serves as a rhetorical opportunity for De Forest to ask his characters to negotiate personal and national transformation—a question that is a crucial component of the cultural problem addressed in the novel.

The civilian response is invested with the familiar confidence that national destiny and personal experience went hand in hand. Dr. Ravenel, a universally sympathetic figure of patriarchal wisdom throughout the novel, tries to assure his daughter and future son-in-law of the certain comfort to be found in uncertain beliefs. Ravenel cites as an example his own evolution on the question of slavery from unconcerned spectator to sworn abolitionist. "I wasn't infallible five years ago . . . the progress of our race from barbarism to civilization is through the medium of constant change. If the race is benefited by it, why not the individual?" (*MR* 63). Ravenel imagines his "old opinions" on slavery as analogous to the snake which symbolically must shed its beliefs like "last year's skins" to survive. Not only is throwing off old ideas inevitable, it is an organic process of the healthy and developing body politic. Speaking with De Forest's permission, Colburne is unconvinced by the metaphor. He remarks that not every change in the nation has been desirable (think, after all, what our Puritan ancestors would say about our Sabbath habits), and so the doctor fashions a different image that could just as easily have been written by a young William James.[49]

"Weak spirits are frightened by this change, this growth, this forward impetus," said the Doctor. "I must tell you a story. I was traveling in Georgia three years ago. On the seat next in front of me sat a cracker, who was evidently making his first railroad experience, and in other respects learning to go on his hind legs. Presently the train crossed a bridge. It was narrow, uncovered and without sides, so that a passenger would not be likely to see it unless he sat near the window. I observed him give a glare at the river and turn away his head suddenly, after which he rolled about in a queer way, and finally went to the floor in a heap. We picked him up . . . and presently the cracker was brought to his senses. His first words were, 'Has she lit'—He was under the impression that the train had taken the river at a running jump. Now that is very much like the judgment of timid and ill-informed people on the progress of the nation or race at such a time as this. They don't know about the bridge; they think we are flying through the air; and so they go off in general fainting fits." (*MR* 63–64)

Cleverly elided together are industrial and ideological change. The history of the nation unfolds just like the lives of its people, and there is no stopping in either "the fifth act in the grand drama of human liberty" (*MR* 445).[50] The technology of the train underscores modernity's approach regardless of the personal doubts of the passengers. In mocking the poor white's discomfort, Ravenel renders personal experience and fear beside the point in a post–Civil War world. Confronted for the first time with the actual loss of soldiers before him, the doctor speaks for the novel's sentimental readers and holds strong in the faith that the metanarratives of progress and assured victory were the only knowledge the nation needed.

The response from the soon-to-be soldier Colburne is markedly different. His epistemology depends on getting his hands dirty, because "on the train of human progress, we are parts of the engine and not mere passengers. I ought to be revolving somewhere. I ought to be at work. I want to do something—I am most anxious to do something—but I don't know precisely what. I suppose that the inability exists in me, and not in my circumstances" (*MR* 64). Rather than the doctor's blind civilian confidence, Colburne seeks that transformative experience that comes only from participation. Colburne's indecisiveness here results in part from an incomplete personal knowledge. He has not at this point entered the war, and Colburne's tone echoes the young De Forest abroad and in boot camp when he had assumed personal ambition and national destiny would energize his resolve. In this scene, De Forest characterizes the soldier as an agent of patriotic conviction only so he can later, on the battlefields, reverse the table as the table was reversed on him. There is no idealistic nation in the novel's foxholes. De Forest's writings testify throughout that there was no larger meaning-making system at all, save perhaps—and only perhaps—the veteran writing his story.

The cultural aftermath of the Civil War invariably wrestled with the problem of too many veterans still living, many of whom needed to voice their individual experiences in some way. When that expression took written form, such as in the now-forgotten words of Franklin H. Durrah, the personal knowledge of the Civil War veteran was met with

the public desire for silence. Bourne could acknowledge and even celebrate the patriotic sacrifices of Union veterans in elaborate tours and
ceremonies, but he did not print and thereby license the soldiers' naked
words themselves. The din of variety would have been overwhelming,
and De Forest knew as much. Both he and Durrah shared the same fate
of being but one soldier among many soldiers. Whereas earlier veterans had written in the hopes of establishing political dignity, soldiers
in light of the Civil War were increasingly skeptical of the coherence of
identity categories.[51] The soldier's record of the Civil War would always
be incomplete. There were innumerable soldiers' stories that would go
unwritten or that would at best be read for a time and then forgotten.

De Forest saw the absence of the veteran experience in the written record as a limitation finally of language and time and analogous
to the difficulty of writing a representative national experience. In an
essay written shortly after *Miss Ravenel's Conversion* entitled "The Great
American Novel" (1868), De Forest weighed in on the contemporary
concern over what was the best and most illustrative American novel.
"Is there, in other words, a single tale which paints American life so
broadly, truly, and sympathetically that every American of feeling and
culture is forced to acknowledge the picture as a likeness of something
which he knows?" After quickly dismissing Irving and Cooper ("These
are ghosts, and they wrote about ghosts, and the ghosts have vanished
utterly") as well as Hawthorne, De Forest briefly considers *Uncle Tom's
Cabin* for the honor, but then finally answers his own question, "We
must answer, Not one!" As was true for the "common" experience of the
soldier, asking for the distinctively "American" novel was, in light of the
Civil War, the wrong question. Veterans had rendered knowledge and
experience radically regional and fiercely antagonistic. "When you have
made your picture of petrified New England village life, left aground
like a boulder near the banks of the Merrimac, does the Mississippian
or the Minnesotian or the Pennsylvanian recognize it as American
society? We are a nation of provinces and each province claims to be
the court."[52] De Forest accepts, as few contemporary writers would, the
fragmentation that the war both reflected and produced.

Readers since 1867 have been almost unanimous in their reception
of *Miss Ravenel's Conversion* as a realistic facsimile of the conditions of
war. De Forest's contemporaries saw a faithful correspondence in his

novel to how the scenes of war looked, not necessarily to how they felt, or to the psychological effects they would produce, but to the "blind ruck of event" itself.[53] Henry James, writing in the June 1867 *Nation,* sidestepped the question of the novel's failure or success as a piece of original fiction (he had in fact found himself frequently distracted by the "characters we find not interesting and with one exception, Carter, not well drawn") and focused instead on the merit to be drawn from what the novel actually was—an authentic and representative example of experience in the military. "[It is the] picture of the military service in the Department of the Gulf, 'a novel of the war,' that we think best of the book. So considered, it deserves more praise, we think, than any of its numerous rivals for popular favor, and is so well worth reading that, though we are constrained to pronounce the work a poor novel, we are quite willing to say that it is a poor novel with a deal of good in it."[54]

One month later, William Dean Howells reviewed the novel with a similar air in the *Atlantic Monthly.* Like James, Howells could only praise the "deal of good" to be found in the novel's inauguration of the soldier as a foundling literary type. "Mr. De Forrest [sic] is the first *to treat the war really and artistically.* His campaigns do not try the reader's constitution, his battles are not bores. *His soldiers are the soldiers we actually know,*—the green wood of the volunteers, the warped stuff of men torn from civilization and cast suddenly into the barbarism of camps, the hard, dry, tough, true fibre of the veterans that came out of the struggle."[55] In the 1880s when both James and Howells were setting down their mature theories of realism, the war and the soldier continued to weigh heavily on their respective approaches. In *Criticism and Fiction* (1891), Howells often refers to Ulysses S. Grant's memoirs as an example of the "simple, natural and honest" standards of the realist mode. Grant's writing style is appreciated for its "unliterariness" that contained a "plebeian plainness at times." Indeed, "there is no more attempt at dramatic effect than there is at ceremonious pose; things happen in that tale of a mighty war as they happened in the mighty war itself, without setting, without artificial reliefs one after another, as if they were all of one quality and degree . . . it is always an unaffected, unpretentious man who is talking; and throughout he prefers to wear the uniform of a private." Howells aligns Grant's status as an ordinary soldier with his success as a realist writer, noting that because Grant was no "genius," nor had any sense of calling to the war, he could write about the experience fairly: "he gives you the facts, and leaves them with you."[56]

His praise of the general reads very much like his praise of De Forest. Indeed, Howells had thought De Forest was the first great American realist, "a realist before realism was named," he wrote in his "Editor's Study" column in *Harper's* in February 1887. He went so far as to call De Forest's *Kate Beaumont* (1871) "as good a piece of realism as I know of . . . worthy of the greatest novelist living in any country," and later, in the "Editor's Study" of September 1887, he boldly placed De Forest on an equal footing with Tolstoy.[57] I doubt any modern critic would make similar grandiose claims today, and yet De Forest's contribution to how civilian realist writers understood the individual in an increasingly hostile world cannot be ignored. The firsthand experience of the soldier translates into a personal knowledge for the reader that, as Dr. Ravenel himself put it, "the age of miracles is over" (*MR* 51).

The age of miracles was over, not just for Dr. Ravenel but also for aging civilian writers who bridged the nation before and after the Civil War. Oliver Wendell Holmes Sr., whose son, the future jurist, was twice injured in the Civil War, grew unnerved by his constant lack of access to the troops. Three decades after penning "The Last Leaf," Holmes wrote in *Soundings from the Atlantic* (1864) how the physical and psychological distance from live battle made the home front unbearably skittish. "Men cannot think, or write, or attend to their ordinary business," he declares, for they are too out of sorts to function. Noncombatants always got word of the war belatedly through newspapers and days-old dispatches publicly posted in town centers. The postponement inherent in these reports made Holmes feel powerless over the war, so he compensated for all the things he did not know by filling in the gaps of time and space with a tragic sense of foreboding: "[A] person goes through the side streets on his way for the noon *extra,*—he is so afraid somebody will meet him and *tell* the news he wishes to *read,* first on the bulletin-board, and then in the great capitals and leaded type of the newspaper . . . When any startling piece of war-news comes, it keeps repeating itself in our minds in spite of all we can do. The same trains of thought go tramping round in circle through the brain, like the supernumeraries that make up the grand army of a stage-show. Now, if a thought goes round through the brain a thousand times in a day, it will have worn as deep a track as one which has passed through it once a week for twenty years." As chapter 3 highlighted, Melville certainly was one of these "supernumeraries" worn out by the traumatic distance of the Civil War. So too was Walt Whitman, whose time among wounded soldiers in the hospitals of Washington corroborated Holmes's account in "My Hunt after 'the Captain'" of the "impossible" task "to individualize" soldiers and their suffering.[58] In "A March in the Ranks Hard-Prest, and the Road Unknown" from *Drum-Taps* (1865), the sea of endless soldiers quickly overwhelms the wound-dresser speaker.

> . . . I sweep my eyes o'er the scene, fain to absorb it all
> Faces, varieties, postures beyond description, most in obscurity,
>   some of them dead;
> Surgeons operating, attendant holding lights, the smell of ether,
>   the odor of blood;
> The crowd, O the crowd of the bloody forms of soldiers—the
>   yard outside also Fill'd;
> Some on the bare ground, some on planks or stretchers, some in
>   the death-spasm
> Sweating . . .

Whitman looks at the wounds and is gladly "fain to absorb it all," whereas the wounded wince at their injuries. A nameless patient in "The Wound-Dresser" endures Whitman's washing of his "amputated hand," yet "His eyes are closed, his face is pale, he dares not look on the bloody stump, / And has not yet look'd on it."[59] The Civil War caused sympathetic spectators, such as Melville, Holmes, Whitman, and Bourne, to alternate between wanting to acknowledge the wreckage and, like the wounded soldier, being unable to look at it at all.

The dizzying crowds of wounded soldiers likewise stunned Nathaniel Hawthorne, who for most of the war lived in New England far away from the sounds and smells of battle. Before his death in 1864, he descended to the war zone for the first and final time. The satiric travelogue of Hawthorne's journey south, published in the April 1862 *Atlantic Monthly* as "Chiefly about War Matters," takes him by train near active sites of battle. In the descent, Hawthorne notices the increasing accumulation of convalescent soldiers outside his cabin window. They cluttered and impeded the roads outside Philadelphia. Between Baltimore and Washington, their numbers grew ever more concentrated. The fractured nation had unexpectedly become overrun with veterans who were fractured themselves.

> Even supposing the war should end to-morrow, and the army melt into the mass of the population within the year, what an incalculable preponderance will there be of military title and pretensions for at least half a century to come! Every country-neighborhood will have its general or two, its three or four colonels, half a dozen majors, and captains without end,—besides non-commissioned officers and privates, more than the recruiting offices ever know of,—all with their campaign-stories, which will become the staple of fireside-talk forevermore. Military merit, or rather, since that is not so readily estimated, military notoriety, will be the measure of all claims to civil distinction. One bullet-headed general will succeed another in the Presidential chair; and veterans will hold the offices at home and abroad, and sit in Congress and the state legislatures, and fill all the avenues of public life. And yet I do not speak of this deprecatingly, since, very likely, it may substitute something more real and genuine, instead of the many shams on which men have heretofore founded their claims to public regard; but it behooves civilians to consider their wretched prospects in the future, and assume the military button before it is too late.[60]

Hawthorne is at once critical of "bullet-headed" soldiers at the same time he is supportive of the "something more real and genuine" that authenticates their place within the "public regard." He is suspicious of military "pretensions" and prescient enough to realize that postwar American politics would be substantially shaped by veterans.[61]

Hawthorne suspected that martial experiences, that "military button" as he called it, would soon form the basis of the nation's governance and that civilians needed to work fast to appropriate military experience before veterans exploited their identity for political gain. In light of the Civil War, there were too many veterans, each with a story to tell, and that reality was a troubling proposition not only for Melville's, Hawthorne's, and Whitman's generation but also for the generation following Reconstruction and its attendant moment of literary realism. On its face, American literary realism at the end of the nineteenth century appears to be sympathetic to military experience, but in truth it is the Trojan horse that allowed such civilian authors as Henry Adams and Henry James to strip veterans of their own military experience and exile them even further to the margins of American citizenship. That cruel trick, in which veteran literary culture lost ownership of its experience once again (as it had during and after the Revolutionary and Mexican Wars), would soon drive veteran authors of the twentieth century out of this world.

Veterans in Outer Space

Beyond 1880

Experience is never limited and it is never complete; it is an immense sensibility, a kind of huge spider-web, of the finest silken threads, suspended in the chamber of consciousness and catching every airborne particle in its tissue . . . The power to guess the unseen from the seen, to trace the implication of things, to judge the whole piece by the pattern, the condition of feeling life, in general, so completely that you are well on your way to knowing any particular corner of it—this cluster of gifts may almost be said to constitute experience.

—Henry James, "The Art of Fiction" (1884)

Anonymously published two decades after *Miss Ravenel's Conversion from Secession to Loyalty,* Henry Adams's *Democracy* (1880) wryly exposed the failures of Reconstruction to form a more perfect union between North and South. Madeleine Lee is "a Philadelphian by birth" who has decided to pass the winter in Washington because "she wanted to see with her own eyes the action of primary forces; to touch with her own hand the massive machinery of society . . . She was bent upon getting to the heart of the great American mystery of democracy and government" (*D* 4, 7). Her Southern husband, "a descendant of one branch of the Virginia Lees" (*D* 4), recently has died when the novel opens, thus leaving her a widow and a "half Yankee" (*D* 15) interested in political ambition: "What she wanted was POWER" (*D* 8). Power, of course, corrupts, especially for Senator Silas P. Ratcliffe, who stuffed ballots for Lincoln during the

Civil War and "would do it again, and worse than that, if I thought it would save this country from disunion" (*D* 61). The novel's political theory is pragmatic if not outright Machiavellian insofar as the ends always justify the means in Adams's appraisal of American life.

Ratcliffe's "worse than that" occurs during the election of 1868, which Ulysses S. Grant would ultimately win, although that outcome was uncertain at the time. The "result of that election would be almost as important to the nation as the result of the war itself," Ratcliffe insists to Madeleine.[1] To ensure victory, he and others in his party spent "freely"— too freely, in fact, and as a result Ratcliffe stole some money and hid his tracks to pay off campaign debts (*D* 190–91). It is the cover-up that ultimately convinces Madeleine not to marry Ratcliffe (a likely presidential candidate for the next election) and to leave Washington with her sister, Sybil, at the end of the novel in order to experience Egypt instead, because "democracy has shaken my nerves to pieces" (*D* 200). Discovering the cover-up disorients Madeleine as it does the reader, both of whom have been confronted with troubling questions throughout the novel. Was Silas P. Ratcliffe all that different from other politicians, even someone as vaulted as George Washington? Moreover, if American politics are corrupt, is that the fault of the politicians themselves, or is their character a reflection of the people who elected them?

The political anxieties that agitate *Democracy* are self-evident, yet for all the novel's intrigue about political corruption and cover-up, I want to suggest by way of conclusion an even greater deceit. Namely, the moment of American literary realism at the end of the nineteenth century that I argued in chapter 4 was rooted in Civil War veteran literature ultimately evolved into a civilian cover-up for the hostile takeover of Civil War veteran experience.

At one key moment in the novel, Madeleine's sister Sybil travels to Arlington National Cemetery with John Carrington, who "at twenty-two . . . had gone into the rebel army as a private and carried his musket modestly through a campaign or two" (*D* 13). Sybil is visiting the former property of Robert E. Lee, the Confederate general but also her relative by marriage, whose land now holds the bodies of the Union dead. The mixture of emotions and loyalties confuses her. "Madeleine dissected her own feelings and was always wondering whether they were real or not," but "Sybil particularly disliked this self-inspection" (*D*

120). Indeed, Sybil is content in her repression until she sees the "white ranks of headstones" for the first time. "Here was something new to her. This was war—wounds, disease, death. She dropped her voice and with a look almost as serious a Carrington's, asked what all these graves meant." Worse, "it suddenly occurred to her as a new thought that perhaps he himself might have killed one of them with his own hand" (*D* 121–22). The possibility of violence titillates her imagination. "Sybil had everything to learn; the story came to her with all the animation of *real life*" (*D* 123; emphasis added). Had Carrington ever killed anyone in the war? He is not sure, although he knows others tried to kill him. "Then Sybil begged to know how they had tried to kill him, and he told her one or two of those experiences, such as most soldiers have had, when he had been fired upon and the balls had torn his clothes or drawn blood. Poor Sybil was quite overcome, and found a deadly fascination in the horror" (*D* 124). The scene implicitly equates "real life" with voyeurism and the so-called insight which imagining other people's trauma might bring. Sybil would not be alone in wanting to hear veteran pain.

Civilian realist authors during the waning years of the nineteenth century became increasingly fascinated with veterans and the putative gravitas of their military experience. Civil War veteran and nouveau riche Silas Lapham dines with "'we non-combatants [who] were notoriously reluctant to give up fighting'" in William Dean Howell's *The Rise of Silas Lapham* (1885). Lapham's personal narrative of wartime experience captivates his civilian crowd as Sybil had been enchanted. "'I don't want to see any more men killed in my time.' Something serious, something somber must lurk behind these words, and they waited for Lapham to say more." The air of veteran reverence similarly follows Basil Ransom as he walks through Harvard's Memorial Hall in Henry James's *The Bostonians* (1886), wherein Ransom "lingered longest in the presence of the white, ranged tablets, each of which, in its proud, sad clearness, is inscribed with the name of a student-soldier." James would write in his preface to *The American* (1907) that "the real represents to my perception the things we cannot possibly *not* know, sooner or later, in one way or another," a sentiment that describes the realist author's encounter with veteran experience more broadly—be it Adams at Arlington, Howells listening to war stories at a dinner party, or James walking through a war memorial.[2] What could be more real, which is to say inescapable, than imagining real people who suffered the real consequences of war?

To imagine, as does Sybil, the "reality of war"—that which cannot *not* be known—is to feel the irresistible sense of importance as Whitman did when he encountered the "significant word UNKNOWN" on anonymous Civil War "monuments and gravestones, singly or in masses."[3] Yet in such an encounter, a transference occurs between such veterans as Carrington, Lapham, and Ransom and their civilian observers, who, in their very imagining of veteran experience, confiscate that very thing. As the epigraph from Henry James suggests, what was yours is now mine—within the world of the texts themselves but also in the very tradition of realistic war narratives that were composed by nonveterans (both Henry Adams and William Dean Howells left for Europe during the years of the Civil War, and Henry James could not fight because of his "obscure hurt" suffered in early 1861).[4] James would write in "The Art of Fiction" that the purpose of art is "to compete with life." Moreover, "the only reason for the existence of a novel is that it *does* compete with life," and if it fails to convince the reader, then the work is a "betrayal."[5] Such competition was not always friendly. Stephen Crane, for one, wanted to win. The most celebrated Civil War novel today, *The Red Badge of Courage,* arose in part from Crane's belief that he could write about the Civil War better than the veteran accounts he was reading in the *Century* and elsewhere. Furthermore, he felt compelled to write a book that "denied the authority of veterans over the battlefield" because they had their chance and had not delivered.[6]

While I do not want to take away from the achievement of *The Red Badge of Courage* or the accomplishments of Adams, Howells, and James, I do want to underscore the inherent paternalism in the civilian realist desire to represent Civil War veterans. The competition between civilian and veteran might have been sympathetic, might even have come from a sincere sense of curiosity about veteran experience and what it was like, but it was also not a fair fight, given the long struggle of nineteenth-century veteran literature. Just as veteran service benefits the civilian nation, so veteran literature benefits civilian literature—in this case, realism. The trap from which veteran Americans could not escape at the end of the nineteenth century was the enduring parasitic nature of civil-military literary relations that failed to improve since Colonel Manly's first complaint in *The Contrast* a century earlier.

Realist literature knew as much, whether consciously or not, and I call realism a cover-up because it denied its guilt over, first, being the victor in the competition between civilian art and veteran life and, second, in not knowing whether its claims to the Civil War's so-called reality were more convincing than veteran accounts. That is to say, a novel such as *Democracy* is often concerned not only with the political failures of Reconstruction but also with the crisis of confidence in civilian experience—the very foundation for what its characters believe to be "real" life. At a gala at the White House, the newly elected president and his wife appear to Madeleine as "two seemingly mechanical figures, which might be wood or wax," little more than "automata, representatives of the society which streamed past them" (*D* 50–51). Their lifeless performance shocks her to the point of near hysterics. "The sight of those two suffering images at the door is too mournful to be borne. I am dizzy with looking at these stalking figures. I don't believe they're real" (*D* 53). While this disbelief is not exactly the same as De Forest's battlefield shock, the impulse is similar insofar as the soldier of the Civil War and the civilian in light of Reconstruction relentlessly feel compelled to test reality—a faculty that proved to be as much a casualty for civilians as for veterans entangled in the trauma of the Civil War.[7]

When trauma does announce itself in *Democracy,* such as when Sybil reveals that Madeleine's husband died "after only one day's illness," only to have "just a week later her little child [die] of diphtheria, suffering horribly," or when Carrington breaks down to reveal that "of his two brothers, one had survived the war only to die at home, a mere wreck of disease, privation, and wounds; the other had been shot by his side, and bled slowly to death in his arms during the awful carnage in the Wilderness," the pain is quickly buttoned up and never spoken of again (*D* 138–39). Why? Because civilian literary realism denies rather than confronts. Adams suggests as much at a political ball near the end of the novel, in which the narrator admits he is describing various women somewhat incorrectly: "The lady just behind the Princess on her left is Mrs. Lee, a poor likeness, but easily distinguishable from the fact that the artist, for his own objects, has made her rather shorter, and the Princess rather taller, than was strictly correct, just as he has given the Princess a gracious smile, which was quite different from her actual expression. *In short, the artist is compelled to exhibit the world rather as we would wish it to be, than as it was, or is, or, indeed, is like shortly to become"* (D 161; emphasis added). Like Sybil at Arlington, realist literature after the Civil War was aspirational ("as we would wish the world to be") rather than steely ("as it was, or is, or indeed is like shortly to become")—a wince rather than an existential encounter with the "things which we cannot possibly *not* know."[8] While it is true that somewhere between the world we have and the world we want is the world we write, I want to challenge realism's cozy relationship with veteran literary culture.

I claim literary realism worked to deny and cover up veteran experience, but plenty of veteran literature since the Civil War has worked within the expectations of civilian realism. The dominant trend for over a century has been to embed the reader in the experience of war, and as a consequence, veteran literature has become more or less synonymous with combat literature and the realism of *What It Is Like to Go to War* (2012), to quote Karl Marlantes's more recent memoir about the Vietnam War. The list of twentieth-century veteran realism is long, including Ernest Hemingway's *A Farewell to Arms* (1929), Norman Mailer's *The Naked and the Dead* (1948), Gustav Hasford's *The Short-Timers* (1979), and Phil Klay's *Redeployment* (2014). An instinct toward verisimilitude has happened on the nonfiction side of literature written by veterans as well, such as in J. Glenn Gray's *The Warriors* (1958), Philip Caputo's *A Rumor of War* (1977), Dave Grossman's *On Killing* (1995), and, more recently, Kayla Williams's *Love My Rifle More than You* (2005) and Colby Buzzell's *My War* (2005). This line of veteran realism since the Civil War is well established, but whereas many modern veteran writers have wanted to go back to the actual battlefield, quite a few have gone to outer space instead. Outer space is a realm that is far from the late nineteenth-century sense of "the real," and it has contributed to a strain of veteran literature that rejects the usual realist way we read veterans today as war's correspondents by instead critiquing the civilian desire to "be there."

Outer space cuts two ways. It is at once relaxing—an imaginative safe harbor where the fantasy of "not Earth" becomes a sort of cover for the

thematic and emotional risks veteran authors take under the guise of science fiction—yet it is also quite taxing—a narrative of exile and rejection
in a nonnational place very far away from the comforts of home. What
was true for the disposable veteran literacy in the nineteenth century is
still true today. Such contemporary charity organizations as "Operation
Paperback" and booksforsoldiers.com encourage deployed troops to
make book requests of their stateside civilian nation. Soldiers, sailors, and
marines often ask specifically for fantasy and speculative fiction. There
are many demands for *Star Wars* and *Twilight*. Comic books and west-
erns. Lots and lots of science fiction. The troops seem to desire nothing
"serious," as a headline for one website makes clear: "Please do not send
any romance, political, or religious books, unless the request specifically
asks you to send."[9] What veterans read and what they write are interre-
lated social practices, yet they are also difficult to illuminate because the
archive of veteran literary life has so often appeared to be ephemeral and
light. A soldier reading a science fiction novel in Afghanistan supposedly does so on his own time as a kind of "mindless escape" and nothing
more, and when he is done reading, the novel gets thrown away or left in
the barracks never to be given much thought again. What I insist here is
that veterans in outer space are not simply doodling or escaping in their
downtime but also working through their imagined and often fractious
relationship with their civilian audiences that traces its fault lines not only
to realism at the end of the nineteenth century but as far back as the early
Republic of chapter 1. Science fiction veteran representation writes itself
as an alien world set apart from the nation it serves, asking us to reconsider how we read and how we relate to the long cultural and literary
history of veterans in the United States.

Events transpire in *Democracy* that compel Ratcliffe, then secretary of
the treasury, to get rid of Carrington by sending him to Mexico on a
government post. Carrington accepts the appointment even though he
is in love with Madeleine and wants to stay: "his mother and two sisters
were struggling for a bare subsistence on a wretched Virginian farm,
and . . . all his exertions barely kept them from beggary" (*D* 138). The
war had ruined his family, and he needs the money. The same was true
of Captain John Carter in Edgar Rice Burrough's popular *Barsoom* se-

ries. An ex-Confederate during the Civil War, Captain Carter made his debut in *A Princess of Mars* (1917), which opens with the question that many nineteenth-century veterans could not adequately answer: With the war now over, what was a veteran supposed to do? "At the close of the Civil War I found myself possessed of several hundred thousand dollars (Confederate) and a captain's commission in the cavalry arm of an army which no longer existed; the servant of a state which had vanished with the hopes of the South."[10]

Implicit in this passage are several important realities for veterans in the lead up to World War I. The first was the bleak economic reality they faced. Carter's Confederate money is now useless, and thus out of necessity and without any clear skill set or market value, he must find a new way to make a living. That anxiety will drive Carter in the winter of 1865 to the Arizona desert to speculate for gold (just as Burroughs had gone to Arizona to speculate on a military career that did not pan out).[11] In Arizona, a band of Apaches drive Carter into a magical cave, where he will quickly be transported to Mars, the site of the main action of the novel and where he will become a hot commodity once again as a soldier (more specifically, a Thark warrior). A second important reality that this passage reveals is existential, namely, that Captain Carter's army "no longer existed" because his Confederate state "had vanished." As pointed out in chapter 4, much of the South after the Civil War quickly calcified into a "Lost Cause," and so too would the identities of its veterans be diminished by a postwar nationalism that preferred reunion and appeasement over divisive memories located in identities such as the Confederate veteran.[12] Whatever else the novel might be— boyhood fantasy, prototype of the superhero who never dies and always gets the girl—*A Princess of Mars* is at its core the story of a stateless, down-on-his-luck veteran who nostalgically longs for a shameful past while at the same time nervously fearing a present that is unwelcoming and a future whose economic prospects are dim.

John Carter's alienation reaches back to the nineteenth century and looks forward to the long twentieth century. To wit, no matter how one feels about Scientology, there is no denying that its extraterrestrial religiosity was imagined in *Dianetics* by its founder, L. Ron Hubbard—a navy lieutenant during World War II. Richard A. Heinlein (*Starship Troopers*), a longtime reader of such pulp dime novels as those of

Burroughs, was also in the navy, and Frank Herbert (*Dune*) was in the Seabees. Isaac Asimov was briefly in the army, as was Vietnam veteran Joe Haldeman (*The Forever War*) and Afghanistan veteran Weston Ochse (*SEAL Team 666*). Veteran authors of the twentieth century again and again ventured into outer space, and while I claim part of the motive in going there is to react against the inhospitable realism of the late nineteenth century, there are other reasons as well that need to be explored in light of the arguments of *Veteran Americans*. Given that the few pages that remain here cannot compress a whole century, I can only offer a sketch of where such an analysis might begin.

When William Mandela, the protagonist of *The Forever War* (1974), returns home after decades of fighting in outer space, the United States is a feral nation that cannot provide basic services for its people. Food is scarce, to the point that a "ration war" has broken out and calories have become the new currency. Crime is high, and the only job growth is in the military-industrial complex: "Wars in the past often accelerated social reform, provided technological benefits, even sparked artistic activity. This one, however, seemed tailor-made to provide none of these positive by-products . . . And in the past, people whose country was at war were constantly in contact with the war. The newspapers would be full of reports, veterans would return from the front; sometimes the front would move right into town, invaders marching down Main Street . . . The enemy was a tangible thing . . . But this war . . . the enemy was a curious organism only vaguely understood, more often the subject of cartoons than nightmares." When Mandela makes contact with the enemy for the first time, he discovers they are more humanlike than he had supposed. He soon realizes "they weren't aliens, I had to remind myself—*we* were."[13] As a protest novel upset with the distance between American veterans and civilians and also with the American impulse to dehumanize the Vietnamese, *The Forever War* disrupts the realist and one-sided (American) approach to narrating the Vietnam War seen in such veteran texts as Robin Moore's *The Green Berets* (1965), Robert Mason's *Chickenhawk* (1983), and Harold Moore's *We Were Soldiers Once . . . and Young* (1992). Journalistic civilian nonfiction such as Michael Herr's *Dispatches* (1977), Sebastian Junger's *War* (2010), and Kevin Sites's *The Things They Cannot Say* (2013) have similarly wanted to embed the reader in the war experience of American troops.

Indeed, the urge to embed civilians in war's "reality" has only increased since Vietnam. Our ongoing engagements in the Middle East and Afghanistan have produced HBO's *Generation Kill* (2008), Sebastian Junger's *Restrepo* (2010), and Mark Wahlberg's *Lone Survivor* (2013)—all variants of a "first-person shooter" genre that assume a veteran subjectivity for the audience in the representation of war. Writing against this problematic sense of togetherness is thirty-year veteran of the military Weston Ochse, whose 2014 novel *Grunt Life* focuses on suicidal veterans of the wars in Iraq and Afghanistan and the ways in which they have been excluded from civil society. The novel opens with Benjamin Mason (the protagonist who suffers from post-traumatic stress disorder [PTSD] after tours in Iraq, Afghanistan, Mali, and Kosovo) on a Los Angeles bridge about to jump.[14] Before he can do so, a mysterious man named Mr. Pink appears and offers an alternative: come work for him along with other suicidal vets who have lost their sense of mission and purpose. It turns out that aliens have long been among us waiting for their opportunity, and an invasion from "the Cray" (as they are called) is imminent. The world needs a secret force to defend it, which is where Mason comes in. He is alienated from civilian society (the main reason he is up on that bridge), and because the world has already pegged him for dead, it will not miss him if he is gone. Mr. Pink plants a drifter's body and sets Mason's house on fire. Problem solved. Mason becomes free and clear to join Task Force OMBRA along with other veterans whom the nation has forgotten.

Ochse's veterans in outer space are there because they are the dustbin of American society. They are the living dead who become revived only by moving to a separate and clandestine world that the rest of America cannot know (it would start a panic if the public knew there were aliens among us), and within that world, they rely on and read one another. To wit, much of Mason's secret underground training involves reading veteran science fiction, notably *Starship Troopers* and *The Forever War*. The latter novel for Mason "perfectly described the inability of a soldier to ever return to civilian life."[15] This failure to reintegrate leads one to ask, What does such a self-awareness on the part of veteran writers of other veteran writers tell us about how veteran literary culture has changed since the nineteenth century, a period in which there was less explicit conversation between veteran authors?

In part, veterans writing science fiction and veterans reading other veterans who write science fiction create a community of positive possibility that can have it both ways—a way to talk about fear, dishonor, and shame without actually talking about fear, dishonor, and shame. Science fiction's narrative conceit of remove and distance might explain why so many science-fiction texts such as *Starship Troopers* (as well as Orson Scott Card's *Ender's Game*) have been on the required reading list for both the U.S. Marine Corps and the U.S. Navy. To quote Robert J. Spiller in describing "the American intervention in Lebanon," the fantasy of science fiction is "not war but like war"—just as veterans in outer space are not veterans on earth but like them.[16] *Veteran Americans* has dealt with the veteran literature of prisoner-of-war narratives, memoirs, adventure pamphlets, newspapers, and novels. Science fiction reveals yet another context in which veterans feel their twoness, to go back to the words of W. E. B. Du Bois from the introduction (the same name, by the way, of a wizened teacher in *Starship Troopers*).

When Dejah Thoris, the Red Martian beauty from Burroughs's *Princess of Mars,* first meets Captain Carter, she is amazed at what she sees: "What strange manner of man are you, that you consort with the green men, though your form is that of my race, while your color is little darker than that of the white ape? Tell me, are you human, or are you more than human?"[17] Science fiction has allowed veteran authors not to have to answer that question "Am I *more,* different, unique?" with a straight or "realistic" narrative because that route perhaps feels dishonest or insincere. I am reminded of *Redeployment,* a collection of short stories by Iraq War veteran Phil Klay, in which a veteran character has returned from the war and enrolled in college only to find that his view of Iraq is incompatible with the liberal civilian students in the class. Heated disagreements ensue. He cannot seem to get them to understand how confused he feels about his relationship to his own military experience.

> The weird thing with being a veteran, at least for me, is that you do feel better than most people. You risked your life for something bigger than yourself. How many people can say that? You chose to serve. Maybe you didn't understand American foreign policy or why we were at war. Maybe you never will. But it doesn't matter. You held up your hand and said, "I'm willing to die for these worthless civilians." At the same time,

though, you feel somehow less. What happened, what I was a part of, maybe it was the right thing. We were fighting very bad people. But it was an ugly thing.[18]

Klay's characters are not in outer space, but they might as well be. Like veteran literature more broadly, veteran science fiction creates an environment in which veteran authors are free from the repugnance of being "less"—those "ugly things" of which Klay speaks that become the fodder for "war porn" (what I would call "realism" by another name)—and in which veteran authors may become conscious actors in charge of their own representation, however speculative and incoherent that representation might be. Whatever else might be said, veterans have relentlessly adapted their writing lives despite the indifference of the civilian world throughout the nineteenth and twentieth centuries and, as Tim O'Brien's words from the first page of *Veteran Americans* remind us, regardless of whether anyone is reading them at all.

Khe Sanh

There it is.

—Karl Marlantes, Matterhorn *(2010)*

Khe Sanh survives today as little more than an overgrown coffee plantation. Few visible traces remain of the U.S. Marine base that withstood the siege from the North Vietnamese Army in the early months of 1968. No barracks. No graves. If you are with people who know their way around, you can find what remains of the base's airstrip by escaping out the back of the official memorial area. The runway's red dirt has been warped into disrepair after years of rain and neglect, although the shape of a landing strip can still be made out if you look for it. The space does not look like a war zone. Hills 881 North and South can be seen in the distance, but they are green and lush now. At your feet, indifferent trash from the plantation's workers litters the ground.

For a small admission fee, you can enter a small outside square cordoned off by a makeshift fence and guarded by a lone state worker that contains a few exhibits of American aircraft shot down during the assault, as well as an aging museum that stands defiantly on the former sites of Charlie Med and Graves Registration. This lone building houses more American materiel captured during the siege, mostly weapons, radios, and uniforms. They are the trophies of the Vietnamese victory, as are the photographs lining the walls. Captions accompanying the images pay tribute to the bravery of the North Vietnamese while downplaying the claims of American honor. A forlorn picture of Lyndon Johnson stands in the midst of the profiles of smiling North Vietnamese heroes. Below, an anonymous curator has written, "What was he thinking?"

For the visitor interested in understanding a bit of the American experience of war, there is little ostensible reason to come to Khe Sanh. As is their prerogative, the Vietnamese have overridden the space with their coffee as well as their patriotism, and the tone of the site's collective memory is certainly one good reason to dissuade a typical Western sightseer. The logistics required in getting there are another. Most tours of the demilitarized zone (DMZ) leave from Hué, Vietnam's ancient cultural capital, or Dong Hoi, a little further north, and the driving time from these cities down Highway 9 (past the Rockpile, past Camp Carroll, past the Ho Chi Minh Trail) to Khe Sanh takes the better part of five hours. Five hours there, five hours back. Most visitors only have a few minutes to experience Khe Sanh if they even decide to embark on the journey, especially if they also want to go further down the road to see Lang Vay Special Forces Camp before turning back. It is a lot of time and work for not a lot of what they probably came there to see, yet despite these toils and these disappointments, Americans (and Europeans, Vietnamese, and a whole host of other nationals) still manage to come each year. Why would anyone come to such a meager and remote spot of war, especially since, to quote Gertrude Stein in a different context, there is no *there* there?[1]

Part of the reason people come is to write and to record their feelings about the war, even though they must know few readers will ever discover their words. In the entranceway to Khe Sanh's museum there is a large table that holds a thick red book. When one book becomes filled, another identical volume takes its place.[2] Most of the entries are written by guests who were not at the siege. They reverberate with emotion, even if their memories often take the form of clichéd slogans. "Khe Sanh is a reminder and monument . . . When will we ever learn?" A Canadian writes simply, "Lest we not forget." A man from Belgium is more frustrated: "Don't let this shit ever happen again." These particular authors of war go by a variety of names—civilian, noncombatant, spectator, literary historian (if I can implicate myself). What they are assuredly not is "veteran," and perhaps as a result of the implicit space between themselves and the military experience they imagine, they write with a sense of hope for the future as well as distance from the past. "Best wishes for the local people!" Depending on who you are and what you want to see at a place like Khe Sanh, such sentiments might come off as earnest. To the veteran voices in the book, these nonveteran authors condescend. They don't get it, and they never will.

"Good afternoon," a United States Marine captain writes on May 5, 2009. "Those who write in this book that didn't serve here need to be careful on what you write. You must have walked the walk before you talk the talk." Two and a half weeks later, "two English people enjoying Vietnam" write that they "admire the Vietnamese for moving on from war but not forgetting the atrocities. The Vietnamese culture is to be loved and [policy]makers must come to see the culture and taste the cuisine. Remember war but do not glorify in it." Below this couple's entry, the scrawl of the same Marine from before has returned: "Atrocities were committed by both sides you dumb ass Englishmen." This Marine has come back, one suspects, because he feels there is a real and enduring fight going on over who gets to represent war and how they get to represent it. He is angry, even though the Englishmen have not been nasty, political, or openly partisan, and yet what they write is less important than the fact that they were writing anything at all.[3] Five short days later, the same Marine returns yet again, his third visit to Khe Sanh in less than a month. "The same dumb asses continue to write in this book. Remember in order to talk the talk, you need to walk the walk." A different Marine from June 12 offers a bit more diplomacy amid the rhetorical sparring. "I fought to assure everyone the right to speak freely, no matter what the opinion or view they may wish to espouse. I have no bad feelings for anything anyone else has felt here, or written here." Even then, the veteran cannot escape his claims to the authority of war and its representation. Remembering his first day at Khe Sanh in

January 1968, this second Marine recalls his feeling separate: "Above the command bunker was a sign which read: FOR THOSE WHO FIGHT FOR IT, FREEDOM HAS A FLAVOR THE DEFENDED NEVER KNOW. I believe that holds true no matter on which side you fought."

That last inscription was written by my father, who was a sergeant in the United States Marine Corps and served in Vietnam from 1966 to 1968. I never conceived this book to be about me or my family, certainly not about Vietnam and its veterans, and least of all about veterans of the nation's more recent wars in Iraq and Afghanistan. At least not explicitly. But insofar as any relationship between author and book can be said to be personal, I wanted to end where in many ways this project took hold of me, in Southeast Asia, where I witnessed my father write in a book that no one would ever read. Freedom has a flavor the defended never know. Lest we not forget. The fundamental civil-military divide that coincided with the origins of the American Republic and became hardened by the literary practices and realities of nineteenth-century print culture has not eased much since. Civilian observers and writers have always struggled between wanting to remember and not wanting to remember (never forget, but let's just *move on* already), and veteran authors have often responded by representing themselves as a forgotten minority who must constantly defend themselves from civilian ignorance and mistreatment (my freedom tastes different from yours). Such are the feelings in just one war book of many and in just one war of many, but they testify to the persistent strains and fault lines in the discussions which we have about military experience and which, in light of *Veteran Americans,* might seem to have always been with us and, ultimately, might seem fated to remain. To make matters worse, these guest book sentiments may easily be dismissed as kitsch, a kind of saccharine narrative that oversimplifies and, when we are in its presence, feels like a violation.

Sybil's visit to Arlington National Cemetery in Henry Adams's *Democracy* reflects the frustrating ambivalence inherent in my own approach to veteran literature that aspires toward sincerity but threatens to fall into vulgarity with every sentence. At Arlington, the crowds of tourists inscribing their feelings in a guest book inside Robert E. Lee's former home rattle Sybil. "'Eli M. Grow and lady, Thermopyle Centre.' Not even the graves outside had brought the horrors of war so near. What a scourge it was! This respectable family turned out of such a lovely house, and all the pretty old furniture swept away before a horde of coarse invaders 'with ladies.' Did the hosts of Attilla write their names on visiting books in the temple of Vesta and the house of Sallust? What a new terror they would have, added to the name of the scourge of God!" (*D* 122). Guest book tourists disgust her because each is—as David Foster Wallace opined—"existentially loathsome, an insect on a dead thing," always remaining "alien, ignorant, greedy for something you cannot ever have, disappointed in a way you can never admit."[4] Sybil recoils at what she takes to be an affront on sacred territory, but she is herself an alien, ignorant, and greedy tourist of war, as perhaps most of us are, as perhaps this very book has been. I go back and forth as to whether Wallace's sentiments describe the ethics of *Veteran Americans*. I cannot say. Yes, but no.

NOTES

Introduction: What We Talk about When We Talk about Veteran Americans

1. Massachusetts had outlawed theatrical productions in 1750 but not New York. For more on context and reception, see Royall Tyler and Cynthia A. Kierner, *The Contrast: Manners, Morals, and Authority in the Early American Republic* (New York: New York University Press, 2007), 1–9; Ada Lou Carson and Herbert L. Carson, *Royall Tyler* (Boston: Twayne, 1979), 28; and Helen Tyler Brown, introduction to *The Contrast: A Comedy in Five Acts* by Royall Tyler, ed. James Benjamin Wilbur (Boston: Houghton Mifflin, 1920), xxix. For a reproduction of the list of subscribers, see *C*, 7–19. Tyler was aware of the play's singular status, billing it as "Never performed . . . a COMEDY of Five Acts, written by a CITIZEN of the United States." The play was not published until 1790 in Philadelphia by Thomas Wignell and Prichard and Hall.

2. Brown, introduction, xxvii. For a fuller portrait of the causes and consequences of Tyler's military beginnings, see Richard S. Pressman, "Class Positioning and Shays' Rebellion: Resolving the Contradictions of *The Contrast*," *Early American Literature* 21, no. 2 (1986): 90–91.

3. Carson and Carson, *Royall Tyler*, 16–17; Brown, introduction, xxv–xxvi.

4. W. E. B. Du Bois, *The Souls of Black Folk*, ed. Henry Louis Gates Jr. (New York: Oxford University Press, 2007), 3.

5. Dave Phillips, "Report Finds Sharp Increase in Veterans Denied V.A. Benefits," *New York Times*, March 30, 2016, https://www.nytimes.com/2016/03/30/us/report-finds-sharp-increase-in-veterans-denied-va-benefits.html. Accessed May 26, 2017.

6. John Evelev, "*The Contrast*: The Problem of Theatricality and Political Crisis in Postrevolutionary America," *Early American Literature* 31, no. 1 (1996): 80, 74–76.

7. Pressman, "Class Positioning," 98.

8. We also get Tyler's own ambivalent (if not self-loathing) response to his particular class status as a "gentleman" veteran, which meant he had a particular cultural cachet that the majority of veteran authors before the Civil War lacked. Regarding

class, *The Contrast* remains conflicted about Shays' Rebellion, in which Tyler participated. The play references the event twice, in Act II. Manly supports the state, whereas Jonathan, his servant, supports the veteran insurgents.

9. Daniel Aaron, *The Unwritten War: American Writers and the Civil War* (New York: Oxford University Press, 1973), xviii–xix.

10. Caleb Smith, *The Prison and the American Imagination* (New Haven: Yale University Press, 2009), 27–52.

11. Paul Foos, *A Short, Offhand, Killing Affair: Soldiers and Social Conflict during the Mexican-American War* (Chapel Hill: University of North Carolina Press, 2002), 6–18.

12. Frederick Douglass delivered "Men of Color, to Arms!" on March 2, 1863. The call would be reprinted in various broadsides.

13. Tim O'Brien, *The Things They Carried* (New York: Broadway, 1990), 232.

14. Alex Vernon, *Soldiers Once and Still: Ernest Hemingway, James Salter, and Tim O'Brien* (Iowa City: University of Iowa Press, 2004), x.

15. Samuel Hynes, *The Soldiers' Tale: Bearing Witness to Modern War* (New York: Penguin, 1997), xiii. Like myself, Hynes analyzes professional writers as well as "one-book men," his main criterion being "whether the book speaks with a voice that is stubbornly distinct, telling us what it was like, for *this* man, in *his* war" (xv). As a consequence of his search for immediacy, general and senior officers are not included. He also rejects "narratives written with the help of another hand" because "they fail my primary test: they lack an individual voice" (xv). See also two of the earliest critical studies of veteran literature, as well as a more recent example, in Charles V. Genthe, *American War Narratives, 1917–1918: A Study and Bibliography* (New York: D. Lewis, 1969); Peter Aichinger, *The American Soldier in Fiction, 1880–1963: A History of Attitudes toward Warfare and the Military Establishment* (Ames: Iowa State University Press, 1975); and Alex Vernon, ed., *Arms and the Self: War, the Military, and Autobiographical Writing* (Kent, OH: Kent State University Press, 2004).

16. First published as "Hiroshima: A Soldier's View," *New Republic*, August 22, 1981, 26–27. Reprinted and quoted here as "Thank God for the Atom Bomb," in Paul Fussell, *"Thank God for the Atom Bomb" and Other Essays* (New York: Ballantine, 1990), 2, 5–6.

17. Vernon, *Soldiers Once and Still*, 25. Vernon does concede that "in asserting that belief, however, I do not mean to suggest that some aspects of their works are inaccessible to those without such experience, only that my own experiences doubtless influence my reading of their texts. Feminist criticism's validation of experiential knowledge in interpretive scholarship I find liberating and fruitful."

18. J. Glenn Gray, *The Warriors: Reflections on Men in Battle* (Lincoln: University of Nebraska Press, 1998), 201.

19. Raymond Williams, "Distance," in *What I Came to Say* (London: Hutchinson Radius, 1989), 40.

20. For the sake of consistency in sentence constructions, I have gendered my pronouns, but this is not to disallow the real presence of women and gender-nonconforming veterans of the United States. Scholarly interest in veteran gender and sexuality has mostly focused on the Civil War and later. In addition to the discussion at the end of the introduction, see also Elizabeth D. Leonard, "To 'Don the Breeches, and Slay Them with a Will!': A Host of Women Soldiers," in *The Civil War Soldier: A*

Historical Reader, eds. Michael Barton and Larry M. Logue (New York: New York University Press, 2002), 69–82; DeAnne Blanton and Lauren M. Cook, *They Fought Like Demons: Women Soldiers in the American Civil War* (Baton Rouge: Louisiana State University Press, 2002); Judith Stiehm, *It's Our Military, Too!: Women and the U.S. Military* (Philadelphia: Temple University Press, 1996); and Steve Estes, *Ask & Tell: Gay and Lesbian Veterans Speak Out* (Chapel Hill: University of North Carolina Press, 2007).

21. While I am most interested in the United States and its veterans, similar lines of argument could apply to other Western nations. The Napoleonic Wars (1799–1815) influenced European literature as diverse as Jane Austen's *Pride and Prejudice* (1813) and Alessandro Manzoni's "The Fifth of May" (1821). Tolstoy was a second lieutenant of an artillery regiment during the Crimean War (1854–55). His military experience helped accelerate *War and Peace* (1869), a retrospective novel set during the Napoleonic Wars. Most conventional military histories are less interested in national specificity. See, for example, John Keegan, *The Face of Battle* (New York: Penguin, 1976); Charles Townshend, ed., *The Oxford History of Modern War* (New York: Oxford University Press, 2005); and Jeremy Black, *War: A Short History* (New York: Continuum, 2009).

22. Thomas Jefferson to John Wayles Eppes, September 9, 1814. Reprinted in Thomas Jefferson, *The Works of Thomas Jefferson,* ed. Paul Leicester Ford, Federal ed., vol. 11 (New York: G. P. Putnam's Sons, 1905), 426 (emphasis added).

23. Quoted in John Phillips Resch, *Suffering Soldiers: Revolutionary War Veterans, Moral Sentiment, and Political Culture in the Early Republic* (Amherst: University of Massachusetts Press, 1999), 2; see also 65–92. George Clinton Jr. echoed Jefferson and Adams, speaking before New York City's Tammany Society in 1798: "In a republic every citizen should be a soldier . . . The means of the national defense should rest in the body of the people" (quoted in ibid., 66). The trajectory of Resch's book traces the changing meaning of "the people's war" in the first fifty years or so of the Republic. "At the turn of the nineteenth century, Americans viewed the Revolution as a people's war won by a virtuous citizenry. Within twenty years Americans conceived the Revolution as a people's war won by the Continental Army" (ibid., x).

24. Peggy Noonan, "We're All Soldiers Now: Survival Tips for the New War," *Wall Street Journal,* November 2, 2001. Available at http://www.opinionjournal.com/columnists/pnoonan/?id=95001413. Accessed May 26, 2017.

25. Paul W. Kahn, *Sacred Violence: Torture, Terror, and Sovereignty* (Ann Arbor: University of Michigan Press, 2008), 35.

26. Evelev, "*The Contrast,*" 79.

27. John A. Casey Jr., *New Men: Reconstructing the Image of the Veteran in Late Nineteenth-Century American Literature and Culture* (New York: Fordham University Press, 2015), 9, 163.

28. Fussell, "Thank God for the Atom Bomb," 16.

29. Vernon, *Soldiers Once and Still,* 36.

30. Drew Gilpin Faust, *This Republic of Suffering: Death and the American Civil War* (New York: Knopf, 2008), xi–31.

31. As of August 31, 2017, there are 1,346,002 Americans in active duty in the armed forces. As of November 4, 2017, there are more than 325,000,000 people living in the United States. https://www.dmdc.osd.mil/appj/dwp/dwp_reports.jsp. Accessed November 4, 2017. https://www.census.gov. Accessed November 4, 2017.

32. Lynne Hanley, *Writing War: Fiction, Gender, and Memory* (Amherst: University of Massachusetts Press, 1991), 26, 31.

33. See Jean Bethke Elshtain, *Women and War* (New York: Basic, 1987); Catherine Clinton and Nina Silber, *Divided Houses: Gender and the Civil War* (New York: Oxford University Press, 1992); Nina Silber, *Daughters of the Union: Northern Women Fight the Civil War* (Cambridge, MA: Harvard University Press, 2005); Helen M. Cooper, Adrienne Munich, and Susan Merrill Squier, *Arms and the Woman: War, Gender, and Literary Representation* (Chapel Hill: University of North Carolina Press, 1989); and Susan Jeffords, *The Remasculinization of America: Gender and the Vietnam War* (Bloomington: Indiana University Press, 1989).

34. Sarah Rosetta Wakeman and Lauren M. Cook, *An Uncommon Soldier: The Civil War Letters of Sarah Rosetta Wakeman, Alias Private Lyons Wakeman, 153rd Regiment, New York State Volunteers* (New York: Oxford University Press, 1995), 1–13.

35. Ibid., 22, 46, 19.

36. Ibid., 58.

37. Ibid., 44.

38. Shirley Samuels, *Facing America: Iconography and the Civil War* (New York: Oxford University Press), 87.

39. Wakeman and Cook, *An Uncommon Soldier,* 44.

40. Male veterans also struggled, like female veterans, not to be co-opted by civilian editorial control. For example, *The Adventures of Louisa Baker,* also known as *The Adventures of Lucy Brewer,* also known as *The Female Marine,* was first published in 1815 and chronicles a fallen woman who joins the marines to escape her life of prostitution in a black neighborhood in Boston. While Nathaniel Coverly Jr. gets credit for its composition, Daniel A. Cohen has argued that it was most likely written by "a hack author in his employ," Nathaniel Hill Wright. To complicate matters, the first-person male narrator frames the text as a female autobiography. As Cohen notes, "It would be a fitting irony for the playful story of a woman disguising herself as a man to have been written by a man presenting himself to his readers as a woman" and, moreover, for that man (Wright) to be passing himself as another man (Coverly). Daniel A. Cohen, ed., *The Female Marine and Related Works: Narratives of Cross-Dressing and Urban Vice in America's Early Republic* (Amherst: University of Massachusetts Press, 1997), 3–5.

41. Herman Mann, *The Female Review: or, Memoirs of an American Young Lady. . . .* (Dedham, MA: Printed by Nathaniel and Benjamin Heaton, for the author, 1797); Mordecai Manuel Noah, *She Would Be a Soldier, or the Plains of Chippewa* (New York: G. L. Birch, 1819). For more on Deborah Sampson, see Alfred Fabian Young, *Masquerade: The Life and Times of Deborah Sampson, Continental Soldier* (New York: Vintage, 2005).

42. Noah, *She Would Be a Soldier,* 59–60.

43. The Civil War in particular produced numerous veteran texts written by women. See Sarah Emma Edmonds, *Nurse and Spy in the Union Army: Comprising the Adventures and Experiences of a Woman in Hospitals, Camps, and Battle-Field* (Hartford, CT: W. S. Williams, 1865), and Belle Boyd, *Belle Boyd in Camp and Prison* (London: Saunders, Otley, 1865). While not a veteran herself, E. D. E. N. Southworth fictionalized female veterans in such novels as *The Hidden Hand* and *Britomarte the Man-Hater.*

44. Jennifer C. James, *A Freedom Bought with Blood: African American Literature from*

the *Civil War to World War II* (Chapel Hill: University of North Carolina Press, 2007), 2.

45. Bernard C. Nalty, *Strength for the Fight: A History of Black Americans in the Military* (New York: Free Press, 1986), 5, 6.

46. Sidney Kaplan and Emma Nogrady Kaplan, *The Black Presence in the Era of the American Revolution* (Amherst: University of Massachusetts Press, 1989), 3–4. Kaplan and Kaplan are quoting Benjamin Quarles, who also insisted that "principle" was the reason why African Americans fought. See Benjamin Quarles, *The Negro in the American Revolution* (Chapel Hill: University of North Carolina Press, 1961), vii. See also Herbert Aptheker, *The Negro in the American Revolution* (New York: International Publishers, 1960), who believes black service is motivated by "the desire for freedom" (5).

47. See William Wells Brown, *The Negro in the American Rebellion: His Heroism and His Fidelity* (Boston: Lee & Shepard, 1867); and William C. Nell, *The Colored Patriots of the American Revolution* (Boston: Published by Robert F. Wallcut, 1855).

48. Thomas Wentworth Higginson, *"Army Life in a Black Regiment" and Other Writings* (New York: Penguin, 1997), 3, 22. Originally published in Boston by Fields, Osgood, and Company in 1870.

49. James, *A Freedom Bought with Blood*, 6–15 (emphasis in original). See also Larry M. Logue and Peter Blanck, *Race, Ethnicity, and Disability: Veterans and Benefits in Post–Civil War America* (New York: Cambridge University Press, 2010), 17; and Donald R. Shaffer, *After the Glory: The Struggles of Black Civil War Veterans* (Lawrence: University Press of Kansas, 2004), 5.

50. William Apess, *"A Son of the Forest" and Other Writings*, ed. Barry O'Connell (Amherst: University of Massachusetts Press, 1997), xiv–xv, 26, 30–31.

51. Susie King Taylor, *Reminiscences of My Life in Camp with the 33rd U.S. Colored Troops, Late 1st South Carolina Volunteers*, ed. Patricia W. Romero (New York: Markus Wiener Publishing, 1988), 135–36.

52. Paul Fussell, *The Great War and Modern Memory* (New York: Oxford University Press, 2013), 11, 15, 37. First published in 1977.

Chapter 1: Revolutionary Captivity

1. See, for example, Moses Coit Tyler, *The Literary History of the American Revolution, 1763–1783*, 2nd ed., vol. 2 (New York: G. P. Putnam, 1898), 228–45. Tyler's study was for the Revolutionary War what Edmund Wilson's *Patriotic Gore* (1962) was for the Civil War, that is, the first comprehensive bibliography and analysis of the Revolutionary War. Within two volumes and well over a thousand pages, only four prisoner-of-war narratives are ever discussed. They are the most prominent and well read of their time: Ethan Allen, John Dodge, Thomas Andross, and Henry Laurens. The first modern compiler of American autobiography was Louis Kaplan, *A Bibliography of American Autobiographies* (Madison: University of Wisconsin Press, 1961). Kaplan consciously excluded "most episodic accounts, such as those relating to Indian captivities, military imprisonments, 'overland' narratives, and escapes from slavery" (v).

2. Rowlandson originally published her experience as a captive under the title *The Sovereignty and Goodness of God*. It would appear under different titles in subsequent editions. Greg Sieminski, "The Puritan Captivity Narrative and the Politics

of the American Revolution," *American Quarterly* 42, no. 1 (March 1990): 35–38.

3. Mary Rowlandson, *The Sovereignty and Goodness of God,* ed. Neal Salisbury (Boston: Bedford, 1997), 54; Linda Colley, *Captives: Britain, Empire, and the World, 1600–1850* (London: J. Cape, 2002), 231.

4. Brett F. Wood, ed., *Letters from France: The Private Diplomatic Correspondence of Benjamin Franklin, 1776–1785* (New York: Algora, 2006), 43–44.

5. Kathryn Derounian-Stodola and James Levernier have traced the development of the "instructional value of the captivity narratives" from Puritan spiritual discipline to Revolutionary and mid-nineteenth-century casus belli (the latter aimed at Indian nations and, like their Revolutionary cousins, little more than "propaganda and outright bigotry" to justify Indian removals). By the time the genre had reached the 1780s and 1790s, the captivity narrative had become, as Michelle Burnham claims, "virtually indistinguishable from sentimental novels." Print culture of the early national period has often been imagined as a vast mélange "of individuals blending their voices *with* each other" in the service of "democratic fellow feeling," a phrase Julia Stern borrows from Adam Smith's 1759 treatise *The Theory of Moral Sentiments.* See Kathryn Zabelle Derounian-Stodola and James Levernier, *The Indian Captivity Narrative, 1550–1900* (New York: Twayne, 1993), 26; Michelle Burnham, "Between England and America: Captivity, Sympathy, and the Sentimental Novel," in *Cultural Institutions of the Novel,* eds. Deidre Lynch and William Beatty Warner (Durham, NC: Duke University Press, 1996), 47–72, quotation on 55–56; and Julia Stern, *The Plight of Feeling: Sympathy and Dissent in the Early American Novel* (Chicago: University of Chicago Press, 1997), 5.

6. Robert J. Denn, "Captivity Narratives of the American Revolution," *Journal of American Culture* 2, no. 4 (Winter 1980): 579. Propaganda, of course, traveled both ways across the Atlantic. See, for example, the British officer Robert Prescott, *A Letter from a Veteran, to the Officers of the Army Encamped at Boston* (New York: Printed by Hugh Gaine, 1774). See also Daniel Williams, *Liberty's Captives: Narratives of Confinement in the Print Culture of the Early Republic* (Athens: University of Georgia Press, 2006), which is a discriminate collection of post-Revolutionary captivity texts that expands the field away from the established captivities of Americans by Native Americans to include "the textual experiences of American prisoners of war, Americans enslaved by North Africans, Africans enslaved by Americans, Americans imprisoned by other Americans, American mariners forced to sail on British warships, Americans taken by pirates, and Americans shipwrecked on desolate, hostile shores" (1). My comment is intended only to show how the veteran prisoner-of-war narrative has not gained its own separate attention.

7. Nathaniel Segar, *A Brief Narrative of the Captivity and Sufferings of Lt. Nathan'l Segar, Who Was Taken Prisoner by the Indians and Carried to Canada during the Revolutionary War, Written by Himself* (Paris, ME: Printed at the Observer Office, 1825), 5.

8. Edwin G. Burrows, *Forgotten Patriots: The Untold Story of American Prisoners during the Revolutionary War* (New York: Basic Books, 2008), 161.

9. John Dodge, *Narrative of Mr. John Dodge during His Captivity at Detroit, Reproduced in Facsimile from the Second Edition of 1780* (Cedar Rapids, IA: Torch Press, 1909), 5.

10. Ibid., 29, 42.

11. Jeremy Black, *War: A Short History* (New York: Continuum, 2009), 10; Samuel P. Huntington, *The Soldier and the State: The Theory and Politics of Civil-Military Relations* (Cambridge, MA: Belknap Press of Harvard University Press, 1985).

12. Lauren Berlant, *The Queen of America Goes to Washington City: Essays on Sex and Citizenship* (Durham, NC: Duke University Press, 1997), 13.

13. Charles Henry Metzger, *The Prisoner in the American Revolution* (Chicago: Loyola University Press, 1971), 32.

14. Burrows, *Forgotten Patriots,* x–xi.

15. These are my estimates, though corroborating tallies appear in Richard Mercer Dorson, *America Rebels: Narratives of the Patriots* (New York: Pantheon, 1953), 1; and Sarah J. Purcell, *Sealed with Blood: War, Sacrifice, and Memory in Revolutionary America* (Philadelphia: University of Pennsylvania Press, 2002), 150. Dorson estimates 200 "narratives," although the number is closer to 500 if we include short sketches and journals. Other helpful collections and bibliographies include John C. Dann, *The Revolution Remembered: Eyewitness Accounts of the War for Independence* (Chicago: University of Chicago Press, 1980); and J. Todd White and Charles H. Lesser, *Fighters for Independence: A Guide to Sources of Biographical Information on Soldiers and Sailors of the American Revolution* (Chicago: University of Chicago Press, 1977).

16. William Widger, "Diary of William Widger of Marblehead, Kept at Mill Prison, England, 1781," *Essex Institute Historical Collections* 73 (1937): 318.

17. Benedict Anderson, *Imagined Communities: Reflections on the Origin and Spread of Nationalism* (New York: Verso, 2006), 33–36.

18. Widger, "Diary," 316–18.

19. Ibid., 347. For further analysis of Widger, see Jesse Lemisch, "Listening to the 'Inarticulate': William Widger's Dream and the Loyalties of American Revolutionary Seamen in British Prisons," *Journal of Social History* 3, no. 1 (Autumn 1969): 1–29.

20. Quoted in Ray Raphael, *A People's History of the American Revolution: How Common People Shaped the Fight for Independence* (New York: New Press, 2001), 102.

21. Letter from Ebenezer Huntington to Andrew Huntington, dated July 7, 1780. Reprinted in Ebenezer Huntington, *Letters Written by Ebenezer Huntington during the American Revolution* (New York: Chas. Fred. Heartman, 1914), 87–88.

22. Russ Castronovo, *Necro Citizenship: Death, Eroticism, and the Public Sphere in the Nineteenth-Century United States* (Durham, NC: Duke University Press, 2001), 4.

23. Bruce Burgett, *Sentimental Bodies: Sex, Gender, and Citizenship in the Early Republic.* (Princeton, NJ: Princeton University Press, 1998), 13 (emphasis in original).

24. I must acknowledge and thank once again the several anonymous readers who at various stages along the way made this book and its argument stronger. This particular point one reader urged me to make more strongly. Less visible footprints from readers' comments have colored my prose throughout.

25. Metzger, *The Prisoner in the American Revolution,* vii–viii, 61. In the centuries of European and Native American contact leading up to the Revolutionary War, Linda Colley notes that "Indian captive-taking was rarely a random business"; rather, it was usually a sensible strategy of revenge for Native American losses sustained by white invaders and also as a way to prevent colonists from reproducing and replenishing their own ranks (*Captives,* 145). Native Americans also took white captives in order to demand ransoms, and such a mercenary tone was quite pronounced in the Barbary captivities that appeared in print alongside

Revolutionary prisoner-of-war narratives in the late eighteenth and early nineteenth centuries. One could look at these Barbary captivity narratives and ask how they differ, if at all, from Revolutionary prisoner-of-war texts. The anonymously published *American in Algiers, or the Patriot of Seventy-Six in Captivity* (New York: Buel, 1797), for example, sounds just as melancholy as Widger: "And does Columbia still disdain to own / A well-try'd Patriot and a free born son? / And has she means within her pow'r to save / Her num'rous offspring from becoming slaves?" (16). Many speakers of Barbary captivities, from *American in Algiers* through Royall Tyler's *The Algerine Captive* (1797), also offered critiques of American society and slavery in particular. See Paul Baepler, ed., *White Slaves, African Masters: An Anthology of American Barbary Captivity Narratives* (Chicago: University of Chicago Press, 1999); and Lawrence A. Peskin, *Captives and Countrymen: Barbary Slavery and the American Public, 1785–1816* (Baltimore, MD: Johns Hopkins University Press, 2009). To these objections it must be noted that Barbary captives were detained and held as capitalist assets rather than as military combatants. The pleas for help from "Columbia" eventually met diplomatic ears. The United States would finally pay ransoms and bring North African captives home. Indeed, paying ransom was an act of political recognition for North African captives in contrast to the "nonpersons" which Revolutionary captivity created according to Burrows, *Forgotten Patriots*, 37.

26. Biographers also highlight that Allen's captivity narrative largely contributed to his contemporary fame. A sampling of conventional readings of Allen's captivity rhetoric would include Stewart Hall Holbrook, *Ethan Allen* (New York: Macmillan, 1940), 113–27; Charles A. Jellison, *Ethan Allen: Frontier Rebel* (Syracuse, NY: Syracuse University Press, 1969), 166–75; and John Pell, *Ethan Allen* (Boston: Houghton Mifflin, 1929), 122–30.

27. Ethan Allen, *A Narrative of Col. Ethan Allen's Captivity, from the Time of His Being Taken by the British, near Montreal, on the 25th Day of September, in the Year 1775, to the Time of His Exchange, on the 6th Day of May, 1778: Containing His Voyages and Travels . . . Interspersed with Some Political Observations* (Boston: Draper and Folsom, 1779), 8.

28. Ibid., 10.

29. Ibid., 13–19.

30. Ibid., 13.

31. Judith Butler, *Frames of War: When Is Life Grievable?* (New York: Verso, 2009), xiv–xvi.

32. Allen, *A Narrative of Col. Ethan Allen's Captivity*, 15.

33. Martin Heidegger, *The Fundamental Concepts of Metaphysics: World, Finitude, Solitude,* trans. William McNeill and Nicholas Walker (Bloomington: Indiana University Press, 1995), 239.

34. Allen, *A Narrative of Col. Ethan Allen's Captivity*, 39, 17, 9, 23, 33, 27.

35. Ambrose Bierce, *Civil War Stories* (Mineola, NY: Dover, 1994), 46.

36. Allen, *A Narrative of Col. Ethan Allen's Captivity*, 22.

37. James Dawes, *The Language of War: Literature and Culture in the U.S. from the Civil War through World War II* (Cambridge, MA: Harvard University Press, 2002), 15.

38. Another example of mixed loyalties is Revolutionary captive William Scudder, *The Journal of William Scudder, an Officer in the Late New-York Line, Who Was Taken Captive by the Indians at Fort Stanwix, on the 23d of July, 1779, and Was Holden a Prisoner*

in Canada until October, 1782, and Then Sent to New-York and Admitted on Parole: With a Small Sketch of His Life, and Some Occurrences of the War, Which Chiefly Happened under His Notice Previous to His Captivity (New York: Printed for the Author, 1794). Scudder's Native American overseer orders him to dress in his old regimental uniform and have a cartel with a group of Tories to gather information about American troop movements. At the end of their session, Scudder finds an opportunity to escape but refuses it: "I told Capt. Robertson, I thought it best for me to go and lodge with my chief—He replied that a bed was provided for me. But as I knew we must start by day-light, and my clothes being none of the neatest, having been so long with the Indians, I prevailed and took my leave, and slept with my chief as usual" (50).

39. Lemuel Roberts, *Memoirs of Captain Lemuel Roberts Containing Adventures in Youth, Vicissitudes Experienced as a Continental Soldier, His Sufferings as a Prisoner, and Escapes from Captivity, with Suitable Reflections on the Changes of Life Written by Himself* (Bennington, VT: Printed by Anthony Haswell, for the Author, 1809), 75.

40. Ibid., 81.

41. June Namias, *White Captives: Gender and Ethnicity on the American Frontier* (Chapel Hill: University of North Carolina Press, 1993), 51–57.

42. Luke Swetland, *A Very Remarkable Narrative of Luke Swetland, Who Was Taken Captive Four Times in the Space of Fifteen Months, in the Time of the Late Contest between Great Britain and America . . . Written by Himself* (Hartford, CT: Printed for the Author, 1780), 2–7.

43. Ebenezer Fox, "The Revolutionary Adventures of Ebenezer Fox of Roxbury, Massachusetts," in *Narratives of the American Revolution as Told by a Young Sailor, a Home-Sick Surgeon, a French Volunteer, and a German General's Wife,* ed. Hugh F. Rankin (Chicago: Lakeside Press, 1976), 101, 99, 117. Originally published in Boston by Charles Fox in 1838.

44. Ibid., 125.

45. Dana D. Nelson, *American Manhood: Capitalist Citizenship and the Imagined Fraternity of White Men* (Durham, NC: Duke University Press, 1998), 6.

46. See, for example, Nathaniel Fanning, *Narrative of the Adventures of an American Navy Officer, Who Served during Part of the American Revolution under the Command of Com. John Paul Jones, Esq.* (New York: Printed for the Author, 1806); and Abner Stocking, *Interesting Journal of Abner Stocking of Chatham, Connecticut Detailing the Distressing Events of the Expedition against Quebec, under the Command of Col. Arnold in the Year 1775 Published by the Relatives of Abner Stocking, Now Deceased* (Catskill, NY: Eagle Office, 1810).

47. Roberts, *Memoirs of Captain Lemuel Roberts,* 82–84.

48. Ibid., 94–96.

49. United States War Department, John C. Calhoun and Henry Clay, *Letter from the Secretary of War: Transmitting a Report of the Names, Rank, and Line, of Every Person Placed on the Pension List, in Pursuance to the Act of the 18th March, 1818, &C. January 20, 1820. Read and Ordered to Lie on the Table* (Washington, DC: Gales & Seaton, 1820), 3. This document includes the names of all soldiers receiving pensions and comprises over 600 pages. Calhoun's brief preface, cosigned by Henry Clay, makes note that the updated list excludes "those who served in corps which, at first, were considered continental, but which, on full inquiry, proved not to be so" (3). Such scrutiny suggests an endemic distrust of veteran pension applicants, which I explore at greater length in chapter 2.

50. John Phillips Resch, *Suffering Soldiers: Revolutionary War Veterans, Moral Senti-ment, and Political Culture in the Early Republic* (Amherst: University of Massachu-setts Press, 1999), 8.

51. Alfred Fabian Young, *The Shoemaker and the Tea Party* (Boston: Beacon Press, 1999), 133.

52. For a discussion of the nation's changing relationship to veterans during and after the Civil War, see Drew Gilpin Faust, *This Republic of Suffering: Death and the American Civil War* (New York: Knopf, 2008); and Theda Skocpol, *Protecting Sol-diers and Mothers: The Political Origins of Social Policy in the United States* (Cam-bridge, MA: Belknap Press of Harvard University Press, 1992).

53. David Perry, *Recollections of an Old Soldier. The Life of Captain David Perry, a Sol-dier of the French and Revolutionary Wars* (Windsor, VT: Printed at the Republican & Yeoman Printing-Office, 1822), iii.

54. For an overview of the struggle over the meaning of the Revolutionary War in the early decades of the nineteenth century, see Purcell, *Sealed with Blood*. In line with Purcell, John Resch has suggested that the nation's neglect of ordinary soldiers after the war was a result of the widespread political belief that the Revolution had been "a people's war won by a virtuous citizenry" (*Suffering Soldiers*, x). Since everyone was expected to sacrifice and serve, no one could claim special status as having sac-rificed more. It followed that no soldier would have any claims to the public welfare.

55. Andrew Sherburne, *Memoirs of Andrew Sherburne: A Pensioner of the Navy of the Revolution, Written by Himself* (Utica, [NY?]: William Williams, 1828), corroborates the account of the horrible conditions on board the *Jersey* and the number of satel-lite hospital ships (107–8). Sherburne had worse things to say about the American "nurses" than did Dring, insinuating they were compensated and "could indulge in playing cards, and drinking, while their fellows were thirsting for water, and some dying" (110–11).

56. Henry Reed Stiles, ed., *Letters from the Prisons and Prison-Ships of the Revolution* (New York: J. M. Bradstreet & Son, 1865), 27–33.

57. Charles Edwin West, *Horrors of the Prison Ships* (Brooklyn, NY: Eagle Book Print-ing Department, 1895), 11, 15.

58. Ibid., 19.

59. Burrows, *Forgotten Patriots*, 223–25.

60. Sherburne, *Memoirs of Andrew Sherburne*, 83.

61. Roberts, *Memoirs of Captain Lemuel Roberts*, 29; Stocking, *Interesting Journal of Abner Stocking*, 32.

62. Judith Hiltner, "'She Bled in Secret': Deborah Sampson, Hermann Mann, and *The Female Review*," *Early American Literature* 34, no. 2 (1999): 190. Mann was a pub-lisher and bookseller. See also Herman Mann, *The Female Review: Or, Memoirs of an American Young Lady. . . .* (Dedham, MA: Printed by Nathaniel and Benjamin Heaton, for the Author, 1797).

63. Deborah Gannett (Sampson), *An Addrss* [Sic] *Delivered with Applause* (Dedham, MA: Printed and Sold by H. Mann, 1802), 9, 24, 27, 28.

64. Joseph Foulke, *Memoirs of Jacob Ritter, a Faithful Minister in the Society of Friends* (Philadelphia: T. E. Chapman, 1844), vii, 13–14. Anticipating criticism that he might have altered the record, Foulke claims "the narrative of Jacob Ritter was, at his own request, committed to writing many years before his decease, and was carefully preserved among his papers" (iii).

65. Conversions to Christianity are often reported in the later Revolutionary captivities from the 1820s and 1830s. Even then, the amount of time spent praising the Lord is often minimal, appearing as background or way of conclusion. See, for example, Perry, *Recollections of an Old Soldier,* and Roberts, *Memoirs of Captain Lemuel Roberts.* Notable exceptions that focus almost exclusively on Christian conversion and service are Thomas Andros, *The Old Jersey Captive; or, a Narrative of the Captivity of Thomas Andros, (Now Pastor of the Church in Berkley,) on Board the Old Jersey Prison Ship at New York, 1781* (Boston: W. Peirce, 1833); Sherburne, *Memoirs of Andrew Sherburne;* Jonathan Burnham, *The Life of Col. Jonathan Burnham, Now Living in Salisbury, Mass. . . .* (Portsmouth, NH: Printed and sold at S. Whidden's Printing Office, 1814); and John Robert Shaw, *A Narrative of the Life and Travels of John Robert Shaw, the Well-Digger, Now Resident in Lexington, Kentucky, Written by Himself* (Lexington, KY: Printed by Daniel Bradford, 1807). Prodigal Son stories at the time were not unique to soldiers. See Jay Fliegelman, *Prodigals and Pilgrims: The American Revolution against Patriarchal Authority, 1750–1800* (New York: Cambridge University Press, 1982), 68–83, 107–16.
66. Foulke, *Memoirs of Jacob Ritter,* 16, 16, 19.
67. Quoted in Caleb Smith, *The Prison and the American Imagination* (New Haven, CT: Yale University Press, 2009), 10.
68. Ibid.
69. Benjamin Rush, "On the Different Species of Mania," in *The Selected Writings of Benjamin Rush,* ed. Dagobert D. Runes (New York: Philosophical Library, 1947), 214–15.
70. See William Blackstone, *A Summary of the Constitutional Laws of England, Being an Abridgement of Blackstone's Commentaries* (London: Printed for the Author, at the Literary-Press, No. 14, Red Lion Street, 1788). Blackstone describes soldiers as a class of men prone to perpetual cursing and swearing who are in need of fines (141); as idle and "wandering soldiers and seamen" (169–71); and as liable to incite mayhem and thus a constant threat to the general peace (182).
71. Mere weeks after the Invalid Pension Act of 1792 was enacted, United States attorney general Edmund Randolph petitioned the Circuit Court of Pennsylvania to approve the pension application for veteran William Hayburn. The Pennsylvania Court (composed of Supreme Court justices riding the circuit) declined to hear the petition, claiming in a jointly written letter to George Washington that the Pension Act unconstitutionally required them to perform duties reserved for Congress. See Hayburn's Case, 2 U.S. 409 (1792). "It is a principle important to freedom that in government, the judicial should be distinct from and independent of the legislative department" (411). Hayburn's Case was only the fourth to be heard by the Supreme Court and the first to declare a law passed by Congress unconstitutional. Civilian courts were unwilling and the laws ill equipped to evaluate the demands of veterans.
72. Abraham Leggett, *The Narrative of Abraham Leggett* (New York: New York Times, 1971), 17.
73. Metzger, *The Prisoner in the American Revolution,* vii–21. Metzger details how during the Revolutionary War, "in an age when the distinction between soldier and civilian was meaningful . . . it was the accepted rule that, on the whole, civilians enjoyed immunity from attack, arrest, and imprisonment" (16). Both sides lacked any true legal system to handle the volume of, and distinctions between, civil and military cases.

74. Henry Tufts, *The Autobiography of a Criminal,* ed. Edmund Lester Pearson (New York: Duffield and Company, 1930), 18, 94, 201, 104, 195, 207, 197, 209, 202. All quotations refer to this edition. The original title of the autobiography was *Narrative of the Life, Adventures, Travels, and Sufferings of Henry Tufts, Now Residing at Lemington, in the District of Maine. In Substance as Compiled from his Own Mouth, printed in Dover, NH by Samuel Bragg.* The 1930 edition edited by Pearson suggests that the text most likely was ghostwritten by a major familiar with Tufts's story (xv). Thomas Wentworth Higginson "discovered" Tufts in the 1880s and helped reissue the volume.

75. Daniel E. Williams, "Rogues, Rascals, and Scoundrels," *American Studies* 24 (Fall 1983): 14, 14.

Chapter 2: Civilian Memories and Veteran Memoir

1. Washington Irving, "The Legend of Sleepy Hollow," in *"The Legend of Sleepy Hollow" and Other Stories,* ed. William L. Hedges (New York: Penguin, 1988), 288. *The Spy* was first published in New York by Wiley and Halsted in 1821.

2. For more on Cooper's tendency toward paranoia and distrust of secret societies, see Robert S. Levine, *Conspiracy and Romance: Studies in Brockden Brown, Cooper, Hawthorne, and Melville* (New York: Cambridge University Press, 1989), 58–103.

3. W. H. Gardiner, "The Spy," *North American Review* 15, no. 36 (1822): 259. Master spy Benjamin Tallmadge corroborates the idea of Washington's double standard, writing that Washington gave him "charge of *a particular part of his private correspondence*" to take back and forth between Arnold and Washington. Benjamin Tallmadge, *Memoir of Col. Benjamin Tallmadge, Prepared by Himself, at the Request of His Children* (New York: Thomas Holman, 1858), 68.

4. H. L. Barnum, *The Spy Unmasked; or, Memoirs of Enoch Crosby, Alias Harvey Birch, the Hero of Mr. Cooper's Tale of the Neutral Ground; Being an Authentic Account of the Secret Services Which He Rendered His Country during the Revolutionary War (Taken from His Own Lips, in Short-Hand) Comprising Many Interesting Facts and Anecdotes, Never Before Published* (New York: Printed by J. & J. Harper, 1828), 162.

5. Many editions of André's court case survive, but see, in particular, John André, *Minutes of a Court Inquiry, upon the Case of Major John André, with Accompanying Documents, Published in 1780 by Order of Congress. . . .* (Albany, NY: J. Munsell, 1865). All quotations refer to this edition. This text was a private reprint not only of the court documents but also of contemporary reactions and correspondence, such as Alexander Hamilton's emotional letter to Henry Laurens (the only American ever held prisoner in the Tower of London). At trial, André testified: "I agreed to meet upon ground not within posts of either army, a person [Arnold] who was to give me intelligence . . . Against my stipulation, my intention and without my knowledge before hand, I was conducted within one of your posts . . . I quitted my uniform and was passed another way in the night without the American posts to neutral ground, and informed I was beyond all armed parties and left to press for New-York" (12). Furthermore, "I am branded with nothing dishonourable, as no motive could be mine but the service of my king and as I was involuntarily an imposter" (13). André's attempt to dismiss his mens rea was significant because he never denied the evidence of the tribunal's case, only the occupation of his mental state when the supposed crimes took place.

6. Ibid., 15, 35. The jury was composed solely of generals and several founding members of the Society of the Cincinnati, among them Major General Nathanael Greene (presiding) and Major Generals Robert Howe, James Clinton, Henry Knox, and Jedediah Huntington. The official record of the trial consists almost entirely of epistolary testimony written both in accusation and defense of André (from both American and British generals).

7. Robert A. Ferguson, *Reading the Early Republic* (Cambridge, MA: Harvard University Press, 2004), 131–45. The quotation appears on 131. Ferguson argues that in the case of André, Washington's silence was necessary in order "to establish the separate high-mindedness of the American army" (137). Rather than recognize André directly, Washington instead denied André's requests for mercy via an exchange with his ranking counterpart in the British army, Henry Clinton. During the trial, Clinton had personally requested leniency for André, yet Washington denied having any official power to grant clemency, claiming that though he was commander in chief of the American army, the matter was outside his jurisdiction. See also André, *Minutes*, 19–26.

8. André, *Minutes*, 55. For more on Hamilton's sentiments, see André, *Minutes*, 48, 53.

9. Hannah Adams, *An Abridgment of the History of New England, for the Use of Young Persons* (Boston: Etheridge & Bliss, 1807), 168–69. Adams's text originally was published in 1799, then edited as a school primer in 1801. Other historians at the time felt obliged to document their impressions of André, including the anguished James Thacher, *A Military Journal during the American Revolutionary War, from 1775 to 1783: Describing Interesting Events and Transactions of This Period; with Numerous Historical Facts and Anecdotes, from the Original Manuscript* (Boston: Cottons & Barnard, 1827), 219–25. For a useful summary of "André texts," see Barnum, *The Spy Unmasked*, 153–62.

10. Tallmadge, *Memoir*, 38–39.

11. Reprinted in William Coyle and Harvey G. Damaser, *Six Early American Plays, 1798–1890* (Columbus, OH: C. E. Merrill, 1968), 20.

12. Anna Seward, *Monody on Major André, by Miss Seward (Author of the Elegy on Capt. Cook), to Which Are Added Letters Addressed to Her by Major André, in the Year 1769* (New York: Printed by James Rivington, 1781), 5–6. John Renfro Davis's folk ballad "The Ballad of John André" (ca. 1822) was similarly sympathetic, and even the military historian Henry Lee in *Observations on Jefferson's Writings* (1832) reminisced about the American commanders' lack of "compassion for the impending fate of Major André." Reprinted in Henry Lee and Robert E. Lee, *Memoirs of the War in the Southern Department of the United States* (New York: University Publishing Company, 1870), 22.

13. William Johnson and Nathanael Greene, *Sketches of the Life and Correspondence of Nathanael Greene: Major General of the Armies of the United States, in the War of the Revolution; Compiled Chiefly from Original Materials*, vol. 1 (Charleston, [SC]: Printed for the Author, A.E. Miller, 1822), 205.

14. Irving, "The Legend of Sleepy Hollow," 273, 289.

15. Caleb Crain, *American Sympathy: Men, Friendship, and Literature in the New Nation* (New Haven, CT: Yale University Press, 2001), 1–10.

16. Max Weber, "Politics as a Vocation," in *From Max Weber: Essays in Sociology*, trans. H. H. Gerth and C. Wright Mills (New York: Oxford University Press, 1946), 78–81.

17. Joseph J. Letter, "Past Presentisms: Suffering Soldiers, Benjaminian Ruins, and the

Discursive Foundations of Early U.S. Historical Novels," *American Literature* 82, no. 1 (March 2010): 31.

18. See Carol Gluck, "Operations of Memory: 'Comfort Women' and the World," in *Ruptured Histories: War, Memory, and the Post-Cold War in Asia,* eds. Sheila Miyoshi Jager and Rana Mitter (Cambridge, MA: Harvard University Press, 2007), 47–77.

19. Sarah J. Purcell, *Sealed with Blood: War, Sacrifice, and Memory in Revolutionary America* (Philadelphia: University of Pennsylvania Press, 2002), 144–60, 6.

20. Alfred Fabian Young, *The Shoemaker and the Tea Party* (Boston: Beacon Press, 1999), 132–42. The quotation appears on 133.

21. John Phillips Resch, *Suffering Soldiers: Revolutionary War Veterans, Moral Sentiment, and Political Culture in the Early Republic* (Amherst: University of Massachusetts Press, 1999), x.

22. David Humphreys, *An Essay on the Life of the Honorable Major-General Israel Putnam: Addressed to the State Society of the Cincinnati in Connecticut* (Hartford, CT: Barzillai Hudson and George Goodwin, 1788).

23. James Fenimore Cooper, *Lionel Lincoln* (London: John Miller, 1825), 37–38; John C. Dann, *The Revolution Remembered: Eyewitness Accounts of the War for Independence* (Chicago: University of Chicago Press, 1980), 65–68. Dann's study is an extensive accounting of Revolutionary pension applications. Both references were brought to my attention by Catherine Kaplan, "Theft and Counter-Theft: Joseph Plumb Martin's Revolutionary War," *Early American Literature* 41, no. 3 (2006): 521.

24. It took the calming presence of George Washington near the end of the war to counteract the Newburgh Conspiracy, whose plot was motivated by widespread unrest over back pay. See Samuel P. Huntington, *The Soldier and the State: The Theory and Politics of Civil-Military Relations* (Cambridge, MA: Belknap Press of Harvard University Press, 1985), 143–48.

25. Though initially published in Hallowell, Maine, by Glazier, Masters, and Company in 1830 as *A Narrative of Some of the Adventures, Dangers and Sufferings of a Revolutionary Soldier,* few original copies exist today. The work was published as *Private Yankee Doodle* by George F. Scheer in a 1962 edition. More recent editions have modified the title further.

26. See Minor Myers, *Liberty without Anarchy: A History of the Society of the Cincinnati* (Charlottesville: University Press of Virginia, 1983), 1–19. See also Tallmadge, *Memoir,* 57–60.

27. Myers, *Liberty without Anarchy,* 17.

28. Joseph Plumb Martin, *Ordinary Courage: The Revolutionary War Adventures of Joseph Plumb Martin,* ed. James Kirby Martin (Malden, MA: Blackwell, 2008), xiii.

29. The "long-term Continental enlistee" was incredibly rare, "probably no more than 1 out of every 250 persons in the Revolutionary populace" (ibid., x).

30. Ibid., xiii. Although Martin did publish anonymously, Hallowell was such a small town that there was no real secret regarding its authorship.

31. Sacvan Bercovitch, *The Puritan Origins of the American Self* (New Haven, CT: Yale University Press, 1975), 134.

32. Daniel B. Shea, "The Prehistory of American Autobiography," in *American Autobiography: Retrospect and Prospect,* ed. John Paul Eakin (Madison: University of Wisconsin Press), 40. See also Daniel E. Williams, "The Common Transactions of

a Private Soldier: Joseph Plumb Martin's View of the Issues and the Battles of the American Revolution," *Studies on Voltaire and the Eighteenth Century* 263 (1989): 273–75. Williams likewise is interested in how "Martin related his experiences from the viewpoint of a common man" (274).

33. Richard Mercer Dorson, *America Rebels: Narratives of the Patriots* (New York: Pantheon, 1953), 3–4. By Dorson's count, most veteran memoirs were published between 1820 and 1840, and indeed many were. As a general rule, the later the memoir, the less reliable its authorship. Some were written "as told to" family members and not published until as late as the twentieth century.

34. Daniel Webster, *The Writings and Speeches of Daniel Webster*, vol. 1 (Boston: Little, Brown, 1903) 235.

35. William Huntting Howell, "Starving Memory: Joseph Plumb Martin Un-Tells the Story of the American Revolution," *Common-Place* 10, no. 2 (January 2010), http://www.common-place-archives.org/vol-10/no-02/howell/. Accessed June 16, 2017.

36. Ibid.

37. Benjamin Franklin, *The Autobiography of Benjamin Franklin* (Mineola, NY: Dover, 1996), 5; Frederick Douglass, *Narrative of the Life of Frederick Douglass* (Mineola, NY: Dover, 1995), 1–2.

38. Jesse Lemisch, "The American Revolution Seen from the Bottom Up," in *Towards a New Past: Dissenting Essays in American History*, ed. Barton J. Bernstein (New York: Pantheon Books, 1968), 3–45; Howard Zinn, *A People's History of the United States* (New York: Harper & Row, 1980).

39. Alfred Fabian Young, *Liberty Tree: Ordinary People and the American Revolution* (New York: New York University Press, 2006), 4. See also Alfred Fabian Young, *The American Revolution* (Dekalb: Northern Illinois University Press, 1976); and *Beyond the American Revolution* (DeKalb: Northern Illinois University Press, 1993).

40. Ray Raphael, *A People's History of the American Revolution: How Common People Shaped the Fight for Independence* (New York: New Press, 2001), 50–103; Charles Royster, *A Revolutionary People at War: The Continental Army and American Character, 1775–1783* (Chapel Hill: University of North Carolina Press, 1979).

41. Charles Patrick Neimeyer, *America Goes to War: A Social History of the Continental Army* (New York: New York University Press, 1996), 25–26. The G.I. Joe comparison to Martin appears in Neimeyer, *The Revolutionary War* (Westport, CT: Greenwood Press, 2007), xi.

42. Martin, *Ordinary Courage*, xiv. James Kirby Martin makes his conclusion after reviewing the most complete bibliography to date of Revolutionary soldier writing, Todd J. White and Charles H. Lesser, *Fighters for Independence: A Guide to Sources of Biographical Information on Soldiers and Sailors of the American Revolution (Chicago: University of Chicago Press, 1977)*. Purcell likewise relies on White and Lesser when she counts twelve soldier memoirs published between 1776 and 1800 and twenty-two between 1801 and 1819 (*Sealed with Blood*, 150). Young also puts the number between 1801 and 1819 at twenty-two in *The Shoemaker and the Tea Party*, 135. Not to retread too much from chapter 1, but my own archival accounting of published veteran writing does not differ drastically. Some commentators such as Fleming propose that Martin wrote from a wartime journal or diary, though such a suggestion is speculation.

43. See, in particular, Nathaniel Segar, *A Brief Narrative of the Captivity and Sufferings of Lt. Nathan'l Segar, Who Was Taken Prisoner by the Indians and Carried during the Revolutionary War, Written by Himself* (Paris, ME: Printed at the Observer Office,

1825). Segar notes how after leaving the service, "I received no pay nor provisions to bear my expenses on my long and tedious journey home" (9). Like Martin, he returns to the issue of missing compensation as the text concludes, insisting that the failure to be paid was the rule and not the exception. "Indeed, the country was not able at that time to properly satisfy the soldiers for their labors in that service. And furthermore, I have had no compensation for the time I was in captivity" (31). During much of his captivity, Segar was housed with almost two hundred American soldiers in a large Canadian camp. He was freed alongside them in a massive prisoner exchange following Cornwallis's surrender in 1782. The last lines of the narrative testify to Segar's sense of injustice: "The loss of time, and the hardships I then underwent, were felt as in the service of my country; and were so considered, as I was *exchanged* as a soldier, taken in actual service, or in time of battle; and, therefore, I always thought, and still think, that I, in *justice*, ought to have received some compensation from my country; but as I have received nothing, it still adds to my calamity, and which has been sensibly felt through life" (31–32).

44. Quoted in Martin, *Ordinary Courage*, xii.

45. Resch, *Suffering Soldiers*, 10. For an account of how "disability" became a contested bureaucratic category for Revolutionary veterans such as Martin, see Laurel Daen, "Revolutionary War Invalid Pensions and the Bureaucratic Language of Disability in the Early Republic," *Early American Literature* 52, no. 1 (2017): 141–67.

46. Kaplan, "Theft and Counter-Theft," 515. As chapter 3 documents, many veterans were quite clear about their financial motives for writing. For example, Captain Samuel Dewees's memoir concludes with a call for contributions: "Shall I state, reader I have done my part—*do thine* . . . Who are they that are prepared to deny him the free boon of a patriotic and generous nature, patronage to the amount of ONE DOLLAR?" John Smith Hanna, *A History of the Life and Services of Captain Samuel Dewees, a Native of Pennsylvania, and Soldier of the Revolutionary and Last Wars* (Baltimore, MD: Printed by Robert Neilson, 1844), 28–29.

47. Resch, *Suffering Soldiers*, 8.

48. Young, *The Shoemaker and the Tea Party*, 133.

49. Raphael, *A People's History of the American Revolution*, 62.

50. Kaplan, "Theft and Counter-Theft," 524.

51. Howell, "Starving Memory."

52. The quotation appears in Kaplan, "Theft and Counter-Theft," 520. Kaplan notes that "by the time of the French and Indian War, New Englanders had begun to think of military service as a 'contractual agreement' between soldier and government, and they protested when they felt their labor was not being properly compensated" (526). See also Frederic W. Anderson, "Why Did Colonial New Englanders Make Bad Soldiers? Contractual Principles and Military Conduct during the Seven Years War," *William and Mary Quarterly* 38 (1981): 395–417.

53. Elaine Scarry, *The Body in Pain: The Making and Unmaking of the World* (New York: Oxford University Press, 1985), 7.

54. Descriptions of Martin's hunger appear twenty times (N 26, 50, 58, 59, 64, 65, 67, 68, 70, 72, 86, 89, 148, 157, 160, 164, 174, 196, 197, 212). Descriptions of extreme thirst occur five times (N 48, 64, 89, 164, 205).

55. What appears to be the only life-threatening affliction is a bout with yellow fever near the end of his service (N 219). Martin also suffered a hospital stay after contracting smallpox, during which time he also contracted dysentery (N 57–58).

56. Thomas Jefferson, *Papers of Thomas Jefferson*, eds. Julian P. Boyd, and L. H. Butter-field, vol. 7 (Princeton, NJ: Princeton University Press, 1950), 105–6.

57. Myers, *Liberty without Anarchy*, 40–41.

58. David Ramsay, *An Oration, Delivered in St. Michael's Church, before the Inhabitants of Charleston, South-Carolina, on the Fourth of July, 1794, in Commemoration of American Independence, by the Appointment of the American Revolution Society, and Published at the Request of That Society, and Also of the South-Carolina State Society of Cincinnati* (Charleston, SC: Printed by W. P. Young, 1794), 12–13.

59. Ibid., 7.

60. Josiah Priest, *The Low Dutch Prisoner: Being an Account of the Capture of Frederick Schermerhorn. . . .* (Albany, [NY], 1839), 5.

61. Christopher Hawkins, *The Adventures of Christopher Hawkins, Containing Details of His Captivity, a First and Second Time on the High Seas, in the Revolutionary War, by the British, and His Consequent Sufferings, and Escape from the* Jersey *Prison Ship*, ed. Charles Ira Bushnell (New York: Privately printed, 1864), ix–x. The preface by Hawkins is dated April 3, 1834.

62. Charles Herbert, *A Relic of the Revolution: Containing a Full and Particular Account of the Sufferings and Privations of All the American Prisoners Captured on the High Seas, and Carried into Plymouth, England, during the Revolution* (Boston: Charles H. Peirce, 1847), 7, 16.

63. Ebenezer Fletcher, *The Narrative of Ebenezer Fletcher: A Soldier of the Revolution* (New York: Printed by Charles Bushnell, 1866), 43–44. See also earlier versions: Ebenezer Fletcher, *A Narrative of the Captivity and Sufferings of Ebenezer Fletcher, of New-Ipswich; Who Was Severely Wounded and Taken Prisoner at the Battle of Hubbardston, Vt. In the Year 1777, by the British and Indians at the Age of 16 Years. . . .* (New-Ipswich, NH: Printed by S. Wilder, [between 1813 and 1828]); and *A Narrative of the Captivity and Sufferings of Mr. Ebenezer Fletcher. . . .* (Amherst, NH: Printed by Samuel Preston, 1798).

64. John Blatchford, *The Narrative of John Blatchford, Detailing His Sufferings in the Revolutionary War, While a Prisoner with the British, as Related by Himself*, ed. Charles Ira Bushnell (New York: Privately printed, 1865), 16. See also an earlier version, John Blatchford, *Narrative, of the Life and Captivity, of John Blatchford. . . .* (New London, CT: [Printed by Timothy Green], 1788).

65. David Perry, *Recollections of an Old Soldier. The Life of Captain David Perry, a Soldier of the French and Revolutionary Wars* (Windsor, VT: Printed at the Republican & Yeoman Printing-Office, 1822), 36–37.

66. See J. Gerald Kennedy, "Anti-Intellectualism: The Comic Man of Learning," *Studies in American Humor* 3, no. 2 (1976): 69–75. The regret over having to kill is a frequent topic of conversation for Sitgreaves and Cooper. See *S* 102, 167.

67. Kaplan, "Theft and Counter-Theft," 515; John G. Cawelti and Bruce A. Rosenberg, *The Spy Story* (Chicago: University of Chicago Press, 1987), 34–54.

68. See, in particular, Dave McTiernan, "The Novel as 'Neutral Ground': Genre and Ideology in Cooper's *The Spy*," *Studies in American Fiction* 25, no. 1 (Spring 1997): 1–20.

69. Letter to André Thompson Goodrich dated June 28, 1820, in James Fenimore Cooper, *Letters and Journals*, ed. James Franklin Beard, vol. 1 (Cambridge, MA: Belknap Press of Harvard University Press, 1960), 44. Subsequent letter to Goodrich dated July 12, 1820, in ibid., 49.

70. Robert S. Levine, *Conspiracy and Romance: Studies in Brockden Brown, Cooper, Hawthorne, and Melville* (New York: Cambridge University Press, 1989), 68.

71. Maria Edgeworth, quoted in McTiernan, "The Novel as 'Neutral Ground,'" 8.

72. James Fenimore Cooper, *The History of the Navy of the United States of America* (Philadelphia: Lea & Blanchard, 1839). Cooper detailed the "distinguished" lives of William Bainbridge, Richard Somers, John Shaw, John Templer Shubrick, and Edward Preble in volume 1, and John Paul Jones, Melanchton Taylor Woolsey, Oliver Hazard Perry, and Richard Dale in volume 2. Perry was Elliott's commander, and Cooper's preference for Perry throughout his writing was a contributing factor to the earlier libel suit provoked by his *History*.

73. James Fenimore Cooper, ed., *Ned Myers; or, A Life before the Mast* (London: Lea and Blanchard, 1843), xii–xiii, x (emphasis added).

74. Writing from Paris to his British publisher Henry Colburn in 1831, Cooper complained, "There is an impudent rogue in America, who pretends to be the original of *The Spy*, and who has even written a book to prove his claim." Cooper was cagey about his denials, however, realizing that the controversy was good for sales. "I never heard of him, until I saw his book advertised, and I should not dislike an opportunity of stating what gave rise of the character—Do the public care enough about these things? How much will you give a volume, or rather a book, for new prefaces, notes and hints explanatory." In Cooper, *Letters and Journals*, vol. 2, 60–61. In his introduction to the 1849 edition of *The Spy*, Cooper talks about how he only wrote the novel after a conversation with "an illustrious participant" of the war, although such a vague reference could be to anyone, not necessarily Crosby or Barnum. When a reader in 1850 asked Cooper whether any of the controversy was true, his response was similarly self-interested. "Never having seen the publication of Mr. Barnum, to which you allude, I can give no opinion of its accuracy. I know nothing of such a man as Enoch Crosby, never having heard his name, until I saw it coupled with the character of *The Spy*, after my return from Europe. The history of the book is given in the preface of Putnam's edition, where you will probably find all you desire to know." In Cooper and Beard, *Letters and Journals*, vol. 6, 212.

75. Barnum, *The Spy Unmasked*, ix, [5].

76. Ibid., ix, ix–x (emphasis in original).

77. Cooper insinuated that the idea for Harvey Birch came from a casual conversation with John Jay years before (during the war, Jay was the head of the New York Committee of Safety, the informal agency responsible for espionage). In 1930, Tremaine McDowell tried to account for the "century of speculation" that Harvey Birch had inspired. Noting that contemporary reviewers believed Birch was "not wholly without historical foundation," McDowell concluded that "Cooper's Harvey Birch . . . is not to be identified with the Enoch Crosby of history." In Tremaine McDowell, "The Identity of Harvey Birch," *American Literature* 2, no. 2 (May 1930): 120. The evidence for his conclusion was reached mostly through historical analysis, during which he discovers there were no fewer than ten spies operating out of Westchester at the time, any one of which could have been to whom Jay was referring.

78. Barnum, *The Spy Unmasked*, xi, x.

79. Crosby certainly enjoyed his brief celebrity. He was in the audience opening night for Charles P. Cinch's theatrical adaptation of *The Spy* at the Lafayette Theatre in New York in 1827. It was at this production that Barnum first "discovered" Crosby.

The enthusiastic reception of *The Spy Unmasked* extended Crosby's public expo-
sure, prompting a second edition in 1831. Following the Pension Act of 1832, Crosby
would cite *The Spy Unmasked* in his application for a federal pension as evidence
of his hardship. The government certainly believed his story. His pension was
awarded, though he only enjoyed it for a short duration. Crosby died in 1835.

80. Asa Greene, *The Debtor's Prison: A Tale of a Revolutionary Soldier* (New York: Published by A. Greene, 1834), 8–9.
81. For more on these differences, see Sigmund Freud, *Beyond the Pleasure Principle*,
ed. James Strachey, intro. Peter Gay (New York: Norton, 1990). Originally published in 1920. Freud looked at "shell-shocked" soldiers returning from World War
I and ascribed the chief reason for their combat trauma (what we would call post-
traumatic stress today) "to rest upon the factor of surprise, of fright" (11), as in the
example where an artillery shell lands close by and startles a soldier who was not
expecting the impact. While I am careful not to argue that a veteran writing in
the early decades of the nineteenth century somehow anticipated psychoanalytic
discourses of the twentieth century, Freud's distinctions help to illustrate the early
American veteran memoirist's situation in hindsight. "'Anxiety' describes a particular state of expecting the danger or preparing for it, even though it may be an
unknown one. 'Fear' requires a definite object of which to be afraid. 'Fright,' however, is the name we give to the state a person gets into when he has run into danger
without being prepared for it; it emphasizes the factor of surprise" (11).
82. Nancy Sherman, *Afterwar: Healing the Moral Wounds of Our Soldiers* (New York:
Oxford University Press, 2015), 49–50 (emphasis in original).
83. Nathaniel Hawthorne, ed., *The Yarn of a Yankee Privateer* (New York: Funk & Wag-
nalls, 1926), 297.

Chapter 3: A Bunch of Veteran Amateurs

1. Ann Fabian, *The Unvarnished Truth: Personal Narratives in Nineteenth-Century
America* (Berkeley: University of California Press, 2002), 6, 50–54, 84, 138.
2. Ibid., 152–54. There are several versions of Cummings's text, including one published in Harrisburg by S. E. Shade that dates to either 1885 or 1887. Unfortunately,
the record is inconsistent.
3. Charles Cummings, *The Great War Relic: Together with a Sketch of My Life, Service
in the Army, and How I Lost My Feet since the War . . .* (Harrisburg, PA: Compiled
and Sold by Chas. L. Cummings, 1890[?]), 1, 7–8.
4. I realize in light of figures such as Roland Barthes and Michel Foucault that there
is a poststructuralist response to the very idea of "the author." I mean the term here
as the person who claims (or disavows) responsibility for the text, rather than who
controls it.
5. Meredith McGill, *American Literature and the Culture of Reprinting, 1834–1853*
(Philadelphia: University of Pennsylvania Press, 2003), 143, 198; Lara Langer Cohen,
The Fabrication of American Literature: Fraudulence and Antebellum Print Culture
(Philadelphia: University of Pennsylvania Press, 2012), 32–66.
6. Michael C. Cohen, "Peddling Authorship in the Age of Jackson," *ELH* 79, no. 2
(Summer 2012): 381, 371; William J. Gilmore, *Reading Becomes a Necessity of Life:
Material and Cultural Life in Rural New England, 1780–1835* (Knoxville: University
of Tennessee Press, 1989), 23.

7. Michael C. Cohen, *The Social Lives of Poems in Nineteenth-Century America* (Philadelphia: University of Pennsylvania Press, 2015), 19. Here and elsewhere, Cohen implicitly critiques American literary criticism's tendency to assume biographies and personalities matter, a proclivity that dates (for me) at least as far back as F. O. Matthiessen's *American Renaissance: Art and Expression in the Age of Emerson and Whitman* (New York: Oxford University Press, 1941).

8. Cohen, "Peddling Authorship," 373.

9. Cummings, *The Great War Relic*, 9–11 (emphasis added).

10. See Fabian, *The Unvarnished Truth*, 40–42, from which I quote here. In Potter, who formed a "fellowship of storytellers" with other "displaced sailors," Fabian saw duplicity as she had with Cummings. "All these [veteran] stories turn on dramas of identity. Who were these men? Were they beggars or entrepreneurs? Were they long-suffering heroes, or practiced liars, innocent victims, or escaped convicts, patriots, or traitors? Each asserted national identity in order to avoid questions about their ambiguous personal identity . . . But American identity was a category as unstable as all the others—not something fixed and permanent, but something claimed and demonstrated."

11. Quoted in David Chacko and Alexander Kulcsa, "Israel Potter: Genesis of a Legend," *William and Mary Quarterly* 41, no. 3 (July 1984): 365.

12. See Bezanson's historical note in Herman Melville, *Israel Potter: His Fifty Years of Exile,* eds. Harrison Hayford, Hershel Parker, G. Thomas Tanselle, and Walter E. Bezanson (Evanston, IL: Northwestern University Press, 1997), 184–87. The quotation appears on 184.

13. Chacko and Kulcsa, "Israel Potter," 367. See also John Filson, *Life and Adventures of Colonel Daniel Boon* (Providence, RI: Henry Trumbull, 1824); and Daniel Boone, *The Adventures of Colonel Daniel Boon, One of the First Settlers at Kentucke: Containing the Wars with the Indians on the Ohio, from 1769 to 1783, and the First Establishment and Progress of the Settlement on That River,* eds. Humphrey Marshall and John Filson (Norwich, CT: Printed by John Trumbull, 1786).

14. Originally published as Israel Potter, *Life and Remarkable Adventures of Israel R. Potter, (a Native of Cranston, Rhode-Island) Who Was a Soldier in the American Revolution* (Providence, RI: Henry Trumbull, 1824).

15. Herman Melville, *Journals,* eds. Howard C. Horsford and Lynn Horth (Evanston, IL: Northwestern University Press, 1989), 43.

16. Ibid., 169.

17. Joyce Adler, *War in Melville's Imagination* (New York: New York University Press, 1981), 79.

18. Melville, Israel Potter, v, v.

19. Adler, *War in Melville's Imagination*, 81–86.

20. Peter J. Bellis, "Israel Potter: Autobiography as History as Fiction," *American Literary History* 2, no. 4 (Winter 1990): 614.

21. Melville, *Israel Potter,* 52.

22. Bellis, "Israel Potter," 613.

23. Israel Potter, *Life and Remarkable Adventures of Israel R. Potter,* ed. Leonard Kriegel (New York: Corinth Books, 1962), 16.

24. Potter's tale of poverty in *Life and Remarkable Adventures of Israel R. Potter* stretches from p. 61 to p. 101.

25. Potter, *Life and Remarkable Adventures of Israel R. Potter,* 63–65, 78–89, 103, 104.
26. Oliver Wendell Holmes, *The Complete Poetical Works of Oliver Wendell Holmes,* ed. Horace Elisha Scudder (Boston: Houghton Mifflin, 1923), 4–5.
27. William F. Hecker, introduction to *Private Perry and Mister Poe: The West Point Poems, 1831,* by Edgar Allan Poe (Baton Rouge: Louisiana State University Press, 2005), xxix. See also Paul Foos, *A Short, Offhand, Killing Affair: Soldiers and Social Conflict during the Mexican-American War* (Chapel Hill: University of North Carolina Press, 2002), 6–18; and Edward M. Coffman, *The Old Army: A Portrait of the American Army in Peacetime, 1784–1898* (New York: Oxford University Press, 1986), 10–22.
28. Hecker, introduction, xli, lxiv–lxv; Coffman, *The Old Army,* 43–45.
29. Samuel P. Huntington, *The Soldier and the State: The Theory and Politics of Civil-Military Relations* (Cambridge, MA: Belknap Press of Harvard University Press, 1985), 234.
30. See Hecker, introduction, xlvi–li. Popular wisdom assumes that Poe was an alcoholic and that he surely must have been expelled from West Point for drunkenness, yet there is no allegation of alcohol in Poe's court-martial. Because alcohol was typically an explicit charge in disciplinary matters at West Point, the absence of any allegation for Poe is striking, suggesting he was kicked out for reasons other than partying. The stated charges were gross neglect of duty (Poe missed some parades and roll calls) and insubordination (he did not attend church despite being ordered to by an officer).
31. Edgar Allan Poe, "The Man That Was Used Up," in *Selected Poems, Tales, and Essays,* eds. Jared Gardner and Elizabeth Hewitt (Boston: Bedford/St Martin's, 2016), 78–79, 86. Originally published in *Burton's Gentleman's Magazine,* August 1839, 66–70.
32. Ephraim Kirby Smith and Robert E. Lee, quoted in Coffman, *The Old Army,* 61–62. See also 86–88.
33. Ibid., 96; Laurence Buell, *New England Literary Culture: From Revolution through Renaissance* (New York: Cambridge University Press, 1986), 3; Leon Jackson, *The Business of Letters: Authorial Economies in Antebellum America* (Stanford, CA: Stanford University Press, 2008), 22.
34. Lawrence Buell, "Autobiography in the American Renaissance," in *American Autobiography: Retrospect and Prospect,* ed. Paul John Eakin (Madison: University of Wisconsin Press, 1991), 48.
35. Quotations appear in Jackson, *The Business of Letters,* 14, 29. See also Kevin Hayes, *Poe and the Printed Word* (New York: Cambridge University Press, 2000). Hayes argues that Poe begrudgingly adapted to the emerging literary marketplaces, such as cheap pamphlet books—a form he detested as unserious but ultimately cooperated with in the publication of "The Man That Was Used Up" and "The Murders in the Rue Morgue" as a pamphlet issued by William H. Graham in Philadelphia in 1843 (90–93)—but he also chose his moments where not to compromise, hence why he made sure his first three poetry collections were published as books and not in a less respected form such as literary periodicals (113).
36. Cohen, *The Fabrication of American Literature,* 5.
37. Poe, *Private Perry and Mister Poe,* 16–19, 28–29. Poe surmised there was no niche for a "native" literature of the United States during the 1830s and 1840s. Instead, the market was saturated with such stale foreign poets as Robert Southey and William Wordsworth.

38. Cohen, *The Fabrication of American Literature*, 18.

39. Albrecht Koschnik, *"Let a Common Interest Bind Us Together": Associations, Partisanship, and Culture in Philadelphia, 1775–1840* (Charlottesville: University of Virginia Press, 2007), 91, 94–95, 96, 150–51.

40. Ibid., 151.

41. Percy Fitz Juan, *The Champagne Club*, December 13, 1834, 13–15. The newspapers and periodicals that follow are largely available through the American Antiquarian Society Historical Periodicals Collection.

42. "Tributes for the Brave," *Literary Harvester: A Semi-Monthly Journal of Literature, Science and the Fine Arts*, July 15, 1842, 63.

43. *U.S. Military Magazine and Record of All the Volunteers, together with Army and Navy*, October 1, 1839, 1.

44. For an example of such fear, see Major J. Swett Jr., ed., "The Militia of the Whole United States," *The Citizen Soldier, a Military Paper, Devoted to the Interests of the Militia*, July 22, 1840, 5. "With these views the stranger would look with astonishment upon the least neglect, or slightest indifference of our citizens toward the institution on which all our hopes and rights depend, without supposing it possible that those, or any of those, who were enjoying its protection over their persons or property, could be secretly plotting to paralyze or amputate this right arm of our common defence. But so it is, and the numbers are not few, who both secretly and publicly put forth their utmost exertions to degrade, disgrace, and render inefficient the Militia of our own country. This spirit is poured from our seminaries of learning, from the pulpit and the bar, and not without effect, for excrescences have been fastened upon the system, which have well nigh caused its dissolution. In order therefore to resuscitate and invigorate the constitutional defence of our country—to render effective our citizen-soldiery—to elevate, and encourage the Militia of our own state, of each state, and of the whole nation,—we propose to publish the Citizen Soldier."

45. Foos, *A Short, Offhand, Killing Affair*, 15.

46. The quotation appears in the *Eclaireur*, August 1, 1854, 1. The anxiety over civilian reach appears in the *Eclaireur*, September 1, 1854, 11–12.

47. *Military Gazette*, January 1, 1859, 1.

48. "Col. William Ward Tompkins," *New York Times*, February 8, 1882, 5.

49. William Ward Tompkins, ed., *Military Journal*, November 22, 1845, 1.

50. "Col. William Ward Tompkins," 5.

51. Alfred Cornebise, *Ranks and Columns: Armed Forces Newspapers in American Wars* (Westport, CT: Greenwood Press, 1993), makes an important distinction between military periodicals and troop newspapers. The first "was well established" by the Mexican War and celebrated both "a preoccupation with the militia as well as the trend toward a growing professionalism in the American military establishment"; the latter "was not as well developed," although the Mexican War allowed for the growth of such newspapers and the penny press (6).

52. Ibid., 10.

53. Ibid., 11. Furthermore, "because the paper strongly supported revolution, the U.S. government ordered its suppression. General Taylor promptly complied and [the editor] was forced to resign. The paper only survived by changing its approach and its name . . . [to] *American Flag*."

54. Robert Johannsen, *To the Halls of the Montezumas: The Mexican War in the American Imagination* (New York: Oxford University Press, 1985), 25.

55. Foos, *A Short, Offhand, Killing Affair*, 21, 4. For a discussion of Manifest Destiny as a contest of "heroic modes" and competing masculinities, see Amy S. Greenberg, *Manifest Manhood and the Antebellum American Empire* (New York: Cambridge University Press, 2005).

56. George Ballentine, *Autobiography of an English Soldier in the United States Army....* (New York: Stringer & Townsend, 1853), v, vii.

57. Edgar Allan Poe, "The Fall of the House of Usher," in *Selected Poems, Tales, and Essays*, eds. Jared Gardner and Elizabeth Hewitt (Boston: Bedford/St Martin's, 2016), 89. Originally published in *Burton's Gentleman's Magazine*, September 1839, 145–52.

58. Nathaniel Hawthorne, *The Scarlett Letter* (New York: Norton, 1962), 31. Originally published in Boston by Ticknor, Reed & Fields in 1850. In his biography of Franklin Pierce, Hawthorne harbored antiveteran sentiments: "The valor that wins our battles is not the trained hardihood of veterans, but a native and spontaneous fire; and there is surely a chivalrous beauty in the devotion of the citizen soldier to his country's cause, which the man who makes arms his profession, and is but doing his regular business on the field of battle, cannot pretend to rival. Taking the Mexican war as a specimen, this peculiar composition of an American army, as well in respect to its officers as its private soldiers, seems to create a spirit of romantic adventure which more than supplies the place of disciplined courage." Nathaniel Hawthorne, *Life of Franklin Pierce* (Boston: Ticknor, Reed, & Fields, 1852), 67.

59. George C. Furber, *The Twelve Months Volunteer, or, Journal of a Private....* (Cincinnati: J. A. & U. P. James, 1848), v–vi, vi.

60. Ibid., vi; Samuel White, *History of the American Troops, during the Late War, under the Command of Cols. Fenton and Campbell....* (Baltimore: Published by the author [D. Edes, Printer], 1829), 3; Benjamin Franklin Scribner, preface to *A Campaign in Mexico, by "One Who Was Thar"* (Philadelphia: James Gihon, 1850).

61. The *"High Private," with a Full and Exciting History of the New York Volunteers, Illustrated . . . Including the Mysteries and Miseries of the Mexican War* (New York: Printed for the Publishers, 1848), 8; Corydon Donnavan, *Adventures in Mexico: Experienced during a Captivity of Seven Months in the Interior—Having Been Captured at Camargo....* (Cincinnati: Published by Robinson & Jones, 1847), iii.

62. There is similarly no stated author in *Encarnacion Prisoners: Comprising an Account of the March of the Kentucky Cavalry from Louisville to the Rio Grande, together with an Authentic History of the Captivity of the American Prisoners....* (Louisville: Prentice and Weissinger, 1848). The narrator is "we" throughout.

63. The *"High Private,"* 25, 34, 42, 46 (emphasis in original).

64. Fictional texts also tended toward the sensational, such as George Lippard's two war novels: *Legends of Mexico* (Philadelphia: T. B. Peterson, 1847); and *'Bel of Prairie Eden: A Romance of Mexico* (Boston: Hotchkiss & Company, 1848).

65. *Life and Adventures of the Accomplished Forger and Swindler, Colonel Monroe Edwards* (New York: H. Long & Brother, 1848), 37.

66. See David S. Reynolds, *Beneath the American Renaissance: The Subversive Imagination in the Age of Emerson and Melville* (New York: Knopf, 1988), 300–308. The quotation appears on 302. The veteran's story is analogous in Melville's career to the tall tale of another likable criminal, Caspar Hauser, who is referenced by Melville in *The Confidence-Man, Pierre, or the Ambiguities*, and *Billy Budd*.

67. Herman Melville, *The Confidence-Man: His Masquerade*, ed. H. Bruce Franklin (Champaign, IL: Dalkey Archive Press, 2006), 13–14, 129, 129, 133–34, 135.

68. Ibid., 135.

69. Reynolds, *Beneath the American Renaissance*, 298–301.

70. Shelley Streeby, *American Sensations: Class, Empire, and the Production of Popular Culture* (Berkeley: University of California Press, 2002), 39.

71. Johannsen, *To the Halls of the Montezumas*, 175–203.

72. Streeby, *American Sensations*, 52–53.

73. Johannsen, *To the Halls of the Montezumas*, 11.

74. Herman Melville, *Correspondence*, ed. Lynn Horth, vol. 14 (Evanston, IL: Northwestern University Press, 1993), 40–41.

75. Herman Melville, "Authentic Anecdotes of Old Zach," *Yankee Doodle*, September 11, 1847, 229. See also editions from July 24 and August 7, 1847.

76. Stanton Garner, *The Civil War World of Herman Melville* (Lawrence: University Press of Kansas, 1993), 388–90. Garner rightfully dismisses the notion that Melville was somehow inactive or cloistered during the Civil War. Melville avidly followed wartime current events and had mulled over composing a cycle of memorial poems soon after the war began. For more on the fraught reconciliatory strategies of *Battle-Pieces*, see Robert Milder, *Exiled Royalties: Melville and the Life We Imagine* (New York: Oxford University Press, 2006), 168–91. Melville dates his composition to the fall of Richmond in his prefatory note to *Battle-Pieces and Aspects of the War* (*BP* 33). *Battle-Pieces* was originally published in New York by Harper and Brothers in 1866.

77. Walt Whitman, *Specimen Days in America* (London: Walter Scott, 1887), 125. *Specimen Days* was first published in Philadelphia by Rees Welsh and Company in 1882.

78. For Mexican War figures, see Foos, *A Short, Offhand, Killing Affair*, 17. Other counts are derived from James Dawes, *The Language of War: Literature and Culture in the U.S. from the Civil War through World War II* (Cambridge, MA: Harvard University Press, 2002), 29–68.

79. Oliver Wendell Holmes, *Soundings from the Atlantic* (Boston: Ticknor & Fields, 1864), 9–10.

80. "My Hunt after the Captain" first appeared in the *Atlantic Monthly*, December 1862. Reprinted in ibid., 46.

Chapter 4: The Real and Written War

1. *New York Pioneer*, December 9, 1840, 1–8. The newspapers and periodicals that follow are largely available through the American Antiquarian Society Historical Periodicals Collection.

2. *The Volunteer*, January 1, 1862, 1.

3. *Soldier's Casket*, January 1, 1865, 3; *Springfield Musket*, December 20, 1864, 1–8; *Soldier's Aid*, March 12, 1865, 89–100; *Sanitary Fair Gazette*, February 24, 1864.

4. *American Volunteer*, November 16, 1865, 1; *Home Mail* (Phelps, NY: [Home Mail], 1874); *Bennett's Reporter* ([Washington, DC], 1857); *Claim Agent* (Washington, DC: Lemuel Bursley, 1870–71); *United States Record and Gazette* (Washington, DC: Darling & Soulé, 1875–77); *Gem of the West and Soldier's Friend* (Chicago: Benson J. Lossing, 1871–75).

5. See William Oland Bourne, *Poems of Hope and Action* (New York: George P. Putnam, 1850); *A Poem before the Literary Societies of the New York Free Academy*, July

25, 1853 (New York: Printed by Edward O. Jenkins, 1853); *Little Silverstring: or, Tales and Poems for the Young* (New York: Charles Scribner, 1853); *Gems from Fable Land: A Collection of Fables Illustrated by Facts* (New York: Charles Scribner, 1853); and *Poems of the Republic* (New York: E. O. Jenkins, 1864). After the war, Bourne would publish *History of the Public School Society of the City of New York* (New York: Wm. Wood, 1870).

6. The foremost objective of the *Soldier's Friend* was to retrain soldiers in their transition back into civilian life. It was by all accounts a successful newspaper, reaching a peak circulation of 60,000 by late 1866. The Huntington Library houses a complete holding of the *Soldier's Friend*, and the papers of William Oland Bourne reside at the Library of Congress. Soldier letters to Bourne at the Library of Congress attest to the prominence of local advertising efforts in recruiting for "Left-Handed Penmanship." R. A. Bain from Marshall, Michigan, writes that he is responding to an advertisement in the *Detroit Tribune*. R. Watson from Pigeon, Michigan, is responding to a notice he saw in the *Michigan Christian Herald*. On the front page of its September 1868 issue, *Soldier's Friend* reprinted the advertisement it had run in *Frank Leslie's Illustrated Newspaper* for the contest. See William Oland Bourne, *The Soldier's Friend* (New York: John A. Gray & Green, 1864–70).

7. "Left-Handed Penmanship," *Harper's Weekly*, July 29, 1865, 467.

8. Decoration Days and other public remembrances began in 1865. For a more complete discussion of the public expressions of veterans, see David W. Blight, *Race and Reunion: The Civil War in American Memory* (Cambridge, MA: Belknap Press of Harvard University Press, 2001), 64–71; and Kirk Savage, *Standing Soldiers, Kneeling Slaves: Race, War, and Monument in Nineteenth-Century America* (Princeton, NJ: Princeton University Press, 1997). My argument agrees with the work of Alan Trachtenberg, who contended that the pervasive visibility of the common soldier diminished the heroic nationalism surrounding him: "The Civil War camera disclosed debris strewn about, weary men, slovenly uniforms—soldiers not as heroes but as soldiers." In Alan Trachtenberg, *Reading American Photographs: Images as History, Mathew Brady to Walker Evans* (New York: Hill and Wang, 1989), 83.

9. Much has already been said about the unprecedented visibility of the war on the public imagination, then and now, in popular and scholarly contexts. For example, see Alexander Gardner, *Gardner's Photographic Sketchbook of the Civil War* (Washington, DC: Philp & Solomons, 1865); Ken Burns, *The Civil War* (Alexandria, VA: PBS Video, 1989); and Franny Nudelman, *John Brown's Body: Slavery, Violence, and the Culture of War* (Chapel Hill: University of North Carolina Press, 2004).

10. "Soldiers Left-Hand Writing," *Harper's Weekly*, April 7, 1866, 211.

11. "Left-Hand Writing," *Harper's Weekly*, November 4, 1865, 691.

12. "Soldiers Left-Hand Writing," *Harper's Weekly*, April 7, 1866, 211.

13. The awards ceremony was written up at some length and expense in the March 1866 issue of *Soldier's Friend*. The following excerpt taken from the first two pages of the issue I quote at length, as the ceremony is the best approximation of how the public consumed these veteran writings. "The hall of the Union Central Committee being generously granted for the purpose, the specimens of penmanship were placed on exhibition for examination by the public. The arrangements and decorations, which were very appropriate and beautiful, were made by the ladies of the Union Relief Committee, who addressed themselves to the work with great interest and zeal. The festooned columns and windows, around which the evergreens mingled in happy

harmony with the red, white, and blue of the flag of the Union, presented a fine appearance, while mottoes and inscriptions, being the names of Grant, Sherman, Porter, Sheridan, Hooker, Thomas, Kilpatrick, Foote, Meade, and Morris, were effectively displayed over the windows . . . On long tables, reaching the length of the hall, one on each side of the room, with ample passage on all sides, were the varied productions of nearly three hundred men who had sacrificed their right arms for the country. Coming from nearly every State of the Union, and in one case, from Canada, from men who had been, or are now, in the service, this remarkable and original display of literary and artistic work was presented in a very effective and truthful grouping of the national colors. On a ground of blue cloth the white manuscripts were laid, and were held in their places by a neat little red tape running the length of the table. At the top of the sheet the number of each manuscript, corresponding with the printed catalogue, was presented in red on a white card, with a red border, while a small red card secured the manuscript at the lower margin. The grouping of colors was characteristic and admired by all who saw the skilful and beautiful display. An additional feature of the exposition was the collection of photographs of the authors, each portrait being placed at the head of the manuscript contributed by the writer. These photographs were not only admired by all, but it brought the visitor into the presence of the honorable members of the Left-Armed Corps who had furnished the tables for this novel and most attractive entertainment" (1–2).

14. "Left-Handed Penmanship," *Harper's Weekly*, July 29, 1865, 467.
15. See "Left-Handed Writing," *Harper's Weekly*, March, 10, 1866, 147. *Harper's* confirmed the elaborate ceremony that the *Soldier's Friend* detailed at length, noting that interested readers could come see "specimens of writing . . . at the hall corner of Twenty-Third Street and Broadway." Still, as far as my research has shown, no printed and bound volume exists in circulation. Soon after the contest's success, the *Soldier's Friend* repeatedly advertised that there would be. The July and August 1866 issues advertised the proposed volume, "Battle Memories of the Left-Armed Corps." William Cullen Bryant had even agreed to write the introduction. The July 1866 issue of the *Soldier's Friend* proclaimed: "It is proposed to publish a MEMORIAL VOLUME, containing the sketches, tales, poems, and war narrative of the Left-Armed Corps, in one handsome octavo volume of five hundred pages. The book will be illustrated with portraits and specimens of Left-Hand Penmanship by men who lost their right arm during the late war" (2). The last mention of the ornate memorial appeared in the final monthly issue of the *Soldier's Friend* in March 1870. Bourne often emphasized the literary talents of his soldiers, beginning most issues with an original poem by a soldier on the first column of the first page. The *Soldier's Friend* was keen to publish prominent noncombatant writers as well, among them Cullen Bryant, George William Curtis, and Charles Eliot Norton.
16. "Left-Handed Penmanship," *Harper's Weekly*, July, 29, 1865, 467.
17. "Left-Hand Writing," *Harper's Weekly*, November 4, 1865, 691.
18. "Left-Hand Writing," *Harper's Weekly*, May 26, 1866, 323.
19. The *Soldier's Friend* published a list of the names of the contributors in November 1865, including a short "sketch from a young colored man, of the Fifth U.S. C. Infantry" (1), but besides these few short and anonymous snippets, no veteran stories from the contest were published. However, Bourne's papers at the Library of Congress show a second contest was held during the last half of 1867. These writings

are all related in the broadest sense by their shared confusion over their compulsion to write something "original" and "literary," which is to say something that other people valued. Soldier Henry Allen professes his humility, "I am no literary genius, and cannot write any manuscript worthy a place in the columns of the 'Soldier's Friend,'" at the same time that soldier William Connor refuses to be meek. His drive to write *something* becomes a compulsion: "In losing my right arm my first thought was to learn to write with the left hand. I commenced practicing with a lead pencil the next day, and in the corner where my bed was located the wall was written as high and as far as I could reach each way." Robert A. Finn, an African American soldier from Ohio, writes of his childhood bereft of a formal education: "I experienced all the disadvantages peculiar to my proscribed race." Consequently, "it is hardly necessary to say that very little can be expected of me, so far a correct composition is concerned." I take Finn to mean by "correct composition" a story acceptable and palatable to a larger public, both in style and content. These veteran texts were not always that, though Franklin H. Durrah, the winner of the contest, writes a fairly "correct composition" in elegant script and is handsomely rewarded for it by Bourne and the contest's judges.

20. Blight, *Race and Reunion*, 45; Nina Silber, *The Romance of Reunion: Northerners and the South, 1865–1900* (Chapel Hill: University of North Carolina Press, 1993).

21. Robert Penn Warren, *The Legacy of the Civil War: Meditations on the Centennial* (New York: Random House, 1961), 54.

22. Ibid., 60–64, 54–58, 76.

23. Pierre Nora, "General Introduction: Between Memory and History," in *Realms of Memory: Rethinking the French Past,* ed. Lawrence D. Kritzman, trans. Arthur Goldhammer, vol. 1 (New York: Columbia University Press, 1996), 1–20; Maurice Halbwachs, *On Collective Memory*, ed. and trans. Lewis A. Coser (Chicago: University of Chicago Press, 1992), 46–51; and Savage, *Standing Soldiers, Kneeling Slaves*, 3–20.

24. Blight, *Race and Reunion*, 172. *Century Magazine* published "hundreds of articles" between 1884 and 1887, "in perhaps the most ambitious attempt ever to retell a war by its leading participants" (174). Among the notable pieces was Mark Twain's "The Private History of a Campaign That Failed" (December 1885). Robert Underwood Johnson and Clarence Clough Buel collected these *Century* veteran writings in their immense four volume *Battles and Leaders of the Civil War.* The first volume was published in 1887.

25. Walt Whitman, *Specimen Days in America* (London: Walter Scott, 1887), 125.

26. Edmund Wilson, *Patriotic Gore: Studies in the Literature of the American Civil War* (New York: Oxford University Press, 1962), 671.

27. John William De Forest, "Our Military Past and Present," *Atlantic Monthly,* November 1879, 572.

28. Wade Newhouse, "Reporting Triumph, Saving a Nation: 'Interesting Juxtapositions' in John W. De Forest's Civil War," *Studies in American Fiction* 32, no. 2 (Autumn 2004): 165.

29. Michael W. Schaefer, *Just What War Is: The Civil War Writings of De Forest and Bierce* (Knoxville: University of Tennessee Press, 1997), 15–17. De Forest's full critical reception is marked by a large gap between his death in 1906 and World War II, during which time *Miss Ravenel's Conversion* was out of print. Van Wyck Brooks came across De Forest's papers at Yale during World War I, but no full-scale interest

in De Forest occurred until 1937, when Bernard DeVoto published "Fiction Fights the Civil War" in the *Saturday Review of Literature*. Besides a doctoral dissertation in the same year, Rebecca Smith Lee, "The Civil War and Its Aftermath in American Fiction, 1861–1899" (Ph.D. diss., University of Chicago, 1937), De Forest faded again until the specter of the war's one hundredth anniversary produced Robert A. Lively, *Fiction Fights the Civil War: An Unfinished Chapter in the Literary History of the American People* (Chapel Hill: University of North Carolina Press, 1957); Wilson, *Patriotic Gore*; and Daniel Aaron, *The Unwritten War: American Writers and the Civil War* (New York: Oxford University Press, 1973). Subsequent scholars have agreed with Schaefer's assessment that the enduring value of the Civil War novel is how it "succeeds in *stimulating and engaging the emotions, the imagination, and the intellect to make the war agonizingly alive in the reader. Its point of view, style, and other techniques make the reader a collaborator* with the author in creating a conception of the Civil War that will enable the reader, long after the fiction ends, *to illuminate his or her experiences*" (emphasis added). David Madden and Peggy Bach, eds., *Classics of Civil War Fiction* (Jackson: University Press of Mississippi, 1991), 8. Robert Antoni argues specifically regarding *Miss Ravenel's Conversion's* representations of battle at Port Hudson and Fort Winthrop that the reader "enters the mind, body, and spirit of De Forest the soldier." Robert William Antoni, "*Miss Ravenel's Conversion*: A Neglected American Novel," *Southern Quarterly* 24, no. 3 (Spring 1986): 58–63. The quotation appears on page 59. I critique this modern transference of veteran experience onto civilian audiences in the conclusion.

30. Gregory S. Jackson, "'A Dowry of Suffering': Consent, Contract, and Political Coverture in John W. De Forest's Reconstruction Romance," *American Literary History* 15, no. 2 (Summer 2003): 277.

31. Wilson, *Patriotic Gore,* 670.

32. See De Forest, "Our Military Past and Future," 561–75. The article is an earnest attempt by an aging veteran to reform the military system. De Forest had learned during the Civil War that soldiers were ambitious, eager, full of vigor—in short, wholly unprepared for the actualities of combat. Expecting another war soon (he thought it would probably happen with Native Americans), De Forest advocated a system of volunteer "citizen soldiers" (562) who would be educated in mandatory military science in the public schools and universities. Realistic preparation was the best antidote to all the toxic and inaccurate descriptions of soldiers he had been reading over the past decade: "But the schools should not be furnished with text-books alone. There should be military histories in their libraries,—not the trashy, misleading ones which prattle of 'billows of Cavalry' and 'infantry standing like rocks'; not such stuff as the world has had about war from a host of ignorant romancers calling themselves historians; but books which show just what war is, and what to do amidst its difficulties" (572).

33. Louisa May Alcott, *Civil War Hospital Sketches* (Mineola, NY: Dover, 2006), 11, 23, 28, 38, 39. Later in 1863, *Hospital Sketches* was published as a book by James Redpath in Boston.

34. Many veterans did publish their experiences in book form decades after the war. An incomplete list would include *Figs and Thistles* by Albion Tourgee (1879), *Tales of Soldiers and Civilians* by Ambrose Bierce (1891), *The Captain of Company K* by Joseph Kirkland (1891), and *Campaigning with General Grant* by Horace Porter (1897). Conversely, civilians were writing war novels contemporaneous with the

war, including Horatio Alger's *Frank's Campaign* (1864), William T. Adams's *Soldier Boy* (1863), and John Townsend Trowbridge's *Three Scouts* (1865). It should also be noted that the prolific novelist and Southern soldier John Esten Cooke published *Surrey of Eagle's Nest* very soon afterward in 1866, and South Carolinian Augusta Evans's *Macaria* (1863) was the best-selling book of the war years, North or South. Their comparisons with De Forest are limited, however, as these cavalier novels lack the type of sober realism I am outlining in *Miss Ravenel's Conversion.*

35. Scholarship has tended to interrogate "war literature by category," which is to say by genre, such as Alice Fahs, *The Imagined Civil War: Popular Literature of the North and South, 1861–1865* (Chapel Hill: University of North Carolina Press, 2001), 8. See also Kathleen Diffley, *Where My Heart Is Turning Ever: Civil War Stories and Constitutional Reform, 1861–1876* (Athens: University of Georgia Press, 1992), 18–39. Sentimental genres such as the "defense of the Old Homestead" that Diffley identifies are largely popular modes of imaginative homogeneity. De Forest, however, is at the moment of *Miss Ravenel's Conversion* serving one master (his war experience) at the expense of another (genre).

36. James W. Gargano, ed., *Critical Essays on John William De Forest* (Boston: G. K. Hall, 1981), 6–7.

37. Wilson, *Patriotic Gore,* 673–76.

38. John William De Forest, *A Volunteer's Adventures: A Union Captain's Record of the Civil War,* ed. James H. Croushore (Baton Rouge: Louisiana State University Press, 1996), 15.

39. Ibid., 2.

40. George J. Ziegler, *The Soldier's Friend; or, Hints for the Physical and Moral Welfare of the Soldiers of the United States* (Philadelphia: [George J. Ziegler, M.D.], 1861), 5, 6. Ziegler was a prominent doctor who is now perhaps best known for his contribution to *Dental Cosmos,* the first professional journal of American dentistry.

41. De Forest, *A Volunteer's Adventures,* 41.

42. Both soldier and citizen shared "the tediums of peace" wherein long stretches of boredom oscillated with quick flashes of excitement. See Wilson, *Patriotic Gore,* 682. Out of the six and a half years he served in the army, De Forest reported only forty-six days of combat. *Miss Ravenel's Conversion* is well over four hundred pages long, and no more than twenty of those are devoted to the battlefield itself. De Forest's aesthetic is frequently informed by his private desire for a conversion experience to counteract the quotidian. We see that desire in his adventures in Europe and then again when he joins the military, and once more when he is forced to reenter civilian life at the war's end. When he was finishing *Miss Ravenel's Conversion* in 1866 while working at the Freedmen's Bureau in Greensboro, North Carolina, De Forest was caught, much like Colburne at the end of the novel, in the transition from military hero to ordinary citizen. In the final pages, one cannot help but read De Forest's own conflicted set of identities in the description of Colburne, now a lawyer, whom the narrator labels a "failure as a soldier" at the same time he is heralded as a "soldier citizen" ready to take on the challenges of Reconstruction (*MR* 468).

43. De Forest, *A Volunteer's Adventures,* 9.

44. Aaron, *The Unwritten War,* 170–71.

45. This straddling of North and South is reflected in De Forest's own biography as well. In 1855 he married a woman from South Carolina whose father taught at the medical college in Charleston, and as mentioned earlier, after the war, De Forest would

work for the Freedmen's Bureau in Greensboro, North Carolina, for several years.
46. Henry James, "Miss Ravenel's Conversion," in *Critical Essays on John William De Forest*, ed. James W. Gargano (Boston: G. K. Hall, 1981), 50. Originally published in the *Nation*, June 20, 1867, 491–92.
47. Edwin Oviatt, "J. W. De Forest in New Haven," in *Critical Essays on John William De Forest*, ed. James W. Gargano (Boston: G. K. Hall, 1981), 40–41. Originally published in the *New York Times*, December 17, 1898, 856.
48. Whitman, *Specimen Days in America*, 124.
49. Warren aligns the vision of the war with pragmatic philosophy (hence my reference to William James) in *The Legacy of the Civil War* when he quotes the historian Sidney Hook's assessment of Lincoln as the quintessential pragmatist: "'To be principled without being fanatical, and flexible without being opportunistic, summarizes the logic and ethics of pragmatism in action'" (18). Similarly, Wilson compares De Forest's stoicism to pragmatic ideals in *Patriotic Gore* when he calls De Forest's style emblematic of a confident "rigidity" (668) that was evident in such other veterans as Thomas Wentworth Higginson and Ambrose Bierce: "All of these writers, then, are positive and disciplined, sometimes trenchant and always concise, as if they were sure of themselves, as if they knew exactly what to think" (654).
50. Dr. Ravenel imagined the Civil War as the ordained culmination of history, divided like a Shakespearean comedy into five acts. "First, the Christian revelation. Second, the Protestant reformation. Third, the war of American Independence. Fourth, the French revolution. Fifth, the struggle for the freedom of all men, without distinction of race and color; this Democratic struggle which confirms the masses in an equality with the few" (*MR* 445).
51. Civil War veterans ultimately reaped many more benefits than did their Revolutionary counterparts. See Theda Skocpol, *Protecting Soldiers and Mothers: The Political Origins of Social Policy in the United States* (Cambridge, MA: Belknap Press of Harvard University Press, 1992), 105–59.
52. John William De Forest, "The Great American Novel," in *Critical Essays on John William De Forest*, ed. James W. Gargano (Boston: G. K. Hall, 1981), 35, 32, 35, 37. Originally published in the *Nation*, January 9, 1868, 27–29.
53. Warren, *The Legacy of the Civil War*, 108.
54. James, "Miss Ravenel's Conversion," 50, 52.
55. William Dean Howells, ["A Review of *Miss Ravenel's Conversion*,"] in *Critical Essays on John William De Forest*, ed. James W. Gargano (Boston: G. K. Hall, 1981), 54 (emphasis added). Originally published in the *Atlantic Monthly*, July 20, 1867, 120–22.
56. William Dean Howells, *Criticism and Fiction* (New York: Hill and Wang, 1967), 43–44, 89.
57. William Dean Howells, *Selected Letters*, ed. George Warren Arms, vol. 3 (Boston: Twayne Publishers, 1978), 170, 170, 196.
58. Oliver Wendell Holmes, *Soundings from the Atlantic* (Boston: Ticknor & Fields, 1864), 5, 6, 46. "My Hunt after 'The Captain'" first appeared in the *Atlantic Monthly*, December 1862, 738–64.
59. Walt Whitman, *Leaves of Grass* (New York: Signet Classics, 2005), 259, 263. The edition of *Leaves of Grass* cited here is from 1892, which included *Drum-Taps* (originally published as its own volume in New York in 1865).
60. Nathaniel Hawthorne, *The Complete Works of Nathaniel Hawthorne*, intro. George

Parsons Lathrop, vol. 12 (Boston: Houghton Mifflin, 1883), 303–4. Originally published in the *Atlantic Monthly*, July 1862, 43–62.

61. For an analysis of Hawthorne's satirical persona in "Chiefly about War Matters," see Randall Fuller, "Hawthorne and War," *New England Quarterly* 80, no. 4 (December 2007): 655–86.

Conclusion: Veterans in Outer Space

1. Published in New York by Henry Holt and Company in 1880, *Democracy* refers to "the Presidential election which took place eight years ago last autumn," which means technically Ratcliffe could be talking about the election of 1872, in which Grant won reelection. But because Reconstruction was well under way in 1872, the stakes then would seem lower than the crucial election of 1868, the first held after the war's end in which "our defeat meant that the government must pass into the bloodstained hands of rebels" (*D* 190).

2. William Dean Howells, *The Rise of Silas Lapham* (New York: Penguin, 1986), 201; Henry James, *The Bostonians* (New York: Modern Library, 2003), 235; and Henry James, *The American* (New York: Oxford University Press, 1999), 10.

3. Walt Whitman, *Specimen Days in America* (London: Walter Scott, 1887), 124.

4. Henry James, *"Notes of a Son and Brother" and "The Middle Years,"* ed. Peter Collister (Charlottesville: University of Virginia Press, 2011), 240. On Henry Adams's and William Dean Howells's relationship with the Civil War, see Daniel Aaron, *The Unwritten War: American Writers and the Civil War* (New York: Oxford University Press, 1973), 93–105, 121–32.

5. Henry James, "The Art of Fiction," *Longman's Magazine* 4 (September 1884), 503–4. James backs away from "compete" in at least one later edition: "The only real reason for the existence of a novel is that it does attempt to represent life." See Henry James, "The Art of Fiction," in *Partial Portraits* (London: Macmillan, 1905), 378.

6. Craig A. Warren, *Scars to Prove It: The Civil War Soldier and American Fiction* (Kent, OH: Kent State University Press, 2009), 22–38. The quotation appears on 36.

7. See, in particular, Louis Menand, *The Metaphysical Club* (New York: Farrar, Straus and Giroux, 2001), 218–32. Throughout his book, Menand traces how the Civil War caused Americans to question the passive confidence they had before the Civil War about their certainty in abstract ideas.

8. For more on the post–Civil War impulse to wince, see James Dawes, *The Language of War: Literature and Culture in the U.S. from the Civil War through World War II* (Cambridge, MA: Harvard University Press, 2002), 9–13.

9. These were my findings during a visit to http://booksforsoldiers.com in June 2015. Such anecdotal evidence is obviously limited, and I would encourage anyone to see the site (if not others) to learn what active duty soldiers want to read.

10. Edgar Rice Burroughs, *Mars Trilogy: A Princess of Mars, the God of Mars, the Warlord of Mars* (New York: Simon & Schuster, 2012), 8. *A Princess of Mars* began in serialization in *The All-Story* in 1912.

11. Erling B. Holtsmark, *Edgar Rice Burroughs* (Boston: Twayne, 1986), 4–5.

12. See, for instance, David Blight, *Race and Reunion: The Civil War in American Memory* (Cambridge, MA: Belknap Press of Harvard University Press, 2002); Nina Silber, *The Romance of Reunion: Northerners and the South, 1865–1900* (Chapel Hill: University of North Carolina Press, 1997); and Coleman Hutchison, *Apples and*

Ashes: Literature, Nationalism, and the Confederate States of America (Athens: University of Georgia Press, 2012).

13. Joe Haldeman, *The Forever War* (New York: St. Martin's, 1997), 119, 138–39, 59.

14. Weston Ochse, *Grunt Life* (Oxford, UK: Solaris, 2014), 11.

15. Ibid., 49–50.

16. Robert J. Spiller, "'Not War but Like War': The American Intervention in Lebanon," in *Leavenworth Papers No. 3* (Fort Leavenworth: Combat Studies Institute, U.S. Army Command and General Staff College, 1958).

17. Burroughs, *Mars Trilogy,* 73.

18. Phil Klay, *Redeployment* (New York: Penguin, 2014), 203.

Epilogue: Khe Sanh

1. Gertrude Stein, *Everybody's Autobiography* (Cambridge, MA: Exact Change, 1993), 298.

2. The following reflections are the result of only one day spent at Khe Sanh in June 2009. Surely other volumes from different months, if not also separate collections from other war memorials, could support or countervail the distinctions I am making. Though my sampling is by no means exhaustive, I would note that guest books from the same month at Quảng Trị and the Vịnh Mốc tunnels read similarly.

3. The rigor of this Marine's voice is compelling, yet it is also somewhat misplaced. Each of these entries is signed "Capt USMC 65–66–69–70." The siege at Khe Sanh happened during 1968. For that matter, the Marine identifies himself in his second inscription as a member of "2/4 (Best in the Corps)," a designation meant to signify the 2nd Battalion, 4th Marines, also known as the "Magnificent Bastards." The 2/4 Marines saw plenty of combat in Vietnam, but they were not at Khe Sanh. The 26th Marines were.

4. David Foster Wallace, "Consider the Lobster," in *"Consider the Lobster" and Other Essays* (New York: Little, Brown, 2005), 240.

INDEX

Page numbers in italics refer to an illustration or an epigraph.

BENJAMIN COOPER teaches English at Lindenwood University in St. Charles, Missouri. Born in Seattle, Washington, and raised in Fairbanks, Alaska, he has received a BA from Davidson College *magna cum laude,* an MA from Northwestern University, and a PhD from Washington University in St. Louis. His scholarship has been supported by a fellowship at the American Antiquarian Society and has appeared in journals such as *Arizona Quarterly* and in edited collections such as a volume from Rutgers University Press about the present generation's relationship with the War on Terror. Professor Cooper currently lives in Brentwood, Missouri, with his wife, Erika Conti, and his daughter, Allegra.